Perspectives in Interdisciplinary and Integrative Studies

Perspectives in Interdisciplinary and Integrative Studies

Edited by Patrick C. Hughes, Juan S. Muñoz,
and Marcus N. Tanner

Foreword by Lawrence Schovanec

Texas Tech University Press

This book is typeset in Minion Pro. The paper used in this book meets the minimum requirements of ANSI/NISO Z39.48-1992 (R1997). ♾

Library of Congress Cataloging-in-Publication Data
Perspectives in interdisciplinary and integrative studies / edited by Patrick C. Hughes, PhD, Juan S. Munoz, PhD, and Marcus N. Tanner, PhD ; foreword by Lawrence Schovanec.
pages cm
Summary: "Collection examining integrative and interdisciplinary scholarship, focusing on the integrative knowledge, theory, methods, and program development and assessment in education"– Provided by publisher.
Includes bibliographical references and index.
ISBN 978-0-89672-937-7 (paperback) – ISBN 978-0-89672-938-4 (e-book) 1. Interdisciplinary approach in education. 2. Interdisciplinary approach to knowledge. 3. Education, Higher–Aims and objectives. I. Hughes, Patrick C. II. Munoz, Juan Sanchez, 1967- III. Tanner, Marcus N.
LB2361.P47 2015
375–dc23
2015012762

15 16 17 18 19 20 21 22 23 / 9 8 7 6 5 4 3 2 1

Texas Tech University Press
Box 41037 | Lubbock, Texas 79409-1037 USA
800.832.4042 | ttup@ttu.edu | www.ttupress.org

For my wife, Jennifer, and our three children,
Jack, Mary Kathleen, and Elizabeth

—Patrick C. Hughes

For my wife, Michelle, and our two children, August and Aiden.

—Marcus N. Tanner

Contents

Illustrations

Foreword

An important challenge of higher education is to educate students who are able to cope with the ever increasing complex problems of the twenty-first century. It is often the case that societal problems and global challenges are so complex that no single discipline can adequately deal with the issues. Consequently, many higher education stakeholders, including state and federal legislators, policymakers, and funding agencies, are encouraging universities to develop a culture that supports interdisciplinary learning and research, as well as greater engagement and collaboration with industry and government.

Although interdisciplinarity is a twenty-first-century imperative, universities are not in alignment with this reality. This is in part due to the traditional disciplinary framework that dominates the organizational structure of higher education. In particular, students focus their studies in a specific major. Faculty members are overwhelmingly hired into a disciplinary department and then progress through the university hierarchy based on their contributions to the discipline, as recognized by scholars in a special field. These impediments to a more integrative approach to education and research have been noted in numerous studies and projects. For example, reports from the National Academy of Sciences make emphatic cases for greater interdisciplinary research and education and graduates capable of transcending academic boundaries. These reports reinforce a theme that has been raised in many other contexts, namely that academic institutional customs often serve to impede interdisciplinary behavior. Project Kaleidoscope, the Association of American Colleges and Universities STEM reform center, while working to advance interdisciplinary teaching and learning environments has also warned that higher education institutions will not create the innovators of the future unless campuses reshape their processes and policies.

In spite of these issues, interdisciplinarity is presently in vogue in academia and has been for some time. On the other hand, the notion of integrative studies has not received the same level of attention. This is somewhat surprising given that scholars of integrative learning and studies have made the case that solutions to complex problems, and a more meaningful curriculum and educational process to prepare students to address such problems, require an approach that is interdisciplinary and integrative. For all of these reasons, *Perspectives in Interdisciplinary and Integrative Studies* is particularly timely and relevant.

This book, which provides theoretical and applied works, will be a valuable resource for scholars and practitioners, especially given the scarcity of texts that address integrative studies as distinguishable from or as an extension of interdisciplinarity. The chapters in the volume provide pragmatic advice as to how interdisciplinary studies and integrative learning can make educational experiences more authentic, providing students with diverse perspectives from within and outside the classroom, along with a synthesis of various disciplinary perspectives.

At a time when colleges and universities are expanding their interdisciplinary and integrative programs, this book should find its way into the hands of administrators who support interdisciplinary education and research, but face academic structures and a culture that serve as an impediment to interdisciplinary behavior. One can hope that the ideas and practices that are represented in *Perspectives in Interdisciplinary and Integrative Studies* could affect faculty and students in ways that will ultimately lead to more engagement with entities outside the academy, in mutual collaboration on complex problems that transcend any one particular discipline.

Lawrence Schovanec, Ph.D.
Provost and Senior Vice President
Professor of Mathematics & Statistics
Texas Tech University
Lubbock, TX
April 2015

References

National Academy of Sciences. 2004. *Facilitating Interdisciplinary Research*. Washington, DC: National Academies Press.

National Research Council. 2014. *Convergence: Facilitating Transdisciplinary Integration of Life Sciences, Physical Sciences, Engineering and Beyond*. Washington, DC: National Academies Press.

Introduction

Expanding Interdisciplinarity: Integrating Life and Learning

Integrative studies is a growing field of scholarship that strives to address many of the evolving accountability, curricular, scholarly, and technological challenges of the twenty-first century in higher education. Integrative studies is a method of synthesis among disciplines that incorporates disciplinary, interdisciplinary, and transdisciplinary research, yet also goes beyond a synthesis of curricular insights by challenging students to integrate their learning into career, future learning, and personal and social spaces beyond their classrooms.

Interdisciplinary approaches have existed in institutions of higher education for decades. Newell (2008) provided an insider's view of the history of interdisciplinary undergraduate education over the past forty years. As interdisciplinary studies were gaining momentum in higher education, Newell and colleagues discovered that students displayed little interest in integrating disciplinary insights, which is the litmus test for interdisciplinarity (Klein and Newell 1997). Repko (2012) viewed integration as the fundamental component to the interdisciplinary research process. Not only is his interdisciplinary research process an integration of Klein's (1990), Newell's (2007), and Szostak's (2002) interdisciplinary processes, but it also is an approach central to interdisciplinarity—creating common ground between fields of study typically centered around a shared complex phenomenon not necessarily considered to be the domain of one field or another and tending to be problem-centered, where the phenomenon or problem, such as a social problem, attracts multiple explanations from multiple fields. Interdisciplinarity is considered "a methodology, a concept, a process, a way of thinking, a philosophy, and a reflexive ideology . . . a means of solving problems and answering questions that cannot be satisfactorily addressed using single methods or approaches" (Klein 1990, 196). Integration is a concept embedded within but that can be separated from interdisciplinarity.

Although integration is central to interdisciplinarity, integrative learning extends interdisciplinarity by teaching students how to make connections between diverse intellectual activities and real-world experiences. In other words, integrative approaches are more additive—cooperative, relational, interactive, and pragmatic—than disciplinary or multidisciplinary, due to the sheer variety of contributing fields. Integrative approaches should be transformative, moving beyond disciplinary and interdisciplinary practices, thereby modifying the processes of inquiry, instruction, research, and curriculum development. Much of the emerging work on integrative learning is attributed to the American Association of Colleges & Universities' (AAC&U) push for new and reformed insights into liberal arts education and its application to life outside the college campus. The AAC&U (2004) defined integrative learning as "fostering students' abilities to integrate learning—across courses, over time, and between campus and community life" (1). An intentionally integrated model would provide the context in which synthesis of student learning would occur (Czechowski 2003).

The guiding principle in preparing this collection was to bring together current theories and methods of practice or application of integrative learning. In this way, this book is decidedly a survey of contemporary perspectives on integrative studies that seem representative, neither exhaustive nor conclusive of the ways integrative studies is being incorporated into and challenged within higher education. Additionally, we hope that this volume invites readers—students and scholars—to consider integrating into their classrooms and research new and unique methods through the development of new programs or through the enhancement of current programs. The contributing authors have provided chapters that represent the emerging discourses about theory, methodology, and application, including one chapter that voices dissent or opposition to integrative scholarship, and assessment of integrative studies. Integrative approaches to course development, pedagogy, and research are highlighted. This edition invites further discussion about how educators apply and advance the principles of integrative learning in their courses, programs, and research studies.

In chapter 1, Julie Thompson Klein argues for a new quadrangulation of disciplinary depth, multidisciplinary breadth, interdisciplinary and transdisciplinary integration, and interprofessional cooperation—connected by integrative learning. Her chapter compares definitions and practices of integration within two historical developments and contends that the connecting link across the quadrangulation is four sets of skills: practicing cognitive flexibility, communicating collaboratively, leveraging integration, and navigating knowledge and information critically. Klein's quadrangle and skill sets support and nudge the prospects for an emerging field of integrative studies. As with all fields, there are epistemologies that comprise theories, methodologies, and applications. In the next few chapters, the contributing authors provide an epistemological foundation for integrative learning.

Although integration has several meanings and applications in various disciplinary and educational contexts, the concept typically entails the synthesis of multiple perspectives. In chapter 2, James Welch, IV, offers a theoretical framework for integrative learning by considering learning theory, cognitive sciences, and neuropsychology. He posits that integrative studies is a broader approach to knowledge that emphasizes the synthetic relationship between academic and experiential learning and that integrative studies can be grounded in theories of learning, cognitive development, and interdisciplinarity. Welch's framework is built upon three foundational principles: integrative nature of the mind, integrative learning engages metacognition, and integrative learning is holistic. Welch asserts that integrative learning necessitates metacognitive awareness of the thinking process itself and provisions students with the cognitive skills for fashioning holistic models that help them make sense of a complex world. Ultimately, synchronizing the internal and external facets of existence is the essential art and craft of this field.

Although Welch provides a convincing theoretical perspective for integrative learning, in chapter 3, Michael Yeo embarks on a critical discourse of the meaning and importance of integration. He calls integrative learning a reform movement, intended to counter the fragmentation of the undergraduate curriculum and bridge the gap between educational institutions and an increasingly complex real world. Granting a redesign of curricula with integration as a goal, students would develop the capacity to better integrate their coursework with life outside the metaphorical walls of the university. Integrated students would be better positioned to "put the pieces together and develop habits of mind that prepare them to make informed judgments in the conduct of personal, professional, and civic life" (AAC&U 2004, 1). While Yeo raises questions of integrative learning as a field because of its lack of epistemic concerns, this volume partly addresses many of the cautions.

Not only do Klein and Welch provide epistemological and theoretical support, but Simeon Dreyfuss and Jennifer Sasser present a model for integrative inquiry in chapter 4. In their model of integrative inquiry, the authors argue that coming to a deeper understanding and creating meaning about complex phenomena is seldom a linear, discrete, or individual process. Rather, constructing environments for integrative learning requires three principles: inviting learners into complexity, inviting learners to be curious about context and their own and others' epistemologies, and inviting learners into conversation and collaboration. This model of integrative inquiry is elaborated using two case studies that provide an institutional example.

The first four chapters thus provide a critical epistemic framework of integrative studies. The authors challenge the notion of integration and integrative learning, provide a theoretical framework for integrative studies, and propose a model for how integrative learning might be applied. In part 2, contributing authors present integrative learning in practice and challenges to assessment.

Marcus Tanner and Charlie Adams in chapter 5 discuss a new program at Texas Tech University that has been designed specifically to address some challenges in typical interdisciplinary programs. Some of the critical challenges that Yeo raises in chapter 3 are addressed through the integrative learning environment at Texas Tech.

One such challenge was to provide a way for students to integrate learning across multiple disciplines and apply that learning in a real-world context. The authors posit that integrative studies curricula develop students' critical thinking skills by giving them a universal understanding of how to work collaboratively to solve complex problems, generate new ideas, and evaluate situations from new and multiple perspectives. Additionally, integrative thinkers are students who see the importance of lifelong learning as a means to conjoin their experiences into a tapestry of knowledge, information, and perspectives that are always evolving and changing. The result is that integrative knowledge gives people the ability to compete in and adjust to a complex and multifaceted world because their all-inclusive learning provides them with insights when other forms of pedagogy may fall short of doing so.

P. Sven Arvidson in chapter 6 examines the concept of integrity as constitutive of integrative programs and articulates the relationship between integrity, autonomy, and discipline in the context of integrative education. By connecting ancient ideas with contemporary thinkers, this chapter articulates a response to how integrative learning can be cultivated through discussing what it could mean to nurture integrity.

Judy Whipps's chapter frames her discussion of models of integrative problem solving in a biographical sketch of Mary Parker Follett. She notes important similarities between interdisciplinary and integrative scholars and Follett, particularly in three areas: (1) understanding integration as a problem-based, active process, directed at resolving a perplexity; (2) embracing diversity: pluralism, multiple perspectives, differences, and contradictions; and (3) the need for creativity to avoid either/or situations and compromise in favor of something new. Further, Whipps advocates for intentional education in integrative thinking. In other words, integrative learning does not simply happen; an intentional process must take place whereby educators teach students to synthesize their learning across curricula and assimilate it into the real world.

Elizabeth Lowham and Annalisa Schilla discuss their intentional process of integrative learning in chapter 8. They report on collaborative and integrative processes and outcomes of a training program funded by the National Science Foundation's (NSF) Integrative Graduate Education and Research Training (IGERT). Based on empirical data, this chapter discusses the challenges and rewards of such graduate training and provides techniques for improving integrative graduate education programs.

The discourse on applied integrative learning continues in chapter 9 as Heather Pinson and Monica VanDieren describe the integrated content and instructional components of a new college course at Robert Morris University. The pedagogy described in this chapter goes beyond interdisciplinary teaching by providing students with intentional and integrative learning experiences based on L. Dee Fink's taxonomy (Fink and Fink 2009; Fink 2003).

Further, Natalie McKnight's chapter 10 describes how professors and students at

Boston University's College of General Studies (CGS) have used e-portfolios to archive, assess, and reflect on their work in a two-year, team-taught, interdisciplinary general education program. In reflective essays, students must support their own developmental assertions by intentionally applying their interdisciplinary learning.

In chapter 11, Michael Kelly, Michael Lange, and Katheryn Wright explore the problems and possibilities delivering an integrative liberal arts experience in a professionally focused undergraduate institution. The authors stress that in a school that focuses on the student as an aspiring career professional, tension often arises between the delivery of job skills and the teaching of broader, critical, and integrative thinking. The degree to which tensions exist varies widely from one professional major to another, based on several factors.

In chapter 12, Philip Craig Morton, Jennifer Shaulis Hughes, and Curtis Craig discuss the idiosyncratic challenges and requirements of assessing integrative learning. They suggest that assessing integrative learning follows the same basic guidelines that are consistent for assessment across all disciplines and identify key issues that administrators and faculty should consider in the development of an assessment plan. In this chapter, the authors describe issues related to accreditation and reaffirmation, strategic planning, tenure and promotion, promoting student success, student engagement and learning outcomes, and navigating institutional politics. They also provide suggestions for addressing these challenges.

We, the editors, contend that integrative studies, as an emerging field, provides for a synthesis of study and life—an application of interdisciplinarity to complex problems. The chapters in this volume show an expansion of interdisciplinarity toward integrative application. Yeo's chapter in the context of this volume is important because he provides a thought-provoking discourse on interdisciplinarity and challenges the idea of integrative studies as an emerging field of study. In this volume, Klein, Welch, and Whipps address many of the epistemic concerns that Yeo raises, supporting for our assertion that integrative studies is an extension of interdisciplinarity. Further, the other chapters describe ways in which integrative curricula is being programmed and assessed in institutions of higher learning. Yeo's chapter should not be thought of as disparate from the other chapters in this volume but rather as a challenge to continue working toward the legitimacy of integrative studies.

References

American Association of Colleges & Universities. 2004. "A Statement on Integrative Learning." http://www.aacu.org/integrative_learning/pdfs/ILP_Statement.pdf.

Czechowski, J. 2003. "An Integrated Approach to Liberal Learning." *Peer Review* 5 (4): 4–7.

Fink, A. K., and L. D. Fink. 2009. "Lessons We Can Learn from the Voices of Experience." *New Directions for Teaching and Learning* 2009 (119): 105–13.

Fink, L. D. 2003. *Creating Significant Learning Experiences: An Integrated Approach to Designing College Courses*. San Francisco: John Wiley and Sons.

Klein, J. T. 1990. *Interdisciplinarity: History, Theory, and Practice*. Detroit: Wayne State University Press.

Klein, J. T., & W. H. Newell. 1997. "Advancing Interdisciplinary Studies." In *Handbook of the Undergraduate Curriculum: A Comprehensive Guide to the Purposes, Structures, Practices, and Change*, edited by Jerry G. Gaff and James L. Ratcliff, 393–415. San Francisco: Jossey-Bass.

Newell, W. H. 2007. "Decision-Making in Interdisciplinary Studies." In *Handbook of Decision Making*, edited by Goktug Morcol, 245–64. New York: Marcel Dekker.

———. 2008. "The Intertwined History of Interdisciplinary Undergraduate Education and the Association for Integrative Studies: An Insider's View." *Issues in Integrative Studies* 26: 1–59.

Repko, A. F. 2012. *Interdisciplinary Research: Process and Theory*. 2nd ed. Thousand Oaks, CA: Sage Publications.

Szostak, R. 2002. "How to Do Interdisciplinarity: Integrating the Debate." *Issues in Integrative Studies* 20: 103–22.

Part 1
Theoretical Perspectives of Integrative Scholarship

Chapter 1

Beyond Interdisciplinarity: Expanding Horizons of Integrative Learning

Julie Thompson Klein, PhD, Wayne State University

The etymological root of the English word *integrative* denotes a process of making something whole, stemming from the Latin noun *integrāre* (Oxford English Dictionary 2013). In modern usage, connotations vary widely: from finding the integral of a function in mathematics, metering flows of electric current, and mixing chemical compounds to achieving racial equality, creating theoretical synthesis in evolutionary biology, and creating a digital mash-up of image, text, and sound. This chapter situates the emerging field of integrative studies in two historical developments: first, in the changing relationship of "integration" and "integrative" education with "interdisciplinarity," and second, in the ascendancy of transdisciplinarity in a more recent history of trans-sector research involving academics and stakeholders in society. Echoing the title of this book, both developments move beyond interdisciplinarity to foster a new quadrangulation of disciplinary depth, multidisciplinary breadth, interdisciplinary and transdisciplinary integration, and interprofessional cooperation. The connecting link across the quadrangle is four sets of skills needed in education as well as research practice: practicing cognitive flexibility, communicating collaboratively, leveraging integration, and navigating knowledge and information critically. Together, the quadrangle and skill sets affirm and extend prospects for a new field of integrative studies.

Integration Redivivus

The emergence of a field that moves "beyond interdisciplinarity," to echo the title of this book, is fraught with historical irony, because the concept of integration preceded the development of interdisciplinarity. Boix Mansilla and Lenoir (2010) consider interdisciplinarity in U.S. education inseparable from integration—but not because they are identical. They "overlap" in the redivivus of revived and renewed connotations. Klein (2005) and Boix Mansilla and

Lenoir (2010) date the term *integration* in education to books on principles of psychology by Herbert Spencer in 1855 and William James in 1896, as well as to Alexis Bertrand's theory of integrated instruction in 1898. In the 1800s, integration also was linked with the role that schools play in promoting social unity and the Herbartian movement's doctrine of correlation, which supplemented the doctrine of concentration on individual subjects by recognizing "natural relations" among them. The meaning of integration expanded in the twentieth century in conjunction with new movements in the curriculum and a major shift in definition. (The following summary is a composite of Boix Mansilla and Lenoir 2010; Klein 2005; and Beane 1997).

The first significant development in the overlapping history of integration and interdisciplinarity was the rise of general education and core curriculum in the opening decades of the twentieth century in K–12 and college. New theme- and problem-based curricula were introduced, and integrative learning was accorded prime value. Over the course of the century, integration was also associated with a number of particular movements. In the 1920s the Progressivists' democratic vision of education centered on students' integration of personal and social concerns, and the project approach was linked with the model of an integrated curriculum. During the 1930s the concept appeared in conjunction with the core curriculum movement again, and then during the 1940s and 1950s with problem-centered cores and life problems. In the closing decades of the century, curriculum integration reappeared in K–12 as a generic term for a mix of approaches that drew on more than one subject or discipline, including thematic studies, multidisciplinary and multisubject designs, integrated units, skills across the curriculum, a social-problems approach to science education, and combined constructs of social studies and whole language. Early childhood educators and proponents of outcomes-based education also argued that sophisticated levels of learning cannot be attained by studying subjects separately, and the movement toward a "brain-based" approach in education furthered the case based on research revealing that the brain is a parallel processor that makes meaning by patterning.

A major shift in meaning also occurred during the 1930s that may be viewed as antecedent to the current emerging field of integrative studies, moving emphasis from the noun *integration* to the adjective *integrative*. This distinction was not a trivial change in wording. It supported the argument for a process- and student-based theory of integration. This idea was reinforced in the 1920s by organismic and Gestalt psychologists' notion of an integrated personality and related processes by which individuals seek unity. A 1935 meeting sponsored by the National Education Association and the 1937 book *Integration,* though, were turning points. Participants concluded that complete unity of knowledge was impossible. Instead, they proposed thinking of *unifying,* not *unified,* approaches. Subsequently, at a 1948 workshop sponsored by the Foundation for Integrative Education, participants distinguished *content integration* (bridging subjects of physical sciences with arts and letters) from *process integration* (the interplay of an individual personality and an environment). They also demarcated *integration* as the synthesizing of accepted postulates from *integrative* building of new conceptual modes capable of producing a holistic experience.

The concept of *interdisciplinarity* also underwent shifts in meaning over the twentieth century. The term is dated conventionally to the opening decades of the century: to the founding of the U.S.-based Social Science Research Council, where it was shorthand for research on societal problems involving two or more of the council's professional societies, and to new curricular movements. Initially, Boix Mansilla and Lenoir (2010) recall, the concept was inscribed in curricular problems under a variety of names, including *coordination, new fields, overlapping projects, interrelated research, borderline research, interpenetration,* and *cross-relationships.* In general education, the terms *integration, synthesis, unity,* and *holism* appeared more often than *interdisciplinarity* (Klein 1996). Boix Mansilla and Lenoir (2010) suggest that John Dewey was the first to advocate academic interdisciplinarity in association with integration. Yet core curriculum was also a prominent locus in two differing models of interdisciplinarity. One was grounded in the legacy of liberal arts, hearkening to the past for unity of knowledge and culture in a theme-based study of a canon of "great" books and ideas. The other model treated historically situated problems of society as a platform for developing integrative understanding of the modern world. The first model still exists, though over time problem-focus and core skills gained greater roles in litanies of desired outcomes.

Over the course of the twentieth century, expanding interest in interdisciplinarity pluralized its meaning across an array of fields. Meanings differed markedly, ranging from comparative literature to sustainability studies, from molecular biology to digital humanities, and from postcolonial studies to clinical and translational science. From the 1980s forward, an increase in integrated approaches to general education also led to greater visibility. As the concept gained credibility, a variety of professional groups developed interdisciplinary theory and practice in their hybrid specialties, notable among them the American Studies Association and the National Women's Studies Association. The Association for Interdisciplinary Studies (AIS) took the most forthright stance on integration as the basis for best practices. In a state-of-the-art account for the *Handbook of the Undergraduate Curriculum*, Klein and Newell (1997) called it the acid test of interdisciplinary studies, and Repko (2008) accorded integration central place in a textbook for students on the interdisciplinary research process, to be achieved by drawing insights from multiple disciplines in order to create common ground.

The concept of integrative studies broadens the definition of *integration* beyond bridging disciplines. It embraces a diverse set of structures, sources, strategies, pedagogies, and learning experiences that cross multiple divides, including high school and college, introductory and advanced levels, general education and the major, theory and practice, campus-based experiences inside and outside the classroom, and academic study and the "real world." Integration might take place in linked courses or in learning portfolios in any class. It might happen in general education, an interdisciplinary field, or a discipline-based capstone seminar. The rise of integrative studies is due in no small part to the partnership of the Association of American Colleges & Universities (AAC&U) and the Carnegie Foundation for the Advancement of Teaching. AAC&U named integrative learning as one of three key themes in the reinvention of liberal education today, alongside breadth and depth. If *synthesis* is a defining keyword of the interdisciplinary studies conception of integration, *connection making* is the keyword of integrative studies. The Integrative Learning Value Rubric acknowledges that some majors, such as interdisciplinary majors or problem-based field studies, appear to inherently evoke characteristics of integrative learning. Yet the Statement on Integrative Learning pluralizes the meaning and the moment (Klein 2005; Schneider 2004; Leskes 2004; Huber and Hutchings 2004; Huber, Hutchings, and Gale 2005).

Boix Mansilla and Lenoir's (2010) characterization of the relationship of interdisciplinarity and integration returns to mind. The concepts are inseparable but not identical. In arguing for a mix of integrative learning and interdisciplinary studies, Newell (2001; 2010) considers the two concepts analogous because they both integrate insights from divergent perspectives for understanding and solving complex problems. Moreover, just as integrative learning is occurring in a range of contexts, interdisciplinarity may occur at multiple points: in interdisciplinary majors, multicultural learning, service learning, learning communities, and collaborative and experiential learning. They may also, Newell adds, have "multiplicative power"; a living/learning community might draw on several disciplines (interdisciplinary study), cultures (multicultural learning), and field experiences (service learning), while using collaborative and traditional formats. To be interdisciplinary, however, requires integrating insights from disciplines. The primacy of disciplines was reinforced recently by the decision to rename the Association for Integrative Studies, founded in 1974, as the Association of Interdisciplinary Studies. The new name, according to the AIS newsletter, reflects expanding international membership of this U.S.-based organization. The argument that the name *integrative* tends to be associated more outside the United States with medicine instead of education is a limited reason, given its use in other fields as well. No mention is made, either, of the claiming of *integrative* in the work of AACU (Association of Interdisciplinary Studies 2013). Yet the AIS name change is a strong affirmation that interdisciplinarity gained greater visibility over the course of the early twentieth century.

Transdisciplinary Momentum

The second development is more recent, although it has already produced a sizable literature. The term *transdisciplinarity* gained visibility in 1972 in a book emanating from the first international conference on interdisciplinary research and teaching (Organisation for Economic Co-operation and Development 1972). Transdisciplinarity was defined as a common system of axioms that transcends the narrow scope of disciplinary worldviews through an overarching synthesis, such as anthropology conceived as the science of humans. Given its prefix, transdisciplinarity was inevitably associated with the historical quest for unity of knowledge. However, the basis for unity is no longer assumed to lie in predetermined postulates. Rather, it emerges in the construction of new paradigms with unifying capacity, including major exemplars of general system theory, feminist theory, Marxism, and sustainability. By the closing decades of the twentieth century, transdisciplinarity also had gained traction in new problem-oriented research. In the United States, a new form of team-based "transdisciplinary science" fostered new methodological and theoretical frameworks for defining and analyzing social, economic, political, environmental, and institutional factors in health and well-being (Rosenfield 1992; Stokols et al. 2008). In Swiss and German contexts of environmental research, the term connoted a new form of research involving stakeholders in society. By the turn of the century, case studies were being reported in all fields of human interaction with natural systems and technical innovations as well as the development context (Klein et al. 2001).

Integration has been central to the latter movement. In the *Handbook for Transdisciplinary Research*, Pohl, van Kerkhoff, Hirsch, and Bammer (2008) call integration "the core methodology underpinning the transdisciplinary research process" (421). There is no universal model, however. Types of integration vary because forms of interdisciplinarity and transdisciplinarity differ in scope, purpose, goals, degree of integration, and relationship to disciplines. Teams also operate in different contexts, including academic, industrial, and governmental settings as well as community organizations and nongovernmental organizations (NGOs). Yet Pohl et al. (2008) identified four primary methods of integration: mutual understanding, theoretical concepts, models, and methods. The main challenges in managing transdisciplinary research, Funtowicz and Ravitz (2008) emphasize, are facilitating mutual learning and shared goal definition in heterogeneous teams. Individuals need to clarify and negotiate differences in disciplinary language, methods, tools, concepts, and worldviews. As a result, managing communication is a central theme in this literature.

Whereas many treatises on integrative education have focused on the individual learner, studies of transdisciplinary collaboration begin with the assumption that social and cognitive integration are tightly interwoven. As a further result, the literature emphasizes methods for fostering integration. Some methods have been widely applied, including systems theory and modeling, Delphi and scenario building, simulation, concept mapping, computer synthesis of data and information flow, and integrated environmental assessment and risk management. Other methods target communication processes, including facilitating common understanding, mental mapping of stakeholder views, consensus conferences, and collaborative learning. McDonald, Bammer, and Deane's (2009) *Research Integration Using Dialogue Methods* identifies fourteen dialogue methods that bring together multiple perspectives for understanding a real-world problem broadly (by integrating judgments) and for understanding particular aspects of a problem (by integrating visions, worldviews, interests, and values). The repertoire of dialogue methods includes hypothesis and model building, integrative assessment procedures, boundary objects and concepts, heuristics, research questions, artifacts and products, mutual learning, and stakeholder participation. Coauthor Bammer has elevated this capacity to a new discipline of integration and implementation sciences aimed at equipping researchers with theory and methods for research integration (www.anu.edu.au/iisn).

Two other recent works add to the repertoire of integrative approaches. Now available in English translation, *Methods for Transdisciplinary Research: A Primer for Practice* examines more than forty methods for knowledge integration and eleven projects that developed, used, and combined them. Elevating integration to a scientific principle, the book identifies three dimensions in which integration is accomplished: communicative, social and organizational, and cognitive-epistemic. The methods and instruments span conceptual clarification and theoretical framing; formulation of research questions and hypotheses; acts of screening, using, refining, and further developing scientific methods; assessment procedures; development and application of models; use of artifacts, services, and products as boundary objects; and procedures and instruments of research organization (Bergmann et al. 2012). A forthcoming book on transdisciplinary sustainability studies takes a step further with case studies of heuristic approaches to complex environmental problems. A heuristic approach eschews commitment to a designated set of methods or concepts in favor of an intuitive though systematic attempt to mobilize and structure cognitive skills by discovering, making sense of, and resolving indeterminate problems. A priori methods, rules of thumb, checklists, and case-based cognitive schemes are useful. However, the integrative process is inventive, not prescriptive (Huutoniemi and Tapio 2014).

The integrative studies movement has focused primarily on bridging academic and other settings while a student is still in college or a university. Models of transdisciplinary education appear both within the curriculum, from early childhood education through PhD level, and in situ, in professional practice and community-based projects through stakeholder workshops, focus groups, symposia and colloquia, training modules, and project-based mutual learning. In both cases, the traditional relationship of content and process is refigured. In establishing criteria for training in transdisciplinary research and community-based learning at the University of Basel, Förster (2000) and colleagues faced the challenge of determining not only what skills and knowledge students needed but also what training concepts and criteria teachers should employ. The underlying philosophy and method that emerged recognize the reciprocal relationship of content and process. Content designates knowledge, principles, and methods of different disciplines as well as inter- or transdisciplinary approaches, fostering analysis of complex problems and familiarity with problem-solving strategies. Process designates knowing how to organize and participate in inter- or transdisciplinary processes and projects and knowing how to communicate across academic disciplines and with external stakeholders. There is no one best method, Förster advises, but rather a "basket of options" (2000, 96).

Any account must acknowledge the disputed status of integration. Lattuca (2001), who prefers *interaction* of disciplines over *integration*, found the dispute to be highest in fields where the term *transdisciplinarity* is associated with critique—especially in humanities and cultural studies informed by poststructuralist and postmodern theories of history, language, and culture. Categorized *as critical interdisciplinarity*, these fields interrogate the existing structure of knowledge and education with the aim of changing them. They include identity fields and self-studies such as women's, Black/African American, indigenous/Native, queer, and disability studies. In self-studies, Vickers (1997) explains that knowledge is mobilized from other sites, including action research designed to transform society and the self as well as knowledge from nonacademic social and political movements. In many projects, moreover, the critique is both antidisciplinary and anti-interdisciplinary. The name *interdisciplinarity* is eschewed in favor of a transgressive transdisciplinarity that jettisons canons of wholeness. Despite their opposition to integration, though, advocates of these practices often integrate multiple methods and concepts in constructing new paradigms and hybrid fields. Teaching how to integrate, then, is a crucial task, whether the context is a classroom or the community.

Quadrangulating Integrative Learning

Together the two movements examined in this chapter underscore the need for a new quadrangulation of disciplinary depth, multidisciplinary breadth, interdisciplinary and transdisciplinary integration, and interprofessional cooperation. Integrative thinking is needed at all points of the quadrangle.

Disciplinary Depth

Interdisciplinarity, transdisciplinarity, and integrative studies all recognize that students need depth of disciplinary content and methods. Yet depth must include traditional approaches as well as a contemporary view of disciplines that incorporates new developments, many of which resulted from interdisciplinary research that produced new understandings of complex objects, such as the gene and identity, and complex concepts, such as life and culture. Integrative thinking is needed for bridging multiple approaches in expanding disciplines.

Multidisciplinary Breadth

Exposure to multiple disciplines is a cornerstone of general and liberal education as well as core curricula in interdisciplinary studies. Integrative studies heightens the need for lifelong learning of new developments across multiple areas, including not only disciplines but also occupational professions, interdisciplinary fields, and other forms of knowledge beyond the academy. Moreover, it entails knowing how to find pertinent knowledge and information that integrate them in order to widen the scope of study and available resources.

Interdisciplinary and Transdisciplinary Integration

Interdisciplinarity and transdisciplinarity both couple depth and breadth in a process of weighing multiple perspectives and generating a synthesis or more holistic understanding. Integrative studies opens a wider range of contexts, including linked courses, theme-based learning communities, and capstone experiences that bridge academic knowledge and the "real world." It also moves further beyond disciplines as the locus of integration to include other forms of knowledge such as new interdisciplinary fields and community-based ways of knowing.

Interprofessional Cooperation

The term *interprofessionalism* is most closely associated with an integrative approach to health care, although engineering also intersects increasingly with physical and life sciences in tackling complex societal problems. A danger lies, however, in the current emphasis on training over education in a fuller sense. The integrative studies movement is fostering a broad-based commitment to reflective learning not possible in isolated modules and coursework. Contextualization is required, as is the capacity to bridge different content and methods.

Four generic skills emerge from situating the emerging field of integrative studies within the two historical developments traced in this chapter and the quadrangulation of disciplinary depth, multidisciplinary breadth, inter- and transdisciplinarity, and interprofessionalism.

Practicing cognitive flexibility. Interdisciplinary studies situates cognitive flexibility in terms of disciplines. The transdisciplinarity movement examined in this chapter accentuates collaboration across social sectors. In each case, though, appreciation of different epistemologies is required in order to identify and integrate relevant resources. Integrative studies expands the temporal and spatial locations of this capacity through lifelong learning and multiple sites of problem solving.

Communicating collaboratively. The ability to work with others has been a striking addition to litanies of desired competencies today in education, the classroom, the workplace, and culture at large. Interdisciplinary studies accentuates the capacity to articulate strengths and weaknesses of disciplinary perspectives. Transdisciplinary teamwork couples that capacity with a social process of mutual learning. Integrative studies fosters those skills across a widening plurality of contexts, where collective intelligence is generated through dialogue and negotiation.

Leveraging integration. Students, teachers, and researchers alike need to be able to generate integration through a process that the Harvard Interdisciplinary Studies Project describes as "weaving together" perspectives into a generative and coherent whole (Boix Mansilla 2010). A host of methods, tools, and models exists for this task. However, integration is always situated. Integrative studies promotes adaptability of modes of thinking and acting across not only multiple but also changing locales.

Navigating knowledge and information critically. The traditional paradigm of literacy assumed a single standard for everyone in reading, writing, numeracy, and oral communication. The growing plurality of knowledge forms and sources has added another essential literacy: the ability to use new technologies to identify pertinent resources dispersed across multiple domains and then use them critically. Integrative studies has opened an expanding sphere of contexts for this new literacy.

A recent call for proposals from the National Socio-Environmental Synthesis Center (SESYNC) underscores the importance of balancing generic capacities and particularities of context in a digital era. The center announced a new focus on interdisciplinary education in funding projects related to interdisciplinary integration. The goal is to understand how students learn to integrate information and concepts and to identify pedagogies that help develop cognitive skills for identifying patterns and integrating knowledge across disciplines. Some of the core questions in the call, it must be said, have long been addressed by scholars of interdisciplinary studies, including pedagogies that foster skills of interdisciplinary integration and the impact of differences in knowledge structures. New initiatives should take account of the accumulated body of theory and practice. Yet SESYNC also aims to situate integration in the context of socioenvironmental problems that present new and unpredictable contexts of problem solving. In order to address related problems, students need to learn to integrate across natural and social sciences as well as large and diverse datasets, raising a further question about the role of cyberlearning tools (see http://www.sesync.org/themes/interdisciplinaryintegration).

Networked information systems are making it easier to find resources across the quadrangle of disciplinarity, multidisciplinarity, interdisciplinarity, and transdisciplinarity, as well as interprofessionalism. Federated search engines along with RSS feeds, adaptive filters, and spiders have increased the capacity for working horizontally across domains of knowledge and information. However, Vickers (2003) cautioned that, in weighing challenges that interdisciplinarians face in the twenty-first century, new tools for navigating and collaborating reinforce the need for guidelines that determine what constitutes reliable knowledge in interdisciplinary work; ease of access and mixing does not equate with quality of use. It is easier to "do" interdisciplinarity technically, Vickers contends, but it is increasingly harder to do well because of the difficulty of evaluating the quality, trustworthiness, and authority of interdisciplinary knowledge claims. The bricolage of cut-and-paste that results, she adds, falls short of the "reliable knowledge" that makes interdisciplinary projects productive. This challenge is not limited to interdisciplinary knowledge. Adjudicating quality of multiple resources and perspectives cuts across the two developments examined in this chapter and the widening sphere of contexts that form the concrete constellations of integrative studies. Metacognitive skills of flexibility, communication and interaction, critical evaluation, and lifelong commitment to learning-to-learn become essential skills for everyone and every purpose.

References

Association for Interdisciplinary Studies. 2013. "Association for Interdisciplinary Studies is Official Name Starting January 1, 2013." *Integrative Pathways*, 34 (4): 1.

Beane, J. A. 1997. *Curriculum Integration: Designing the Core of Democratic Education*. New York: Teachers College Press.

Bergmann, M., T. Jahn, T. Knobloch, W. Krohn, C. Pohl, and E. Schramm, eds. 2012. *Methods for Transdisciplinary Research: A Primer for Practice*. Frankfurt: Campus Verlag.

Boix Mansilla, V. 2010. "Learning to Synthesize: The Development of Interdisciplinary Understanding." In *The Oxford Handbook of Interdisciplinarity*, edited by R. Frodeman, J. T. Klein, and C. Mitcham, 288–306. Oxford: Oxford University Press.

Boix Mansilla, V., and Y. Lenoir. 2010. "Interdisciplinarity in U.S. Schools: Past, Present, and Future." *Issues in Integrative Studies* 28: 1–28.

Förster, R. 2000. Criteria for Training in Transdisciplinary Practice. In *Transdisciplinarity: Joint Problem Solving among Science, Technology, and Society*, edited by R. Haeberli, R. W. Scholz, A. Bill, and M. Welti, 93–97. Zurich: Haffmanns Sachbuch Verlag AG.

Funtowicz, S., and J. Ravetz. 2008. "Values and Uncertainties.: In *Handbook of Transdisciplinary Research*, edited by G. Hirsch et al., 361–68. Frankfurt: Verlag.

Huber, M. T., and P. Hutchings. 2004. *Integrative Learning: Mapping the Terrain*. Washington, DC: Association of American Colleges & Universities.

Huber, M. T., P. Hutchings, and R. Gale. 2005. "Integrative Learning for Liberal Education." *Peer Review* 7 (4): 4–7.

Huutoniemi, K., and P. Tapio. 2014. *Transdisciplinary Sustainability Studies: A Heuristic Approach*.

Organisation for Economic Co-operation and Development. 1972. *Interdisciplinarity:*

Problems of Teaching and Research in Universities. Paris: Organisation of Economic Co-operation and Development.

Klein, J. T. 1996. *Crossing Boundaries: Knowledge, Disciplinarities, and Interdisciplinarities.* Charlottesville: University of Virginia Press.

———. 2005. "Integrative Learning and Interdisciplinary Studies." *Peer Review* 7 (4): 8–10.

Klein, J. T., W. Grossenbacher-Mansuy, R. Häberli, A. Bill, R. Scholz, and M. Welti, eds. 2001. *Transdisciplinarity: Joint Problem Solving among Science, Technology, and Society.* Boston: Birkhauser.

Klein, J. T., and W. H. Newell. 1997. "Advancing Interdisciplinary Studies." In *Handbook of the Undergraduate Curriculum: A Comprehensive Guide to Purposes, Structures, Practices, and Change*, edited by J. G. Gaff, J. L. Ratcliff, and Associates, 393–415. San Francisco: Jossey-Bass.

Lattuca, L. 2001. *Creating Interdisciplinarity: Interdisciplinary Research and Teaching among College and University Faculty.* Nashville: Vanderbilt University Press.

Leskes, A. 2004. "Foreword." In *Integrative Learning: Mapping the Terrain*, edited by M. T. Huber and P. Hutchings, iv–v. Washington, DC: Association of American Colleges & Universities.

McDonald, D., G. Bammer, and P. Deane. 2009. *Research Integration Using Dialogue Methods.* Australia: Australian National University E Press.

Newell, W. H. 2001. "Powerful Pedagogies." In *Reinventing Ourselves: Interdisciplinary Education, Collaborative Learning, and Experimentation in Higher Education*, edited by B. L. Smith and J. McCann, 196–211. Boston, MA: Anker Press.

———. 2010. "Educating for a Complex World: Integrative Learning and Interdisciplinary Studies." *Liberal Education* 96 (4). http://www.aacu.org/ liberaleducation/le-fa10/ LEFA10_Newell.cfm.

Oxford English Dictionary. 2013. S.v. "integration." http://www.oed.com/.

Pohl, D., L. van Kerkhoff, G. H. Hirsch, and G. Bammer. 2008. "Integration." In *Handbook of Transdisciplinary Research*, edited by G. H. Hadorn et al., 441–71. Bern, Switzerland: Springer.

Repko, A. F. 2008. *Interdisciplinary Research: Process and Theory.* Thousand Oaks, CA: Sage.

Rosenfield, P. L. 1992. "The Potential of Transdisciplinary Research for Sustaining and Extending Linkages between the Health and Social Sciences. *Social Science and Medicine* 35 (11): 1343–57.

Schneider, C. G. 2004. "Practicing Liberal Education: Formative Themes in the Reinvention of Liberal Learning." *Liberal Education* 90 (2): 6–11.

Stokols, D., et al. 2008. "The Science of Team Science: Overview of the Field and Introduction to the Supplement." *American Journal of Preventive Medicine* 35 (2S): S77–S89.

Vickers, J. 1997. "Unframed in Open, Unmapped Fields: Teaching and the Practice of

Interdisciplinarity." *Arachne: An Interdisciplinary Journal of the Humanities* 4: 11–42.

———. 2003. "Diversity, Globalization, and Growing Up Digital: Navigating Interdisciplinarity in the Twenty-First Century." *History of Intellectual Culture* 3. http://www.ucalgary.ca/hic/issues/vol3.

Chapter 2

Theories of Integrative Learning

James L. Welch, IV, PhD, University of Texas–Arlington

"Integration" is a liberally utilized concept in multiple disciplinary and educational contexts. The language of integration is used inconsistently across campuses, and the phrase *integrative learning*, along with the basic principles of its application, have attained little common meaning (DeZure, Babb, and Waldmann 2005). Nonetheless, the diverse body of scholarship on integrative learning reveals broad commonalities that supply some cohesion to the subject. According to the "Statement on Integrative Learning" (Carnegie Foundation and American Association of Colleges & Universities 2004), "Integrative learning comes in many varieties: connecting skills and knowledge from multiple sources and experiences; applying theory to practice in various settings; utilizing diverse and even contradictory points of view; and, understanding issues and positions contextually." Schneider (2003) has described integrative learning as an umbrella term for a complex set of capacities, including the arts of connection, reflective judgment, and considered action. It engages "intentional learners" who approach knowledge contextually and are adept at complex problem solving. Integrative learning helps students develop a sense of social responsibility and civic engagement, learning a skill set that will enable them to bring about healthy communities. These characteristics cover a great deal of ground indeed.

Integrative learning is inevitably such a broad subject, amenable to so many contexts. Integration, as a phenomenon, appears to be a fundamental aspect of the operation of the human mind and the way we organize the world around us. This chapter attempts to make some sense of this expansive context by examining general applications of integration in various disciplines. The work of Piaget and Bloom demonstrate the importance of integration in foundational theories of education. An exploration of the integrative nature of the mind in cognitive science and neuropsychology provides further insights into a working theory of integrative learning. From these insights emerge three principles:

1. Integrative nature of the mind.
2. Integrative learning engages metacognition.
3. Integrative learning is holistic.

These principles by no means provide an exhaustive foundation for integrative theory. A proper theory of integrative learning must establish a set of foundational precepts, scientifically and philosophically grounded, that are coherent and generalizable. Such an ambitious enterprise is beyond the scope of this chapter. Similarly, the social aspects of integrative learning and the importance of social constructivist theories of education are also outside of the present focus. The primary intention here, instead, is to provide a broad context for the facets of integrative learning theory revealed by investigating the way the human mind processes its lived experience.

Integration in Multidisciplinary Contexts

To put the subject into perspective, a few examples of the ways integration is utilized in a variety of disciplinary contexts begin to illustrate the basic connotations of the concept. This brief and selective survey helps map the terrain for integrative learning, allowing us to triangulate fundamental commonalities. Historically, integration has been used in a social and political sense, specifically as a means of overcoming racial and ethnic segregation. Studies of successfully integrated neighborhoods show that bridging differences comes from interactions in structured situations, where positive interracial contact promotes greater understanding, trust, happiness, and well-being for individuals and their communities (Oliver 2010). In engineering, *process integration* describes "a holistic approach to process design, retrofitting, and operation that emphasizes the unity of the process" (El-Halwagi 2012, 35). Process integration examines the flow of mass and energy through a system by examining how all of its components should be optimally interconnected.

In religious education, Komaladi (2012) advocates platforms that allow engagement with students espousing other belief systems that promote the common good. Integration is seen as a means to bring mind, heart, and action together toward a solution to social issues such as poverty, environmentalism, and social justice. An early example of integrative learning in secondary education was Watershed, a program where gifted students were taken on field trips that allowed them to integrate their classroom curriculum with experiences in nature. The program was based upon a whole learning approach intent on "the total reintegration of knowledge." Its instructors claimed that the program provided "more contexts and connections for facts and thus more avenues for their retrieval and application in different situations" (Springer 1994, 12–13). Watershed was designed to give students a great deal of control over their own classroom activities—allowing them to take responsibility for their own results and providing the freedom to organize their own tasks. Learning was seen as a cooperative venture through teamwork and shared responsibility.

Integrative medicine is an approach to health and healing that combines traditional and alternative treatment styles and addresses all aspects of the patient, including their social and environmental context. Integrative medicine draws upon the innate capacity of the human body for healing and resilience. It views patients holistically, as mental, emotional, and spiritual beings situated in meaningful social relationships. Further, integrative medicine emphasizes the importance of lifestyle and cultural influences on a patient's health decisions. Finally, integrative medicine stresses the critical role of the doctor-patient relationship. This relationship is based not merely on compassion but a sense of mutual responsibility. The doctor needs to be attentive to the individual needs and circumstances of the patient who, in turn, is an active participant in assessing and directing the path to well-being (Weil 2009). Integrative medicine views health as embedded in a complex system of factors that is best appreciated holistically. This "dynamic balance of biopsychosocial and spiritual influences . . . requires that mind, body, emotions, and spirit are explored to understand best how to facilitate positive change" (Rakel and Jonas 2012, 167).

Sensory integration "is the neurological process of organizing sensory inputs for function in daily life" (Isbell and Isbell 2007, 29). The central nervous system automatically processes information gathered through the body in order to plan and organize behavior and make adaptive responses to the environment. This interaction between brain and environment establishes a reaction, interaction, and learning cycle that is dynamic and accumulative. "The elements of the cycle are: sensory intake, sensory integration, planning and organising, adaptive behaviour and learning, and feedback" (Reynolds and Reynolds 2010, 3). According to this perspective, integration of sensory input, or neuro-efficiency, is fundamental to the thinking process and for correcting learning disabilities.

These disparate perspectives on integration reveal fundamental linkages.

Integration is best structured within a conducive environment. Integrative learning requires scaffolding—creating a space in which learners are encouraged to confront differences in an atmosphere of mutual trust and respect, a space that actively cultivates holistic interactions. Process integration is an example of holistic thinking, comprehending how all the facets of a system work together, enabling one to assess their performance and make adjustments. For religious education, the concept of integration is used to connect the spiritual to the communal, demonstrating that integration is a means to bridge contrasting value systems. The Watershed program shows that integrative learning enables students to make connections and think for themselves as a natural approach to teaching and learning at all levels. In integrative medicine, one can easily replace references to *doctor/patient/healing* with *teacher/student/learning* and find a direct correlation with integrative learning: Students have a natural capacity for learning; they must be treated as complex mental, emotional, and cultural beings, ensconced in a wider society/environment; their lifestyles also have an impact on study habits and learning objectives; and a strong teacher-student relationship is of critical importance. Although sensory integration is of primary concern at the earliest stages of education, its insights reveal that fundamental operations of the brain are concerned with synthesizing inputs from diverse sources into a more holistic form. This cursory glance over the multidisciplinary uses of integration lends depth, nuance, and coherence toward framing the proposed principles of integrative learning theory.

Integration in Educational and Developmental Theory

Integrative learning can productively draw from theories of education and childhood development. Two frequently cited works in integrative learning literature are Piaget's *Psychology of the Child* and Bloom's *Taxonomy of Educational Objectives*. Although they are prominent figures in educational theory, Piaget and Bloom by no means constitute a comprehensive examination of the subject. A brief survey of their work here provides examples of the importance of integration in theories of learning development. An examination of the principles laid out in *Psychology of the Child* demonstrate deep processes of assimilation between consciousness and experience, as well as the organizational structures derived from this relationship (Piaget and Inhelder 1969). Almost from birth, the human mind begins to incorporate "reality data" into its inherent neurological structures. This assimilation is a rudimentary form of integration, occurring naturally and unconsciously from the earliest stages of mental development. The mind then develops a sense of relationships, "structures of ordering and assembling that constitute a substructure for the future operations of thought" (Piaget and Inhelder 1969, 13). As these organizational schemes become more sophisticated, thought detaches from action, and the child acquires the ability to view the world in terms of symbolic representations. At this stage, language comes into prominence as an incredibly sophisticated semiotic system established and reinforced socially. For Piaget, these semiotic systems are the basis of intelligence.

After eighteen months, the child gradually experiences "decentering" from subjectivity and begins to understand the world as permanent objects, each independently experiencing external causal forces. This enables a new dimension for integrative thinking. As the sense of decentering becomes deeper, it allows for a more complex interaction with the world, including its social, affective, and interpersonal aspects:

> What is most striking about this long period of preparation for and formation of the concrete operations is the functional unity . . . that binds cognitive, playful, affective, social, and moral reactions into a whole. . . . We see the unfolding of a long, integrated process that may be characterized as a transition from subjective centering in all areas to a decentering that is at once cognitive, social, and moral. This process is all the more remarkable in that it reproduces and develops on a large scale at the level of thought what has already taken place on a small scale. (Piaget and Inhelder 1969, 128)

Each developmental stage is a more sophisticated and complex version of earlier stages. In this evolutionary perspective, Piaget holds that all stages of development are inherently holistic, integrating and fusing new functions into a cohesive complex system.

Piaget identifies three basic factors of mental development, all of which are important to integrative learning. The first is the physiological aspect, or the organic growth and maturation of the nervous and endocrine systems. The second factor is the influence of hands-on experiences, where a child learns by interacting with the physical world and observing the results. The third factor concerns social interaction and transmission in which the individual both contributes to and receives useful information from activities of interdependence and cooperation. Children do not simply understand the world through the instruction of adults; instead, they must reconstruct adult understanding for themselves. Piaget's work describes mental development as arising from the synthetic interaction between the social and ontogenetic aspects of the human mind and the way in which the mind regulates itself through a process of disturbance, compensation, and adjustment that is both retroactive and anticipatory. These aspects of Piaget's work indicate that the mind begins integrating at an early age and that metacognition and holistic organization are fundamental processes of mental development.

Bloom's *Taxonomy of Educational Objectives* emphasizes integration as the penultimate of cognitive skills (Bloom 1956). This point has long served as a legitimation of integrative and interdisciplinary studies (see Newell 1999; Repko 2012). Like Piaget, Bloom's *Taxonomy* views simpler behaviors as components of more complex behaviors, stages building upon each other to create more complex, inclusive structures. Learning is based upon critical and reflective thinking skills through which we recognize appropriate information and techniques from previous experiences to apply to novel situations. Education is about the ability to see patterns in the world around us and create meaning from experience. At early stages, this involves breaking material down into its constituent parts, classifying them, understanding the relationships between elements, and recognizing the organizational principles of a structure. Synthesis, as the *Taxonomy* refers to the process of integration, involves the "putting together of elements and parts so as to form a whole. This is a process of working with elements . . . combining them in such a way as to constitute a pattern or structure not clearly there before" (Bloom 1956, 162). This involves creativity "within the limits set by particular problems, materials, or some theoretical and methodological framework" (162) to yield a new product that is clearly more than the sum of its parts. Integrative understanding may involve the formulation of a plan to be carried out or the formation of a new set of abstract relations discovered or deduced from the original understanding in which experiences are organized to form a conceptual structure.

Of particular interest to instructors, Bloom's *Taxonomy* mentions the motivational possibilities of synthesis activities in engaging students through the personal satisfaction of creating something unique to their own thought processes. Integrative learning allows students the latitude to put their personal ideas, emotions, and experiences into their work. Integration leads to creativity, which is at the top of the *Taxonomy*'s hierarchy. Creative efforts require a great deal of freedom for students to determine their own purposes and procedures. Sufficient time must be provided to allow students to familiarize themselves with the task at hand, "exploring different approaches, interpreting and analyzing relevant materials, and trying out various schemes of organization" (Bloom 1956, 173). The process of integration assumes that "*every* experience involves a combination of parts of previous experience with the present experience in such a way that the organism is permanently changed, however slightly" (165). Integrative learning—by emphasizing the way students relate ideas, methods, and values in problem-solving environments—contributes to the retention and generalization of knowledge.

The work of Piaget and Bloom lend weight to the assertion that integration is essential to learning development. Their work emphasizes the application of metacognition, which allows consciousness to assess its own functioning, and the principle of holism as fundamental to the way the mind organizes the world. The brief survey of these two important figures demonstrates that integrative learning has a deep history in theories of education.

The Integrative Nature of the Mind

Bloom's *Taxonomy* (1956) describes the brain and central nervous system acting as a vast organizing system, involving conscious, subconscious, and unconscious processes. The nature of the brain described by neuroscience and cognitive psychology helps provide foundational elements for integrative learning theory. The human mind operates through a very sophisticated process of making sense out of sensory impressions. All sensory input travels through the central nervous system and reaches a thick net of nerves at the top of the spine called the reticular activating system (RAS), which controls arousal, attention, and awareness. This extends into the medulla, which is the primitive core of the brain (the site of our fight-or-flight instincts). According to Berger (2002), "Only that information that the RAS considers appropriate for further processing—because it is essential, unusual, potentially dangerous, action-provoking, interesting, arousing, etc. . . . will pass through the gate and be forwarded to other levels of the brain for further processing" (38). In other words, information must make a significant impression on our nervous system in order to enter the higher levels of consciousness.

The next stage of sensory processing is the limbic system, which assesses emotional responses and acts as another gateway to deeper parts of the brain, including the endocrine system and the neocortex. The limbic system "appraises virtually all incoming information, calling for responses ranging from immediate and instantaneous (to a life-threatening situation) to relaxed (to a pleasant and non-threatening situation)" (Berger 2002, 40). In a relaxed state of mind, stimulus coding takes place in the hippocampus, which "tags" information according to time sequence—providing us with a temporal sense—and determines whether information is significant enough to be stored in permanent memory. Information can then pass onto the neocortex, where storage, synthesis, and actual consciousness take place. The neocortex is divided into two hemispheres connected by the corpus callosum, lobes that process sensory information, and the cerebellum, which coordinates motor functions.

Our capacity for metacognition, which is another important element of integrative learning, originates in the neocortex—specifically, the frontal lobe—"the main function of which is to monitor functions and organize, coordinate, maintain and update information facilitating goal-direction and self-regulation" (Tarricone 2011, 109). The frontal lobe organizes and integrates information into meaningful mental representations. It possesses an executive function that allows for monitoring, conscious control, goal setting, and planning—essential for complex problem solving involving novel solutions to unprecedented situations. The frontal lobe enables self-awareness, which allows for the regulation and coordination of the other aspects of consciousness, including memory.

The human mind possesses integrative functions that have evolved to process information from multiple sources simultaneously and synthesize that information into meaningful, complex patterns. Despite the layers of processing and areas of specialized functions, the whole brain is involved in behavior and thought (Berger 2002). Recent models of brain structure describe it in terms of a dynamic-functional anatomy, emphasizing connections between functional structures and the brain's overall plasticity. In this approach to neuroanatomy, structure and function influence each other in flexible and adaptive ways. Disciplines like cognitive and affective neuroscience

> focus on those neural processes that allow [the mind] to integrate and coordinate neural activity across different regions implicating complex neural networks in predominantly functional terms. Such coordination and organization of neural activity may for instance be achieved by plastic changes allowing neural activity to adapt to the respective challenges and tasks required. Another such mechanism recently discussed is the synchronization of neural activity across different brain regions by coordination of their frequency. (Northoff 2008, 228)

The integration of neuronal activity across different regions of the brain allows for complex functions to occur, such as emotion or cognition. These "connectionist" models view consciousness as the coordinated activity of "the entire neural ensemble comprising the brain" (Levy 2003, 208). Knowledge arises from the nature of connectedness—not the state of individual regions of the brain. Consciousness is distributed not only throughout the brain but also the entire mind/body complex and perpetually undergoes the synthesis of cyclic processes of sensory input, instinctual/emotional reaction, meaning making, experience, decision, memory, reflection, and knowledge. The neural structure of thought is in a constant state of revision as new inputs arrive and are processed. Experience influences the structure of consciousness as much as consciousness influences our experiences (Levy 2003).

Brain-based learning is a recent movement in education that applies a neurological understanding to classroom instruction.[1] Understanding the way the brain processes information grants insights into how integrative learning occurs and how it can be enhanced. The human brain consists of a disproportionately large amount of uncommitted cortex unassigned to any specific neurological function, thus granting us unprecedented flexibility and capacity for learning. According to the principles of brain-based education, meaningful learning requires students to "process information in their own way, along their own time line, and in relation to their own perceptual maps. Sorting, analyzing, and drawing conclusions in the context of one's own life are what makes information stick" (Jensen 2008, 178).

Meaning is created by relevance, emotion, and context. Relevance arises from the way neurons in the brain make connections. Intense emotions trigger neurotransmitters that act as signals to the brain to create attention and emphasis. Here, emotion and cognition are interdependent—meaning arises when neural connections achieve a kind of critical mass, forming connections within the context of previous experiences. Perception is the result of the brain constructing mental maps, which categorize and differentiate information into patterns:

> The cortex is both a pattern maker and a pattern detector. The ability to make meaningful sense out of countless bits of data is critical to understanding and motivation. Since the brain's craving for meaning is automatic, patterning occurs all the time. Each pattern that is discovered can then be added to the learner's perceptual maps. (Jensen 2008, 182)

Neurons are involved in pattern recognition through the way that they connect and resonate with each other. Thus, perceptual maps are neural fields that can shift, rearrange, and reorganize into new fields. The desire to form meaningful patterns is innate and common to children and adults. According to this approach, we naturally and primarily perceive the world in holistic, integrative terms. The physiological nature of the human brain reveals that it is integrative in its structure and operation—continually integrating the world around it. Therefore, findings of neuroscience and cognitive psychology support the principle that integrative learning reflects fundamental characteristics of the human mind.

Two Interrelated Processes

From the integrative nature of the mind, metacognition and holism emerge as two primary processes involved in integrative learning. Like all aspects of consciousness, these processes are interconnected and codependent. Metacognition focuses upon the way integrative learners frame their own minds, while holism describes the way learners organize the complex problems they face and incorporate their educational experience into all aspects of their lives. These two dimensions of integrative learning, internally and externally oriented, must be coordinated together in order to make integrative learning effective. Scholarship on integrative learning consistently emphasizes the importance of metacognition and holism. Integrative education facilitates the "development of reflective and intentional learners who will be able to make meaning of and bring coherence to the disparate paths they take through college and into their lives beyond graduation" (DeZure et al. 2005, 26). According to Huber and Hutchings (2004), integrative learning educates the *whole* person, allowing students breadth of perspective, the ability to make connections across multiple domains and to develop a coherent understanding of the world both within and outside of higher education. Newell (1999) notes that integrative learners acquire such cognitive skills as "critical thinking, reflexive thinking, seeing issues in context, being creative, tolerating ambiguity, maintaining an open mind, and identifying and challenging assumptions," along with affective skills that increase "their empathy and compassion, their respect for difference, and their ability to work in a team" (Newell 1999, 19). According to Klein (2005), in integrative learning "students are engaged in 'making meaning.' Application of knowledge takes precedence over acquisition and mastery of facts alone, activating a dynamic process of question posing, problem posing and solving, decision making, higher-order critical thinking, and reflexivity" (10). All of these cognitive skills and educational objectives employ some combination of metacognition and holism.

Lowy, Bloksberg, and Walberg (1973) provide a comprehensive description of the connection between these two facets of integrative learning and the way they can be mutually incorporated into the educational environment:

> "Integration" refers to both an end state and a process. When conceived of as an end state it implies the attainment of completion, the linking together of parts into a useful, meaningful whole. This takes place within the student, so to speak, and in the final analysis it is a psychological phenomenon. As a process, however, integration refers to the means used to achieve this state of wholeness. We have, there, the concept referring to both an end-product and the means to achieve this end-product. . . .

> The issue for education then becomes how to organize the learning experiences into courses, field experiences, and other areas of educational life in order to maximize the cumulative effect of all learning experiences toward the goal of achieving a state of wholeness or completion; that is, integration. (vii–viii)

Metacognition and holism are involved in a synthetic dialectical relationship between structure and process. However, in order to better incorporate metacognition and holism into the development of integrative learning theory, I explore these concepts individually in some depth.

Integrative Learning Engages Metacognition

The importance of metacognition to integrative learning cannot be understated, as it plays a critical role in planning, goal setting, self-evaluation, memory, learning, and academic success (Huber and Hutchings 2004; Sperling, Richmond, Ramsay, and Klapp 2012). For integrative learning, the need for students to become *intentional learners* capable of making connections for themselves specifically engages metacognition. As Huber, Hutchings, and Gale (2005) declare, "Helping students to become more self-aware and purposeful—more intentional—about their studies is a powerful idea, and it is, in our view, the key to fostering integrative learning" (6). According to the Committee on Behavioral and Social Sciences and the Education National Research Council (2003), "Teaching practices congruent with a metacognitive approach to learning include those that focus on sense-making, self-assessment, and reflection on what worked and what needs improving. These practices have been shown to increase the degree to which students transfer their learning to new settings and events" (10). In describing student portfolios, Flower and Rhodes (2005) identify the necessity for "student reflections on their own learning in the context of the general education goals" (22).

Vermunt and Vermetten (2004) call for "process-oriented" teaching aimed at promoting "learning to learn"—enabling learning patterns that focus on knowledge production and application, thereby transferring control of the educational process from teachers to students. This approach links self-diagnosis of student learning and preconception of study habits with individually tailored teaching methods, creating "a powerful way to activate students to reflect on their own way of learning and on alternative possibilities" (378). Their research in this very intentional style of learning indicated positive effects on learning outcomes. Process-oriented teaching demonstrates that it is "indeed possible to influence student learning patterns in such way that . . . their level of deep processing and self-regulation increases" (380–81).

Doğanay and Demir (2011) also emphasize the importance of metacognition to learning:

> Learning requires the active participation of the learners in their own learning by interacting with the environment. What enhances this active participation of learners is metacognition. Metacognition is a thinking system. It is the act of learning to learn, focusing, step by step planning what is going to be done, evaluating every phase of the learning process, and making the necessary arrangements accordingly. (2036)

Metacognitive skills improve questioning skills, develop social skills, enhance cognitive regulation and time management, and develop critical thinking and problem-solving skills; they are essential to academic success (Doğanay and Demir 2011). Sperling et al. (2012) found that metacognition is a "significant predictor" in science achievement and overall GPA scores (5).

In their revision of Bloom's *Taxonomy*, Anderson and Krathwohl (2001) place metacognitive knowledge as its own category of educational objectives. They explain their rationale for this decision at some length:

> Although behaviorist psychology models generally excluded ideas such as consciousness, awareness, self-reflection, self-regulation, and thinking about and controlling one's own thinking and learning, current cognitive and social constructivist models of learning emphasize the importance of these activities. Because these activities focus on cognition itself, the prefix *meta* is added to reflect the idea that metacognition is about or "above" or "transcends" cognition. Social constructivist models also stress self-reflective activity as an important aspect of learning. In this case, both cognitive and social constructivist models agree about the importance of facilitating students' thinking about their own thinking. Accordingly, we have added this new category to the Taxonomy to reflect current research and theory on the importance of metacognitive knowledge in learning. (43)

They contend that students need not only self-awareness but, more importantly, the ability to gauge the accuracy of their self-knowledge.

For Anderson and Krathwohl (2001), metacognitive knowledge includes awareness of cultural norms and other types of situational learning. Therefore, metacognition enables learners to navigate the complexities of relativistic social and educational environments. Vermunt and Vermetten (2004) found that intentional learning increased students' associations between various learning styles and strategies and helped them develop a high sense of internal coherence among learning components, especially for older learners. The implication is that through intentional learning techniques, students come to assert increasingly more control over their own learning process, which in turn amplifies its generalizability to other domains. Furthermore, Vermunt and Vermetten (2004) found that students with a more relativistic viewpoint had a higher affinity for metacognitive learning styles, such as "deep processing, self-regulation, construction of knowledge as a conception of learning, and a personally interested learning orientation" (374).

Understanding the complex facets of metacognition helps deepen integrative learning theory and practice. Tarricone (2011) attempts to draw the various literatures on metacognition together into an overall schema of its various characteristics and applications. Metacognition includes reflection—the ability to form stimulated connections from previous experience to bear upon similar problems—which helps spur new learning and solve novel complex problems. The reflective process many times includes a kind of internal dialogue, wherein one's mind is speaking to itself. In this state, learners are reliant upon their own metacognitive processes for planning, monitoring, goal setting, and problem solving. Introspection, self-knowledge, self-awareness, and reflection are all components of metacognition and are necessary for complex problem solving. "Complex problem contexts challenge and stimulate self-doubt. Doubt about knowledge and the efficacy of strategies stimulates reflection. This instigates the search for and development of effective problem-solving strategies" (Tarricone 2011, 26).

Metacognition is also involved in critical thinking skills. "Critical reflection generally occurs during challenging, demanding, stimulating and engaging situations, which draw in and depend upon higher-order, inductive processes affected by beliefs, values, judgments, reasoning and inferences. This inductive process involves challenging one's own thinking, especially in problem-solving situations" (Tarricone 2011, 29). Critical reflection promotes personal transformation by creating an internal dialectic that critiques prior knowledge and evaluates new knowledge. It involves reasoning, judgment, and analysis—not only of experience and knowledge but also the very strategies and processes from which knowledge is acquired and assessed. Critical thinking can be developed through the use of concept mapping. Concept maps provide scaffolding for metacognitive questions and reflective education, promoting self-reflection through critical evaluation of connections between concepts. These characteristics reflect the earlier theories of Piaget and Bloom; metacognitive knowledge develops in complex problem-solving situations.

Another aspect of metacognition is *metamemory*, an evaluation of the way memories are stored and accurately retrieved. "This introspective knowledge enables the selection, evaluation and modification of strategies during problem solving" (Tarricone 2011, 83). The ability to recall pertinent information and develop effective mnemonic strategies in a conscious and deliberate way is essential for complex problem solving. The regulation and organization of knowledge from memory facilitates task sequencing and time management skills. These processes are "stimulated in complex, demanding memory task situations especially where there is task and strategy novelty, difficult and complex sequencing and execution of actions" (Tarricone 2011, 105).

The metacognitive faculty of self-regulation is of particular importance to integrative learning. Students use metacognition to recognize the effectiveness of their own learning, allowing them to adjust learning strategies and monitor their levels of motivation (Sperling et al. 2012). Metacognitive experiences allow us to retrieve and apply problem-solving strategies. Self-regulation involves consciously and voluntarily reviewing mental processes, including metacognitive processes themselves, in order to select strategies effectively and develop better problem-solving skills.

> The centerpiece of metacognitive theory is strategy selection and use. Not only are specific strategies essential for effective learning and problem solving, they also provide the context for training higher-level planning and executive skills explicitly as well as representing the basis for restructuring attributional beliefs and enhancing self-efficacy. (Tarricone 2011, 146)

Metacognition allows problem solvers to reflect on the specific elements of the task at hand, recall strategies that have (or have not) worked in similar situations, and match strategies to the task in order to facilitate problem solving in different contexts. "Both knowledge of task objectives and knowledge of strategies interact and depend upon each other for successful task outcomes" (Tarricone 2011, 151).

Intentional (i.e., self-regulated) learners are more dedicated and engaged with their own learning processes—more focused, goal-oriented, persistent, and aware of their own beliefs and volitions. "A high level of self-regulated learning is reliant upon a strong sense of self, including self-control, self-efficacy, self-esteem, self-attainment and self-actualisation" (Tarricone 2011, 168). Self-regulation processes include feelings of knowing or ignorance, and judgments about memory. "Such judgments then give rise to cognitive control processes such as selection of type of processing to be performed, how much study time will be given to different materials, selection of retrieval search strategy, and finally termination of search" (Roberts et al. 2012, 86). Students able to regulate their own learning acquire more flexible thinking and better study skills. A high level of metacognitive skills also has been shown to increase teacher performance and effectiveness (Doğanay and Demir 2011).

Metacognition, for all its benefits, is not an easy thing to master. For example, depression can be described as a breakdown of metacognition, where one fails to accurately assess his or her own emotional and physical experience or where one's judgment of self or others is distorted in an extremely negative direction (Northoff 2008). Furthermore, metacognitive activity can lead to a sense of intellectual vertigo, a feeling of uncertainty that many students find uncomfortable or even unbearable. The tension caused by this decentering can cause cognitive dissonance. "To change or remove the perceptual guidelines can result in deep loss, abandonment, or chaos. This process can be painful and strongly resisted until a new order with a sense of security is developed" (Caple 1995, as cited by Newell 1999, 18). Metacognition can cause integrative learners to question deeply held religious, political, or cultural beliefs as well as accustomed judgments about class, race, or gender issues. "Most threatening of all are challenges to the perspective of one's culture, because they call into question the entire system of meaning by which students make sense of the world" (Newell 1999, 22).

This study of metacognition supplies a working understanding of its characteristics, along with a rationale for its importance to integrative learning theory. Our ability to monitor and adjust our own thinking processes empowers the integration of experience into meaningful patterns of understanding. Integrative learning provides a solution to the vertigo that arises from metacognitive awareness by asserting that "learning how to learn" essentially deepens our capacity to make sense of the world and positively navigate our way through it. Furthermore, the integrative approach to the world finds comprehensive stability through holism.

Integrative Learning Is Holistic

Holistic thinking progresses from the either/or thinking of dualism to the relativism of multiple mutually valid points of view, eventually attaining a sense of cohesion in the face of uncertainty (Huber et al. 2005). Holism is the capacity for complex, changing systems to possess dynamic equilibrium and patterns of self-organization. It describes the ways in which the mind and the world mutually and reflexively organize themselves. In other words, internally and externally, consciousness and reality possess holistic characteristics. The true power of holism comes from the manner in which this relationship is realized.

Holism has long been the hallmark of integrative learning. In an early article on interdisciplinarity, Bailis (1984–1985) surveyed the basic formulations of holism. Wholes are conceived of as emerging from the association of parts or from the organizational principles that hold parts together. Holistic thinking rejects analysis and mechanistic approaches to knowledge because these approaches separate the parts of a complex system and isolate them for individual investigation. Holism instead examines phenomena in terms of their relational properties. Altering any aspect of a holistic system affects all the parts of the system, along with its overall operation. All facets of a holistic system are dynamically interdependent. According to theories of holism, emergent characteristics arise that are not reducible to the properties of the interacting parts, which can display entirely different characteristics depending on how they are arranged or organized. Holistic thinking involves developing a conceptual framework that accounts for interrelational and emergent properties of whole systems.

However, Bailis (2002) cautions that integration often occurs across domains that are different—if not incommensurable. In order to compensate for this, integrative work involves various strategies of holism and reductionism. Integration creates overarching conceptions of knowledge applied to specific complex problems, or "highly generalized treatments of the fields comprising a domain of knowledge" (7). The purpose of integration is to develop formulations that allow complementary connections between the partial knowledge of more specialized fields. Integrative strategies involve "strongly reductionist approaches in which apparently different phenomena are represented as manifestations of the same underlying processes. Once grasped, such representations constitute syntheses in the sense of allowing the same or similar understandings of very different classes of things" (7). Holism provides a way of finding common ground within the conceptual clash of knowledge domains by identifying underlying principles that mutually frame the contending domains.

Because the purpose of integration is to synthesize diverse perspectives into a cohesive whole, it conceptually benefits from theories of complexity. Complex adaptive systems theory examines the way diverse and semiautonomous agents within a system learn from interacting within each other in nonlinear relationships that in turn affect the state of the whole system (McDaniel and Lanham 2010). These systems are by nature unpredictable and uncertain, forever shifting their internal and external relationships. Agents in a system continually self-organize and coevolve with their environment. "Emergent properties are dynamic characteristics of a system that are created through the interactions among agents over time. Because of the way in which these properties emerge over time, they cannot be explained through analysis and understanding of its parts" (McDaniel and Lanham 2010, 57). As the system changes, agents within it must continually reevaluate their positions, which leads to learning and changes the dynamics of the system. Holistic systems are characterized by *dynamic equilibrium*—the ability to maintain cohesion while undergoing constant change.

Podd'iakov (2012), drawing from the theories of Vygotsky, describes holistic thinking as essential to mental development and the structure of the mind:

> The mind is born as a holistic entity, undergoes intensive complication, and develops during childhood and adolescence without loss of holism at any phase of this development. A temporary loss of holism in some sphere of a child's mind results in developmental crises that are overcome by restoring this holism. (64)

During childhood activities, the main function of the mind is to connect facets of experiences into a meaningful and coherent whole, proceeding from simple, homogeneous structures to more complex organizational patterns that show the relationship between increasingly sophisticated internal elements. Integrative processes create holistic systems by mapping out in "broad strokes" the horizons of experience and developing an ongoing structural context by which we are able to judge and make sense of the world as we explore it. Educational experiences in and out of the classroom should be consistent and mutually reinforcing, allowing students to transfer knowledge across various domains of their experience. This kind of integrative environment produces the synergistic effects that are characteristic of complex systems (Newell 2007).

Contextuality is another holistic aspect of integrative learning, involving a holistic understanding of how classroom instruction can be meaningfully applied to life and work outside the university.

> Contextuality, conflict, and change are the defining parameters of this kind of learning. Contextuality is a different metaphor of knowledge and education than unity, which assumed consistent, logical relations within a linear framework with the expectation of achieving certainty and universality. Contextuality accepts the contingent character of knowledge and action. Students need to tolerate ambiguity and paradox if they are to take grounded stands in the face of multiple and sometimes conflicting perspectives. The relational skills they gain also foster the ability to adapt knowledge in unexpected and changing contexts. (Klein 2005, 10)

Programs such as the Integrated Learning Project attempt to restore curriculum from its fragmented nature to allow students to make connections between their various courses and with their outside lives (Arcario, Eynon, and Clark, 2005). Integrative learners are expected to adapt skills acquired in the classroom to situations in the workplace, community, or other aspects of personal life (Humphreys 2005). In order to understand something, students need to make connections between new and prior knowledge, integrating it with existing schemas and cognitive frameworks. "Since concepts are the building blocks for these schemas and frameworks, conceptual knowledge provides a basis for understanding" (Anderson and Krathwohl 2001, 70).

Establishing context often involves interpretation in which one representation form can be translated to another, finding correspondence between two or more ideas or experiences. Thus, creativity is an important aspect of holistic thinking. Creativity "involves putting elements together to form a coherent or functional whole . . . Students make a new product by mentally reorganizing some elements or parts into a pattern or structure not clearly present before" (Anderson and Krathwohl 2001, 84). As opposed to understanding how elements fit together in a preexisting whole, creativity involves developing a novel structure, pattern, or product. Creativity is associated with the processes of generating, planning, and producing. In order to create, a student must produce a product—the quality of which is primarily judged by the student's own goals and desires.

Holism enables integrative learning to restore a sense of equilibrium to the dynamic, ever-changing relationship between consciousness and reality. It allows learners to make connections between the very divergent aspects of their lives and place those connections into a cohesive, interconnected web of understanding. This holistic web can be seen as a goal of integrative learning, teaching students to make sense of the world in a much more sophisticated and productive manner than conventional teaching methods can produce.

Philosophical Conclusions

A deeper understanding of the integrative nature of the mind, along with the processes of metacognition and holism presented here help establish the importance of these principles for integrative learning theory. These principles rest upon epistemological and ontological assumptions. The assumption that the human mind is essentially integrative is founded upon the assertion that the human mind developed through evolutionary processes over eons of interactions with the world around it. Through biochemical processes, the human brain produces an electrical field that allows us to respond effectively to our environment. This field is integrative in nature and interacts with the world integratively. If human consciousness was inherently dysfunctional and unable to interact adequately with the world, it would not have survived the trial and error of evolutionary development. Yet our consciousness is a remarkably successful adaptation. Through our natural capacities for abstract reasoning, symbolic representation, and other integrative faculties, we have come to deeply understand a great deal about the world and the principles that guide it.

> Consciousness is a powerful reality processor, able to extract a torrent of information from the senses and organize it into a complex, dynamic web of associations, of thoughts, feelings, memories, and understandings of how it all works together. The mind is fluid and dynamic, constantly reassessing the world in its struggle to adapt. (Welch 2012, 118)

The integrative nature of the mind is an essential adaptation to the world and a reliable method for producing knowledge.

However, the assumption that the human mind reliably integrates the world around it is made problematic by metacognition. Our ability to reflect on our own experiences, to control the way we assess and organize reality, creates a kind of disjunction between our thoughts and the world. As brilliant as we can be, human beings are quite capable of delusion, misinterpretation, and miscalculation. If we were purely instinctual creatures and confined to more direct and immediate responses to our environment, our evolutionary development would have been restrained to a life of stimulus and reaction. However, with metacognition, we are able to create a subjective distance between consciousness and reality and to construct versions of reality that adhere to an internal epistemological order. Metacognition thus generates a paradox: Our ability to reflect upon our own thoughts has the potential to both distract us from reality and deepen our understanding of it. Fortunately, this is not an either/or proposition; these two facets of metacognition form a holistic synthesis. Metacognition is a complex skill that can be cultivated and honed into a powerful approach to knowledge. Our ability to decenter metacognitively actually is necessary to integrative thought. The awareness of our own thought processes and the ability to evaluate our notions of truth grant us an incredible amount of control over our inherited instincts and cognitive processes. Metacognition allows us to evaluate our own delusions and center knowledge through integration. Integrative learning provides a sophisticated method to reorient ourselves to the way our minds naturally make sense of reality.

Finally, the nature of holism provides a way of describing the integrative character of both the mind and the world. Holism maintains a dynamic equilibrium in complex systems and appears to be a fundamental way the universe organizes itself. The cosmos is an incredibly chaotic place, created in an explosion of energy so intense that contemporary physics cannot explain it. Yet, from this explosion, the laws of nature emerged; organizational patterns developed into a universe of form in motion, coherent and comprehensible. At its basis is the principle of holism and the capacity to form order from chaos. These patterns allow the cosmos to make sense. Holistic patterns are never strictly deterministic; rather, they arise and transform within the interaction of cohesive principles. Far from being reductionistic, holism creates a space of dynamic equilibrium in which complexity thrives. Because both the human mind and the world it inhabits seem to mutually possess holistic characteristics, this supplies an epistemological avenue for understanding.

Synchronizing the internal and the external aspects of being is the essential art and craft of integrative learning. Integrative learning is an approach to life, which offers its practitioners the promise of mastering their own consciousness and the ability to productively understand the world in all its dynamic complexity. In order to place such goals in context, the ancient concept of wisdom is worth revisiting here. "Wisdom is the synthesis of all avenues of insight—rational, experiential, intuitive, physical, cultural, and emotional—it breaks down all boundaries between categories of knowledge and returns them to holistic understanding. Wisdom creates equilibrium among these faculties, minimizing their individual weaknesses and achieving synergy" (Welch 2007, 149–50). Wisdom helps provide a conceptual basis for integrative learning theory, synthesizing the principles of integrative nature, metacognition, and holism.

References

Arcario, P., B. Eynon, and J. E. Clark. 2005. "Making Connections: Integrated Learning, Integrated Lives." *Peer Review* 7 (4): 15–17.

Anderson, L. W., and D. R. Krathwohl. 2001. *A Taxonomy for Learning, Teaching, and Assessing: A Revision of Bloom's Taxonomy of Educational Objectives.* New York: Longman.

Bailis, S. 1984–1985. "Against and for Holism: A Review and Rejoinder to D. C. Phillips." *Issues in Integrative Studies* 3: 16–41.

———. 2002. "Interdisciplinary Curriculum Design and Instructional Innovation: Notes on the Social Science Program at San Francisco State University." In *Innovations in interdisciplinary teaching,* edited by C. Haynes, 3–16). Phoenix: Oryx Press, American

Council on Education.

Berger, D. S. 2002. *Music Therapy, Sensory Integration, and the Autistic Child.* London: Jessica Kingsley.

Bloom, B. S. 1956. *Taxonomy of Educational Objectives: The Classification of Educational Goals.* 1st ed. New York: Longman.

Carnegie Foundation and Association of American Colleges and Universities. 2004. "Statement on Integrative Learning." https://www.aacu.org/integrative_ learning/pdfs/ ILP_Statement.pdf.

Commission on Behavioral and Social Sciences and Education National Research Council. 2003. *How People Learn: Brain, Mind, Experience, and School.* Washington, DC: National Academy Press.

DeZure, D., M. Babb, and S. Waldmann. 2005. "Integrative Learning Nationwide: Emerging Themes and Practices." *Peer Review* 7 (4): 24–28.

Doğanay, A., and Ö. Demir. 2011. "Comparison of the Level of Using Metacognitive Strategies during Study between High-Achieving and Low-Achieving Prospective Teachers." *Educational Sciences: Theory and Practice* 11 (4): 2036–43.

El-Halwagi, M. 2012. *Sustainable Design through Process Integration.* Amsterdam: Elsevier.

Flower, M. J., and T. L. Rhodes. 2005. "Integrative Learning, E-Portfolios, and the Transfer Students." *Peer Review* 7 (4): 21–23.

Huber, M. T., & P. Hutchings. 2004. *Integrative Learning: Mapping the Terrain.* Washington, DC: Carnegie Foundation for the Advancement of Teaching.

Huber, M. T., P. Hutchings, and R. Gale. 2005. "Integrative Learning for Liberal Education." *Peer Review* 7 (4): 4–7.

Humphreys, D. 2005. "Why Integrative Learning? Why Now?" *Peer Review* 7 (4): 30–31.

Isbell, C., and R. Isbell. 2007. *Sensory Integration: A Guide for Preschool Teachers.* Beltsville, MD: Gryphon House.

Jensen, E. 2008. *Brain-Based Learning: A New Paradigm of Teaching.* Thousand Oaks, CA: Corwin Press.

Klein, J. T. 2005. "Integrative Learning and Interdisciplinary Studies." *Peer Review* 7 (4): 8–10.

Komaladi, L. 2012. "Building Deep Christians: Mind and Heart in action." *Common Ground Journal* 9 (2): 23–31.

Levy, D. A. 2003. "Neural Holism and Free Will." *Philosophical Psychology* 16 (2): 205.

Lowy, L., L. M. Bloksberg, and H. J. Walberg. 1973. *Teaching Records: Integrative Learning and Teaching Project.* New York: Council on Social Work Education.

McDaniel, Jr., R. R., and H. J. Lanham. 2010. "Sustainable Development: Complexity and the Problem of Balance." In *Pragmatic Sustainability: Theoretical and Practical Tools,* edited by S. Moore, 51–66). London: Routledge.

Newell, W. H. 1999. "The Promise of Integrative Learning." *About Campus* 4 (2): 17.

———. 2007. "Decision-Making in Interdisciplinary Studies." In *Handbook of Decision*

Making, edited by G. Morcol, 245–64. New York: Marcel Dekker.

Northoff, G. 2008. "Neuropsychiatry." *European Archives of Psychiatry and Clinical Neuroscience* 258 (4): 226–38. doi: 10.1007/s00406-007-0783-6.

Oliver, J. E. 2010. *The paradoxes of integration: Race, Neighborhood, and Civic Life in Multiethnic America*. Chicago: University of Chicago Press.

Piaget, J., and B. Inhelder. 1969. *The Psychology of the Child*. New York: Basic.

Podd'iakov, N. 2012. "The Domination of Integration Processes in the Development of Preschool-Age Children." *Journal of Russian and East European Psychology* 50 (2): 64–74.

Rakel, D., and W. Jonas. 2012. "Creating Optimal Healing Environments." In *Integrative Medicine*, edited by D. Rakel, 156–214. Philadelphia: Elsevier.

Repko, A. 2012. *Interdisciplinary Research: Process and Theory*. 2nd ed. Los Angeles: Sage.

Reynolds, C., and K. S. Reynolds. 2010. *A Study of the Effectiveness of Sensory Integration Therapy on Neuro-Physiological Development*. Dubai: British Institute for Learning Development.

Roberts, W. A., N. McMillan, E. Musolino, and M. Cole. 2012. "Information Seeking in Animals: Metacognition?" *Comparative Cognition and Behavior Reviews* 7: 85–109.

Schneider, C. G. 2003. "Liberal Education and Integrative Learning." *Issues in Integrative Studies* 21: 1–8.

Sperling, R. A., A. S. Richmond, C. M. Ramsay, and M. Klapp. 2012. "The Measurement and Predictive Ability of Metacognition in Middle School Learners." *Journal of Educational Research* 105 (1): 1–7. doi: 10.1080/00220671.2010.514690.

Springer, M. 1994. *Watershed: A Successful Voyage into Integrative Learning*. Westerville, OH: National Middle School Association.

Tarricone, P. 2011. *The Taxonomy of Metacognition*. New York: Psychology Press.

Vermunt, J., and Y. Vermetten. 2004. "Patterns in Student Learning: Relationships between Learning Strategies, Conceptions of Learning, and Learning Orientations." *Educational Psychology Review* 16 (4): 359–84. doi: 10.1007/s10648-004-0005-y.

Weil, A. T. 2009. "Why Integrative Oncology?" In *Integrative Oncology*, edited by D. Abrams and A. Weil, 46–78. Oxford: Oxford University Press.

Welch, J. 2007. "The Role of Intuition in Interdisciplinary Insight." *Issues in Integrative Studies* 25: 131–55.

———. 2012. "Interdisciplinarity and the Question of Being." *Issues in Integrative Studies* 29: 99–127.

Chapter 3

No Integration without Differentiation: A Critical Look at Integrative Studies

Michael Yeo, PhD, Laurentian University

Integrative learning has become something of a watchword for a variety of specific innovations in higher education today and the rallying cry for a veritable educational reform movement. Klein (2005) certainly is correct to note that integrative learning is not new. However, as it has emerged in the past decade or so, largely due to the impetus of the Association of American Colleges & Universities (AAC&U) and shaped by its work,[1] integrative learning is at least distinct, even as it echoes and resonates with older ideas and reform movements.

Expectations are high. Among other things, integrative learning is championed as a solution to the fragmentation of the undergraduate curriculum and a way of bridging the gap between academic coursework and an increasingly complex real world. The hope is that by revising curricula in view of the goal of integration and developing in students the capacity to better integrate their courses with one another and to integrate their academic life with life and the world beyond, students will be better positioned to "put the pieces together and develop habits of mind that prepare them to make informed judgments in the conduct of personal, professional, and civic life" (American Association of Colleges & Universities and Carnegie Foundation, 2004).

Notwithstanding the enthusiasm for integrative learning today and the considerable innovation that is happening in its name in various colleges and universities, the term itself is not well defined. The AAC&U and Carnegie Foundation (2004) "Statement on Integrative Learning" is helpful in referring to the goal of "fostering students' abilities to integrate learning—across courses, over time, and between campus and community life," but this tells us little about what integrative learning is, much less how to put it into practice. In their nationwide review of integrative learning initiatives, DeZure, Babb, and Waldmann (2005) report finding "that campuses do not use the language of integration consistently" and that "the phrase 'integrative learning' has limited common meaning" (24). This finding was reinforced by self-reports from many of the 139 colleges and universities they looked at, which admitted "with candour that they are still actively grappling with the meaning of integrative learning" (28). The authors also found that concepts associated with integrated learning initiatives, such as *learning community*, *capstone*, and *first-year experience*, were applied differently by different institutions (24).

One could make too much of definitional uncertainty since, notwithstanding the "limited common meaning" of the term, DeZure, Babb, and Waldmann discern a reasonably consistent pattern of common and recurrent themes associated with integrative learning. Beyond this, one would probably search in vain for a definition that would give unity to the diverse range of initiatives occurring in the name of integrative learning. Any such candidate definition would purchase precision and specificity at the price of stifling experimentation and excluding some initiatives inspired or animated by the term. The alternative is to embrace the generality of the term, recognizing, as the AAC&U and Carnegie Foundation Statement (2004) puts it, that "Integrative learning comes in many varieties: connecting skills and knowledge from multiple sources and experiences; applying theory to practice in various settings; utilizing diverse and even contradictory points of view; and understanding issues and positions contextually." This is the approach that Klein (2005) takes in defining integrative learning as

> an umbrella term for structures, strategies, and activities that bridge numerous divides, such as high school and college, general education and the major, introductory and advanced levels, experiences inside and outside the classroom, theory and practice, and disciplines and fields. (8)

Nonetheless, the lack of a common meaning for integrative learning and the diversity of varieties that exist under this umbrella complicates theorizing about it. Such theorization that has occurred has been rather cursory and, for the most part, issued from an advocacy position committed to advancing integrative learning as a cause and movement. In this chapter, I raise some key theoretical questions and concerns about integrative learning as it emerges today by critically comparing and contrasting it with interdisciplinarity.[2] Interdisciplinarity is instructive not only because it shares many affinities with integrative learning but also because it has a longer institutional history and a more developed body of theoretical literature.[3]

Any generalizations I make in questioning integrative studies, although evidenced in recurrent tendencies and trends, will no doubt fail to do it justice.[4] However, recognizing the diversity of integrative learning initiatives and of the undevelopedness of theorizing about it to date, such criticism—as may be explicit or implicit in the questions and concerns I raise—is not intended categorically. No doubt none of my concerns will resonate with all integrative learning initiatives and theorizations, and some concerns will resonate more with some than with others. Regardless, to integrative learning advocates, such questioning may seem critical and negative. Indeed, it is. However, my questions and concerns are primarily theoretical and, even if not quite on the mark, intended to contribute to theorizing about integrative learning. As concerns advocacy, one would expect that the integrative learning movement would be able to prove the merits of its cause better and develop in a manner that is most fully integrative by questioning its fundamental suppositions and incorporating, or at least considering, the negative, however inadequately expressed.

Integrative Learning and Interdisciplinarity: Obvious Commonalities

Integrative learning and interdisciplinarity have much in common. Both have inspired and galvanized contemporary reform movements in higher education. In diagnosing what is wrong with much of higher education, proponents of both emphasize the problem of the fragmentation or compartmentalization of knowledge in increasingly specialized disciplines and subdisciplines that speak different languages and, in a sense, project different and incommensurate worlds. As reform movements, both seek to create institutional space for learning that opens onto a shared world, reality, or problem that is only partially and therefore inadequately understood from the vantage point of this or that discipline. Integrative learning and interdisciplinarity both face the challenge that the division of knowledge into disciplines is entrenched institutionally in divisions of power, with disciplinary departments being vigilant about preserving and protecting their territory under conditions of scarcity and competition for often dwindling resources.[5]

More importantly from a theoretical point of view, integration is central to both. This is, of course, obvious in the case of integrative learning, in which the word itself, in its adjectival form, modifies the term *learning*. However, the term *integration*, or the cognate term *synthesis*, also figures essentially in standard definitions of interdisciplinarity.[6]

Other commonalities between integrative learning and interdisciplinarity could be enumerated, and the ones I have enumerated warrant more careful elaboration than I have given them. However, important differences and points of contrast also exist. Consideration of these will be more useful than commonalities for probing the theoretical assumptions and foundations of integrative learning.

What Is Integration?

Does *integration* mean the same thing for interdisciplinarity as for integrative learning? An obvious difference comes into view if we ask for each what is supposed to get integrated. In interdisciplinarity, what gets integrated are disciplines, or more precisely, some body of work (concepts, methods, lines of analysis, conversations, interpretative frames, etc.) issuing from disciplines, interdisciplines, or fields of study. What is taken or borrowed from the disciplines includes diverse and heterogeneous elements relevant to whatever phenomenon is under study. More complete knowledge of the phenomenon is gained from these multiple knowledges, each of which contributes something useful or revealing. Interdisciplinarity brings the disciplinarity elements into interaction or interrelation, as contrasted with multidisciplinarity, which merely combines them in an additive way: interdisciplinarity *integrates* disciplinary elements to produce a knowledge that is more than the sum of its parts.

Terminologies that characterize integration in interdisciplinarity vary and are somewhat imprecise. The metaphor of dialogue certainly is helpful and instructive (multidisciplinarity, by contrast, would be a series of monologues), but other terms—such as *synthesis*, *synergy*, and *transformation*—are helpful also. In any event, the core idea in interdisciplinary theory is that the work of integrating disciplines is supposed to achieve a new and more adequate knowledge of the phenomenon under study, knowledge that could not be achieved by the disciplines considered separately or even combined together additively.

Integrative learning goes beyond interdisciplinarity in that it seeks to integrate not only disciplines with other disciplines but also disciplines with life perspectives and reality outside the academy. What does *integration* mean in this context? Leaving interdisciplinarity aside for the moment, there is a sense in which learning in virtually any discipline involves integrating life experience. One would be a poor student of literature who did not bring his or her life to bear in the reading of literature and the literature being read to bear on his or her life. Likewise, one could hardly come to understand the sociology of the family, for example, if one did not flesh out its concepts and theories with one's experience of being in a family, and one could not be said to understand it at all if one could not bring its concepts and theories to bear upon one's own family experiences. Integration in this sense can require considerable stretching, but if this is what integration means, surely it is essential even in disciplinary learning. No disciplinarian could get along without it. Calling such learning *integrative* would accord well with the ordinary usage of the term, but that would only amount to giving a new name to disciplinary learning as it has always been practiced. In this meaning, integrative learning would hardly make sense as a call for reform. If the phrase *integrative learning* is to mean something more than this, it would be better to reserve some other term, such as *application*, to capture the way in which learning even in a disciplinary sense involves moving back and forth from life to text and text to life.[7] The question would then remain: What does it means to speak of integrating disciplinary knowledge and life experience?

An alternative approach would be to suppose that what is to be integrated with disciplinary knowledge is not one's life experience as such, or not just that, but rather something like nondisciplinary or extradisciplinary perspectives or insights. For example, in this sense we could speak of integrating knowledge of this or that disease as it would be analyzed and codified in some discipline (for example, in biology, sociology, economics, rhetoric, or philosophy of medicine) with the insight and perspective of some group, such as those who live with the disease or who care for those who do. For virtually any matter that could be a subject of disciplinary study or object of disciplinary knowledge—from aardvarks to zebras, aphasia to Zoroastrianism—one could identify some individuals or group or community with a perspective.

Certainly there is value in extradisciplinary perspectives, and in some cases knowledge of them may even be indispensable to acquiring an adequate knowledge of a subject matter. However, here also it is not clear that integration is the right term or whether it requires us to go beyond disciplinary learning and inquiry. For example, a cultural anthropologist seeking to understand how knowledge is transmitted from one generation to another in a given culture would be leaving much of importance out of the account and probably could not undertake such a study at all if he or she did not achieve at least some rudimentary understanding of the perspective (or perspectives) of people living in that culture. However, in such a case it would be odd to say that the anthropologist was integrating knowledge from his or her discipline with perspectives from the culture under study. To begin with, there is the question of how best to gain the desired knowledge of cultural perspective, which involves choosing among or drawing from methods for getting at perspectives in the discipline (or to be borrowed from other disciplines) and interpreting or coding the data. In a sense, learning these perspectives would be analogous to learning another discipline but with the important difference that the anthropologist would be drawing from his or her discipline to develop knowledge of those perspectives. The anthropologist would not be *integrating* these perspectives—at least not in the first instance—but rather *studying* them, using whatever methods best did the job.

A more promising possibility for specifying the meaning of integration when disciplines are to be integrated with extradisciplinary perspectives is to think of them as knowledges or ways of knowing: not the knowledge of a perspective as acquired by disciplinary methods but the perspective itself (however it comes to be known) considered as being or containing knowledge. For example, along these lines one could speak of integrating indigenous knowledge concerning some matter (e.g., the migration of birds, the healing properties of plants, or resilience) with knowledge of the same matter in disciplines such ornithology, botany, or medicine. This would resonate with interdisciplinary integration conceived on the model of dialogue.[8] However, elevating nondisciplinary perspectives to the epistemic status of knowledges leaves open important questions, such as how these perspectives are to be known and in precisely what sense they constitute knowledges. Additionally, elevating such perspectives to the status of knowledges or ways of knowing could mean erasing, leveling, or minimizing the importance of distinct epistemic features of disciplinary knowledge and ways of knowing and of disciplinary methods and controls designed to validate knowledge claims and screen out falsity and prejudice.

What Guides the Selection of the Disciplines to Be Integrated?

Another path for questioning the meaning of integration in integrative learning is opened up if we consider how and why disciplines to be integrated are selected and with a view to what end. Whereas interdisciplinarity seeks to integrate some select disciplines, integrative learning seeks to integrate all of the disciplines—or at least some significant subset—that figure as pieces in a student's curriculum (and the curriculum with reality beyond the curriculum). The key thing here is the principle of selection. In interdisciplinarity, the disciplines to be integrated are selected in virtue of their potential to contribute to a more complete knowledge of some complex theme, question, or problem at issue. The pursuit of this knowledge is primary, and contributory relevance to it guides the selection of disciplines. Integration is not an end in itself but rather a necessary means to the end of gathering knowledge that otherwise could not be acquired or acquired as completely, even if developing the capacity to integrate has benefits beyond the immediate epistemic objective. This quality of being purpose-driven informs the often-used metaphor of *borrowing* when discussing interdisciplinary learning: One borrows with a purpose in mind, in view of which one selects what one needs to borrow.

In the case of integrative learning, integration, and development of the capacity for integration to be applied in other contexts, integration itself, or integrative capacity, is the goal—not knowledge. It is not so much that disciplines are selected for integration based on contributory relevance to specific knowledge goals as it is that, with integration and developing the capacity for it as the goal, disciplines that de facto are available in the curriculum are connected or brought into relation with one another. This may occur under any number of arrangements, such as introducing new courses specifically designed to establish connections among existing ones; revising existing courses so as to include in them elements, modules, or modes of assessment designed to encourage connection making with other courses; incorporating experiences in service learning; and using pan-curricular tools like e-portfolios to foster connection-making overall. The metaphor of borrowing is not quite apt.

Of course, interdisciplinary programming and integrative learning sometimes overlap and shade into one another. Many integrative learning initiatives cluster courses that are tied to a theme and selected for their contributory relevance to it. This makes good pedagogic sense, and to the extent that an initiative does this, it may be indistinguishable from interdisciplinary programming. Even so, integration, and not knowledge related to the chosen theme, is primary; one theme might do just as well as any other, provided it is at least equally useful for the purpose of connecting available courses and developing in students the capacity to integrate. Moreover, such theme-based integrative learning falls short of the ambitious goal of integrating the pieces in the overall curriculum and that curriculum with reality beyond. To be sure, in view of resource constraints, interdisciplinary programming too may be limited to cobbling together a heterogeneous roster of existing courses linked more or less tangentially to a theme that is itself chosen because it is the best fit possible with available courses. To this extent, the program formed will fall short of what it might look like if, as would be ideal, contributory relevance alone guided the selection of courses in view of the chosen theme. Thus, even in cases where integrative learning and interdisciplinarity appear virtually indistinguishable, in idea and pedagogy each is quite distinct. Even as integrative learning seeks to go beyond interdisciplinarity, it may be that the most effective and pedagogically sound way for it to achieve its goals is to model it on interdisciplinarity, as appears to be the case in some measure at least for integrative learning initiatives that cluster courses around a unifying theme.

What Is the Value of Disciplines and Disciplinarity?

In some ways, the term *interdisciplinarity* is misleading because seldom does it involve anything so ambitious as appropriation of disciplines in their entirety. Rather, it typically involves only some select disciplinary concepts, tools, methods, or conversations, making no pretense to depth or breadth of disciplinary knowledge beyond what is being borrowed and used for the purpose at hand. Moreover, the term *discipline* should be interpreted inclusively enough to include not just the standard disciplines but also emerging fields of studies and interdisciplines organized in a coherent way around some knowledge theme, which are essentially like disciplines insofar as they approach their subject matter in a disciplined and analytically rigorous way.

Disciplinary analysis is as essential to interdisciplinarity as is integration. Disciplines to be integrated are not chosen arbitrarily; instead, they are thought to have something to contribute to a more holistic understanding of a knowledge theme that guides the inquiry. Work in the relevant disciplines is purposively relative to that knowledge goal. And if it is true that the knowledge interdisciplinarity pursues exceeds and is not available from the standpoint of any one of the selected disciplines, it is also true that the integrated knowledge that emerges would be impossible without the contribution from each of the contributing disciplines.

Interdisciplinarity thus essentially involves two movements: an analytic, disciplinary movement in which work proceeds through the disciplines, examining this or that piece and breaking things down and pulling things apart as is characteristic of each of the selected disciplines, and a synthetic, interdisciplinary movement in which pieces thus analyzed are put together or integrated to yield a new and fuller knowledge of the phenomenon studied. Absent sufficient rigor in the differentiating, analytic movements of disciplinarity, such integration as could occur is bound to be shallow or superficial, like Hegel's (2005/1807) famous "night in which all cows are black" (94). The relationship between disciplinary analysis and interdisciplinary integration, one might say with Hegel, is dialectical.

Of course, just because integrative learning does not in name or by definition indicate a dialectical relationship between disciplinarity and integration, this does not mean that it cannot also be understood dialectically. The AAC&U Statement on Integrative Learning (2004) does point out that the disciplines provide a "foundation" for integrative learning, and the foundation metaphor is open to being understood dialectically. However, integration is typically foregrounded in integrative learning, as the term itself indicates. In the literature, disciplinarity often appears more as a problem to be solved (e.g., fragmentation or lack of perceived relevance) by integration than a resource essential for its meaningful occurrence. The passage through disciplines is the hardest part of interdisciplinary work, given the specificities in terminology, concepts, theories, and methods that differentiate one discipline from another. When integration as such is the goal, and not interdisciplinary knowledge, disciplinary specificities may seem more like impediments to be tolerated ("if only they could all speak the same language!") than as enabling ever more comprehensive, albeit demanding, integrations and, therefore, something for which to be thankful.

Additionally, insofar as the goal of integrative learning is integration across an entire curriculum—or even among some subset of courses grouped together on an ad hoc basis—immersion in this or that discipline will lack the focus and purposiveness that come from the pursuit of a thematic knowledge in some select disciplines. Such thematically-guided purposiveness is what precisely guides and disciplines the disciplinary, analytic moment of interdisciplinarity. It focuses the learner or knowledge seeker on what in the discipline is useful or needs to be borrowed for the knowledge purpose at hand. For nonspecialists at least, to the extent disciplinary learning is purpose-driven with a view to acquiring knowledge concerning some interdisciplinary knowledge theme or question, chances are greater that the immersion in the discipline will be more insightful and that such knowledge that emerges will be relevant and suited for integration with other knowledges the student is working through, and indeed with life and reality outside the academy. As concerns any other disciplines outside the interdisciplinary program that may be included in a given student's course load, it is always possible that some integration will occur serendipitously. Regardless, relaxation of the imperative to integrate can be freeing and conducive to an appreciation not only of the complexity of disciplinary analysis but also of the vastness and variety of disciplines beyond those the student is expected to navigate with a view to integration. The student may also benefit from gaining a sharper understanding of what integration is, what its challenges are, and where it is expected. If everything is to be integrated, integration and the rigors of disciplinarity essential to it may mean something so general as to mean nothing precise at all.

Why Is Integration Valued?

Integration can be valued for any number of reasons; depending on the reasons, the response to the questions and concerns I have posed may differ. As I have elaborated interdisciplinarity, the relationship between integration and knowledge has been a recurrent theme. Knowledge seeking is what motivates interdisciplinarity, and the reason for disciplinary borrowing as well as the integration of what is borrowed. Knowledge seeking is what guides the selection of the disciplinary elements to be integrated, the reason why passage through disciplinarity is necessary, and why such passage through a single discipline is not sufficient. In other words, interdisciplinary integration is valued primarily for epistemic reasons because it is essential to knowledge acquisition (learning) and production with respect to complex phenomena that cannot adequately be grasped from within any single discipline, much less absent such discipline. Such knowledge, in turn, may be valued for any number of reasons, whether for its own sake as an end in itself or, as increasingly so today, because it is instrumental to the solution of some practical problem.

In the literature on integrative learning, integration is also promoted for its epistemic value, at least as it is linked to learning and pedagogy. Integrative learning, after all, is about promoting and facilitating learning, and learning is surely about knowledge (i.e., knowledge seeking, knowledge acquisition, knowledge transmission, and even research to the extent that learning overlaps with searching and researching). However, the epistemic (and even pedagogical) value of integration is considerably less foregrounded or pronounced than it is in the literature on interdisciplinarity. Nonepistemic values having to do with social, economic, and political pressures; constraints; and ideologies receive comparatively greater emphasis.

Schneider (2003), at the time president of the American Association for Colleges & Universities (as mentioned, its work was a major catalyst for the contemporary integrative learning movement), sets the stage for her laudatory exposition of integrative learning by noting the "new, economically driven tension between Americans' interest in higher education and shrinking budgets in the states and in our campuses" (2). The college degree, she observes as she presents statistics on the expansion of college enrollment, "is rapidly becoming what the high school diploma became 100 years ago—THE widely sought and generally expected passport to both economic mobility and contributing citizenship" (2). Digging a little deeper in student demographics in an approbative exposition elaborating the rallying work of the AAC&U, Huber, Hutchings, and Gale (2005) note that the proportion of older students returning to the educational system is growing and that more and more students have "families and jobs that necessarily take precedence over their school work" (6). The challenge of changing student demographics is likewise foregrounded, and more graphically illustrated, in an article by Arcario, Eynon, and Clark (2005). Speaking frankly of the challenges they face in their mission to serve "students who have been traditionally underserved by the educational system," they report "significant under-preparation in key academic areas" among their students, noting that "in 2002 . . . 90 percent of entering students required at least one developmental skills course in reading, writing, or mathematics" (15).

In these expositions, two of which are written by leading proponents, the value of integrative learning is linked in a pronounced way to problems essentially rooted in changing student demographics and external social needs or demands. Integrative learning is lauded and promoted largely as a way of addressing emerging social challenges for which existing academic programming is inadequate. Yet other works on integrative learning could be cited that follow along similar lines. This emphasis suggests that the movement toward integration may be driven less by epistemic values than by the need to adjust to a growing student population that, for various reasons, is poorly served by the status quo curriculum and unable to fit in. Integrative learning is valued and championed not so much because it is an advance in its own right in pedagogy beyond older models (although this is also claimed) as because it is a better way of addressing challenges arising from changing demographics and resource constraints.

The integrative learning literature highlights that the value of integration is linked prominently not only to challenges posed by changing demographics but also to broader societal needs, demands, goals, and ideologies. Schneider (2003), reinforcing the work of the AAC&U, praises integrative learning as a means of developing in students "a strong sense of social responsibility and civic engagement" (5). Humphreys (2005) lauds it as being "essential to prepare students to deal effectively both with complex issues in their working lives and the broader challenges facing society today and in the future" (30), adding that "the business community, too, is calling for integrative capacities in employees" (31).

In these works, as a matter of emphasis at least, the value and importance of integration seems to have less to do with the goal of knowledge as such (or even of knowledge as instrumental to nonepistemic goals). Instead, the focus seems to be on goals such as enhancing the experience and success of a growing number of students for whom the traditional curricula is a bad fit and who are unlikely to succeed in it, developing integrative capacity as a generalized skill useful for purposes beyond the academy, and preparing students overall to integrate themselves better into a rapidly changing world as good and productive citizens.

The relative primacy of epistemic reasons for valuing integration in interdisciplinarity may be due in part to its more pronounced and essential connection to disciplinarity, disciplines being essentially modes of knowledge production. Moreover, the contemporary interdisciplinarity movement has encompassed not just curricular academic programming but research, and not just knowledge transmission and acquisition but knowledge production. There is interdisciplinary teaching and learning, and there is also interdisciplinary research. Institutional and political dynamics are different for each, as are the theoretical issues posed, but overlap and interaction do exist. Both have to do with knowledge seeking. As the two have developed more or less in tandem in higher education settings, the association of interdisciplinary programming with interdisciplinary research has reinforced the orientation of interdisciplinarity to knowledge and strengthened its epistemological theorizing.

Integrative learning, in contrast, is fundamentally about education only. Of course, integrative learning may have implications for research, and research may be incorporated into its academic programming. Leading theorists and many others engaged in the integrative movement are also accomplished researchers. Nonetheless, unlike interdisciplinarity, integrative learning has only a teaching or academic programming arm. There is no integrative research movement advancing integration as a mode of knowledge production in the sense that there is one for interdisciplinary research. As an educational reform movement only, integrative learning may thus be more susceptible, and need to be more responsive, to external pressures and constraints than does interdisciplinary programming.

No doubt such difference as exists here is one of degree. Interdisciplinary programming is certainly subject to the same sorts of expectations, demands, and constraints as is all academic programming today. However, interdisciplinary programming's essential connection to the disciplines, its association with interdisciplinary research, and its orientation to knowledge have anchored it more securely in the traditional epistemic purposes of higher education. In some measure, this anchoring has afforded it a greater measure of prestige in institutional politics and a stronger negotiating position vis-à-vis the economics and politics of educational reform.

To be sure, proponents of interdisciplinary programming also praise its nonepistemic virtues and benefits to justify and make the case for investment in it in the context of intense competition for dwindling resources. So too do proponents of interdisciplinary research and especially so-called instrumental interdisciplinarity. But if instrumental interdisciplinarity is valued primarily for its usefulness in society as a means to some external end, what makes it useful is the knowledge it produces. Likewise, what makes interdisciplinary programming useful is its way of organizing disciplinary knowledge to be integrated in view of some complex phenomenon to be known and learned about—in other words, determining which knowledge may in turn be more or less important for broader social purposes.

Valuing an approach to academic programming—or research, for that matter—for epistemic reasons is not necessarily incompatible with valuing it for its extrinsic benefits. Certainly higher education does need to address frontally the challenges of serving a growing student body less well-prepared for the rigors of academic work and able to invest less time and effort in studies relative to other interests and demands in their lives. Proponents of integrative learning should be commended for taking on these challenges, and if developing integrative skills and capacities in students will better prepare them also to integrate in the job market and as productive citizens, all the better. In principle, it is possible that integrative learning (or some other educational reform yet to be articulated) could prove itself both as an epistemic advance in pedagogy—a superior way of organizing the curriculum for knowledge seeking and transmission—*and* the most fitting solution to pressing practical problems and demands.

However, to say the least, a significant tension here needs to be acknowledged concerning the relationship of higher education to broader societal needs and goals. Everyone agrees that higher education must be responsive to external goals in some measure, if for no other reason than to justify funding and to offer students something more than the joys of knowledge in return for the time, sweat, toil, and money they invest in their education. The challenge is that to the extent that educational institutions justify and promote themselves in terms of social ends, however noble or laudable those ends may be, they risk compromising epistemic ideals and a certain freedom or independence—tenuous, fragile, and limited, to be sure—protective of knowledge seeking that is virtually constitutive of the modern university. Of course, higher education today encompasses a wide variety of types of institutions with different charters and mission statements, which place more or less value on knowledge, freedom, and independence, relative to serving socially defined roles and goals. Regardless, at some point, service to externally defined social goals—whether the production of "good" citizens or well-integrated workers—can displace or render illusory traditional epistemic ideals that ultimately and essentially define institutions of higher education and in virtue of which they distinctly stand apart precisely as institutions of knowledge.[9]

As a movement in higher education facing many of the same pressures and constraints as integrative learning, interdisciplinarity has foregrounded epistemic ideals in negotiating a space for itself (precarious, to be sure) and aligned itself with the emphatically epistemic traditions of the disciplines and of research, making the case that knowledge is and can be instrumental to meeting many social needs and demands. In negotiating its space, the integrative learning movement would be well-served by giving greater attention and emphasis to epistemic ideals and aligning itself more with interdisciplinarity. Likewise, theorists of integrative research seeking to set its theoretical foundations would do well to borrow from the considerable foundational work that has been done in interdisciplinary theory.

Conclusion: The Limits of Integration

In some strains of interdisciplinarity, there is a hope for or dream of some ultimate integration that would synthesize not just this or that set of disciplines or disciplinary knowledges but all disciplines and all knowledges in a grand synthesis. Some such idea is what the philosopher Hegel intended with the term "absolute knowledge." One could argue that fulfilling this dream (or even the resolute undertaking to fulfill it) would be more like a nightmare. Regardless, such an ambition has little to do with the actual interdisciplinary programming and research that occurs today, which sets itself considerably more modest goals.

Certainly integrative learning has no such grand ambitions, but insofar as it aspires to integrate all of the disciplinary and interdisciplinary work across a given curriculum, it sets itself up for failure. Undoubtedly, the diversity of disciplines can be overwhelming for students and experienced in fragments. To the extent students are able to make connections aided by institutional scaffolding and connection-making tools like e-portfolios, that is a good thing. However, being realistic and humble about what is possible is important. If expectations are not set modestly and the challenge of achieving even some degree of disciplinary rigor is not duly recognized, there is a danger of promoting a shallow or superficial integration that is illusory. The pieces thus connected will not have been sufficiently differentiated to begin with, and their specific differences will have been annulled. As interdisciplinary theorizing would have it, the diversity and depth of disciplines is not a problem to be grudgingly tolerated but rather a rich source of necessary resources for knowledge seekers and producers, which should be celebrated as such.

Concerning integrating the academic curriculum with life and reality outside the academy, depending on what this is taken to mean, it would be difficult to imagine how any sort of academic programming—disciplinary, interdisciplinary, or integrative—could not embrace this goal as matter of good pedagogy, not to mention honest and fair delivery to students of value for money. However, caution is in order here, too. If a measure of remoteness and detachment from the concerns of everyday life and demands of the real world can be an impediment to learning, it may nonetheless also be necessary for its meaningful occurrence. The metaphorical walls that separate the academy from the real world, so often disparaged today in offhanded ways, also delimit and protect a virtual space for learning. Within this metaphorical space, students can gain some refreshing respite from the push and pull of everyday life and feel free to inquire in a way that would not otherwise be possible. In this regard, disconnecting may be even more important than connecting. And in the context of nonepistemic goals such as producing a certain kind of citizen or worker, perhaps there also needs to be a place for standing out or standing apart as well as for fitting in. No doubt that developing a suitably modest capacity to integrate is good. However, perhaps this should go hand in hand with a humble appreciation for the vastness of both the known and the unknown and with a tolerance for ambiguity, recalcitrant difference, and that which resists integration or remains left over or left out.

References

American Association of Colleges & Universities. 2002. “Greater Expectations: A New Vision for Learning as a Nation Goes to College.” http://www.greaterexpectations.org/.

———. 2004. “A Statement on Integrative Learning.” http://www.aacu.org/integrative_learning/pdfs/ ILP_Statement.pdf.

———. 2012, Summer. “AAC&U Receives Grant for New Integrative Learning Project.” *Liberal Education* 98 (3): 5.

Arcario, P., B. Eynon, and J. E. Clark. 2005. “Making Connections: Integrated Learning, Integrated Lives.” *Peer Review* 7 (4): 15–17.

Carp, R. M. 2001. “Integrative Praxes: Learning from Multiple Knowledge Formations.” *Issues in Integrative Studies* 19: 71–121.

Chandler, J. 2009. “Introduction: Doctrines, Disciplines, Discourses, Departments.” *Critical Inquiry* 35: 729–46.

Dezure, D., M. Babb, and S. Waldmann. 2005. “Integrative Learning Nationwide: Emerging Themes and Practices.” *Peer Review* 7 (4): 24–29.

Eaton, J. S. 2007. "Assault on Accreditation: Who Defines and Judges Academic Quality?" *Liberal Education* 93 (2): 2–4.

Frodeman, R., J. T. Klein, and C. Mitcham, eds. 2012. *The Oxford Handbook of Interdisciplinarity*. Oxford: Oxford University Press.

Gadamer, H. 1975. *Truth and Method*. Translated by G. Barden and J. Cumming. New York: Seabury Press.

Hegel, G. W. F. 2005/1807. "Hegel's Preface to the *Phenomenology of Spirit*." Translated by Y. Yovel. Princeton, NJ: Princeton University Press.

Huber, M. T., C. Brown, P. Hutchings, R. Gale, R. Miller, and M. Breen, eds. 2007. "Integrative Learning: Opportunity to Connect." Public report of the Integrative Learning Project sponsored by the Association of American Colleges & Universities and the Carnegie Foundation for the Advancement of Teaching, Stanford, CA.

Huber, M. T., P. Hutchings, and R. Gale. 2005. "Integrative Learning for Liberal Education." *Peer Review* 7 (4): 4–7.

Huber, M. T., P. Hutchings, R. Gale, R. Miller, and M. Breen. 2007. "Leading Initiatives for Integrative Learning." *Liberal Education* 93 (2): 46–51.

Humphreys, D. 2005. "Why Integrative Learning? Why Now?" *Peer Review* 7 (24): 30–31.

Klein, J. T. 1990. *Interdisciplinarity: History, Theory, and Practice*. Detroit: Wayne State University Press.

———. 2005. "Integrative Learning and Interdisciplinary Studies." *Peer Review* 7 (4): 8–10.

Moran, J. 2010. *Interdisciplinarity*. 2nd ed. London: Routledge.

Newell, W. H. 2008. "The Intertwined History of Interdisciplinary Undergraduate Education and the Association for Integrative Studies: An Insider's View." *Issues in Integrative Studies* 26: 1–59.

———. 2010. "Educating for a Complex World: Integrative Learning and Interdisciplinary Studies." *Liberal Education* 96 (4): 6–11.

———, ed. 1998. *Interdisciplinarity: Essays from the Literature*. New York: College Board.

Repko, A. F. 2012. *Interdisciplinary Research: Theory and Practice*. 2nd ed. Los Angeles: Sage.

Schneider, C. G. 2003. "Liberal Education and Integrative Learning." *Issues in Integrative Studies* 21: 1–8.

Chapter 4

Enacting Integration: Two Case Studies, Three Principles

Jennifer Sasser, PhD, and Simeon Dreyfuss, MA, Marylhurst University

Between the third and fourth weeks of the Embodiment in Later Life course, Velda fell in a parking lot after grocery shopping, fracturing her hip and wrist. We moved our next three class sessions to the nursing home where she was recuperating. Tiny (she protests this description), white haired, sparkly eyed, and very genteel (as well as quite spunky—you should see what happens when her ire gets raised!), Velda was the heart of our learning community, our touchstone, because she'd lived so much life—at the time of her accident, she was only a few weeks away from her ninetieth birthday—and had been through so much, and, this is crucial, had *reflected upon* her experiences, good and bad and everything in between. She brought an open heart and mind to every class session, took responsibility for her own learning, and also communicated to her co-learners about what she wanted to contribute as well as what she needed from the rest of us in order to do her best work. The Embodiment in Later Life seminar, one of the two case studies of an integrative approach to scholarly work and life we offer in this chapter, is a collaborative inquiry course in which we explore various theoretical and empirical texts and engage in critical self-reflection, experiential learning practices, and hybrid forms of writing about what it means to travel through the life course, especially the later part of the life course, with/in a particular body. Imagine holding such a seminar in an institutional setting, with all its textures, smells, sounds—one resident begged plaintively for help—and odd body-care busyness, where a singular member of our learning community was recovering from the unplanned gift of a new hip!

We start with this example because of our strong belief that integrative scholarship always occurs within a particular historical, personal, and interpersonal context. The goal of integrative work is not only the scholarship we produce, but more so, the cultivation of a certain quality of mind. It is a sensibility that affects how we think, how we work and teach, and indeed, how we inhabit our own lives. One of the principles of integrative thinking we explore in this chapter is that integrative work necessarily involves inviting curiosity about our contexts. What are the cultural, historical, and deeply personal reasons we frame issues and questions in the ways we do? What are the consequences of those framings? And what might we *not* be seeing: what might get left out of the picture because of the particular ways we view complex reality? In posing such questions, we believe, we must also be both curious and explicit about the perspectives we ourselves bring to the conversation. The structure of this chapter reflects this belief.

To continue our opening illustration, holding our class in such an environment and under such circumstances was complicated, challenging, and transformative for all involved. Velda was certainly on the extreme end of the life-course spectrum, and her classmates were all somewhere in what we've decided in the (post)modern Western world to call "midlife." As for me (Jennifer), the instructor, I was in my mid-forties, the youngest among our community of learners. We all had some important things in common: To a person, we had each served as a paid or family caregiver to an elder, worked in some capacity in the field of gerontology, and had spent time in elder-care facilities. But never had we had the experience of actually holding class in such an environment! Our sessions were even more emergent than they normally were, as we never knew how Velda might be feeling and I had to improvise our learning activities not only to account for Velda's state but also to accommodate the comings and goings of Velda's caregivers—nursing assistant, occupational therapist, discharge nurse—and friends and family. As well, I found I had to be sensitive to the collective vibe of her classmates. For example, midway through our first session at the nursing home, we discovered that the mother of one of Velda's classmates had actually lived out her final days there, just down the hall from Velda's room; this particular student didn't realize until being back in that environment how many unacknowledged feelings—regret, anger, and sadness—she had about the decision to place her mother in an institutional setting. At our second session at the nursing home, another student who seemed to give the impression of always being in command of everything, always seeming so solid and confident, tearfully shared with us one of her most closely held secrets (something her closest family and friends didn't know), around which she had enormous shame, regarding the series of unexpectedly life events that had led her in midlife to end a long career and a significant relationship, and return to school to study gerontology.

These are but two of the many poignant moments and unexpected experiences that emerged during our weeks holding class at the nursing home—

and then at Velda's home for one week while she was recuperating. Being immersed in the nursing home environment for three-hour class sessions, not surprisingly, was intense and triggered some raw feelings for all of us. This unanticipated learning experience required me to practice being present with as much of my whole self as I could in order to allow and hold space for the expression of complicated feelings in a way that was in service to our individual and collective learning. We were engaging in real-time gerontology, beholding and respecting whatever emerged, thinking (and feeling) together the connections (and disconnections) between the theoretical insights and empirical findings we were reading about, the "official" curriculum, and the subtle and surprising nature of what we were experiencing and witnessing firsthand.

As our opening example illustrates, human reality and lived experience are complex and emergent. As such, learning and teaching about human reality and lived experience are complex and emergent as well. So, too, are the insights we share in this chapter. We don't aim to offer solid, fixed guidelines for or conclusions about what constitutes integrative learning. Rather, we intend to explore together as comrades and with readers some strong albeit provisional principles that dwell at the heart of what we try to do as educators and scholars committed to integrative learning and teaching. In addition, we want to ponder some questions about the challenges involved in enacting these principles—not only in our work but also lifewide as human beings committed to our own singular paths of developing wholeness and integrity. To wit, in envisioning, choreographing, and enacting potentially integrative learning environments, we foreground three principles:

1. We invite learners into complexity.

2. We invite learners to be curious about context and their own and others' epistemologies.

3. We invite learners into conversation and collaboration.

As we unfold this chapter, our approach is to foreground two case studies and extract from them a deeper exploration of these three principles.

Institutional (and Personal) Contexts

Before proceeding, it seems important, given our commitment to being curious about contexts, to provide some information about who we are as authors and about the institutional context for the seminars that serve as our case studies. We are both on the faculty of Marylhurst University, a Catholic liberal arts university in the Portland, Oregon, metropolitan area. Marylhurst is small in size (currently about sixteen hundred students) and serves a multigenerational student body, ranging in age from nineteen to ninety (the average age is thirty-eight). Students represent life-course experiences and stages as varied as Velda's or, in contrast, that of a traditional-aged, previously homeschooled student experiencing his first full-on institution-based learning, as well as every stage and experience in between. Completing a degree is, for our students, no doubt a priority for which they have cleared space in their lives but often not first or even second in order of importance, coming behind the needs of families, communities, and earning a living. Our faculty is about 70 percent adjunct, practitioners in the fields in which they teach. In short, Marylhurst is on the bleeding edge of many of the changes broadly affecting higher education. In addition, for a small school, we have an unusually large number of programs that might be described as integrative or interdisciplinary, including areas of study such as digital humanities, human studies, culture and media studies, gerontology, art and music therapy, food systems and society, graduate and undergraduate interdisciplinary studies, and arguably our MBA in sustainable business.

We both began our time at Marylhurst as adjunct faculty, working our way to full-time, on-campus faculty and academic administrator positions, serving during a time of tremendous change and growth, and playing key roles both as insiders and outsiders.

Simeon has had a career as an experiential educator, having worked for several years as a freelance journalist and field associate for a national nonprofit, starting service-learning programs in middle schools in the late 1980s and early '90s. He served on the faculty and then directed Marylhurst's prior-learning assessment program; he led the team redesigning the university's general education program into the outcome-based liberal arts core in 1998. Additionally, he served as the program's director for fifteen years, up until another general education redesign that took effect in the fall of 2013, as well as his ongoing position as the chair of undergraduate interdisciplinary studies, the largest undergraduate major by headcount at the university. He designed and managed the online Marylhurst academic portfolio, designed the university's first online course evaluation system, and oversaw the degree audit and advising system during the twelve years it moved in slow stages from a paper-and-pencil system to one available online and integrated with university's central data system. He has served on numerous committees, including a decade as chair or cochair (with Jennifer) of the assessment committee and is now cochair of the faculty policy and practices committee.

For Jennifer, learning and education have served and still serve as major organizing principles for her life, providing a sense of personal agency, hope, stability, and even liberation in the face of experiences that largely make no sense (especially to the much younger Jennifer): early and ongoing experiences with extreme physical pain and emotional trauma, her younger brother's severe hearing and visual impairment caused by a shared congenital disorder, transient economic insecurity throughout her childhood, and significant family system turbulence. Serious study in music and dance (thanks to a benefactor grandmother) throughout the first half of her life course also served as an important avenue for making meaning about and nonverbal self-expression of feelings, thoughts, and dreams that seemed impossible, outsized, and even dangerous. So perhaps it isn't surprising that Jennifer's scholarship has involved cross-disciplinary inquiry and practice regarding issues of embodiment, deep human development, and transformational learning across the life course, especially in later life; intentional aging and radical gerontology; and the connections (and disconnections) between professional knowledge and practice and personal experiences. Jennifer joined the adjunct faculty in the Master of Arts in Interdisciplinary Studies program at Marylhurst in 1997, a year after completing her PhD and the birth of her daughter (and shortly before unexpectedly commencing life as a divorced, single mom). Since 1998 she has served as chair of the Human Sciences Department, a large undergraduate department that houses majors in psychology, social sciences, and a certificate in gerontology, as well as a unique interdisciplinary major: human studies. In addition to administrative responsibilities, most of her work-life time is devoted to advising and mentoring students; designing and teaching cross-disciplinary, integrative, collaborative inquiry courses; critical theorizing about gerontology, writing, and praxis; and serving on numerous committees regarding general education, educational assessment, faculty governance, and faculty development.

Ideas in Time

The other context we wish to be curious about at the front end of this conversation concerns higher education's evolving understanding about integrative learning; our point here is to observe both the particular historical moment in the unfolding conversation about integration at which this chapter is crafted, and to observe the fundamentally emergent nature of understandings about integrative sensibility. As Julie Thompson Klein has observed, the idea that integration is a necessary part of deep learning is hardly new. She reports that an internal report for the Association of American Colleges & Universities' (AAC&U) working group on integrative learning "traced the underlying ideas of connection and synthesis to ancient philosophy" (Klein 2005, 8) and goes on to describe how our collective understanding of integration and integrative learning has evolved over the last 120 years.

We note the 1979 founding of the Association for Integrative Studies. The name was changed to the Association for Interdisciplinary Studies in 2012, in part responding to a deepening common understanding of the differences between interdisciplinary and integrative study that this volume explores. Its journal, *Issues in Integrative Studies*, has served as an important venue for the conversation about the nature and legitimacy of interdisciplinary and integrative scholarship. The histories collected in Augsburg and Henry's *The Politics of Interdisciplinary Studies* (2009) make clear that interdisciplinary degree programs often survive on the margins of the academy—the site of innovative scholarship and teaching, popular with students, but too easily cut or merged into more traditional disciplinary departments at times of economic pressure.

The current scholarly conversation about integrative studies grew out of a conviction that higher education at the end of the twentieth century was an atomized enterprise (American Association of Colleges & Universities 2002; Czechowski 2003). A March 2004 AAC&U statement on integrative learning read,

> The undergraduate experience can be a fragmentary landscape of general education courses, preparation for the major, cocurricular activities, and "the real world" beyond the campus. But an emphasis on integrative learning can help undergraduates put the pieces together and develop habits of mind that prepare them to make informed judgments in the conduct of personal, professional, and civic life. (qtd. in Huber and Hutchings 2004, 13)

The goal of scholars advocating this new emphasis on integrative learning was to prepare for the needs of twenty-first-century learners. As Veronica Boix-Mansilla wrote,

> Learners of the present and the future must be agents of their own learning, critical inquirers, able to collaborate, able to apply higher-order thinking skills to real life problems, to manage cultural complexity and to make meaningful connections across disciplines. . . . Integrative learning enables students to focus on multidimensional issues in their full complexity. It invites them to weigh, apply, and combine disciplinary insights to move beyond naïve views. Most importantly it enables them to bring

> the very forces changing the planet—from climate change to globalization, from the digitalization of everyday life to the ethics of global health and medical technologies—into the classroom for detailed interdisciplinary exploration. (2008, 31)

This idea that integrative learning invites students to engage life's complexities is one of the themes of this chapter and one that comes up frequently in the literature. Various writers (Arcario, Eynon, and Clark 2005; Himbeault Taylor 2011; Kuh 2008; Leonard 2012; Mahoney and Schamber 2011) have observed the potential of integrative learning techniques to transform students' lives. These articles explore particular educational tools such as portfolios, internships, service learning, first-year seminars and experiences, learning communities, or writing-intensive courses. They observe, particularly for nontraditional and immigrant communities, that encouraging students to reflect on the connections between their academic work and their lived experiences transforms the way that students perceive their lives. In this chapter we explicitly make the case that integrative work is fundamentally transformative, not only for our students, but also for anyone taking seriously the principles we explore, including ourselves.

Less common in the literature are discussions of how one might actually design learning experiences and environments that help learners understand and appreciate the nature of complexity. Even theories of interdisciplinary work tend to seek clarity rather than complexity. The most common models of interdisciplinary research (Klein 1990; Newell 2001; Repko 2011) all include a stage in which the goal of the researcher is to resolve conflicts between disciplinary insights and create common ground. This goal is fundamentally different from an intentional decision to enter into and behold complexity, and different from seeking ways to think about and understand the complexity of lived experience in a way that is true to that experience. As Simeon wrote in a previous essay,

> Sometimes . . . there is no singular integrated understanding, no common ground, or at least the things we most need to think about are the ones that resist the discovery of common ground. . . . Sometimes we must seek ways to think and talk about insights that stubbornly refuse to integrate. We need to find ways to tell stories big enough to embrace differences in a way that honors the separate visions and experience at their core. (Dreyfuss 2011, 81)

Indeed, in a later writing, Klein observes that for what she calls integrative interdisciplinarity, "Students are engaged in 'meaning making.' Application of knowledge takes precedence over acquisition and mastery of facts alone, activating a dynamic process of meaning making, problem posing and solving, decision making, higher-order critical thinking, and reflexivity" (2005, 10). She goes on to say,

> Contextuality, conflict, and change are the defining parameters of this kind of learning. Contextuality is a different metaphor of knowledge and education than unity, which assumes consistent logical relations within a linear framework with the expectation of achieving certainty and universality. Contextuality accepts the contingent character of knowledge and action. (2005, 10)

Again, we pick up and explore these themes in this chapter, focusing on examples of how one might structure a learning environment to accomplish these goals. The goal of the courses we describe in the two case studies we offer is not so much to resolve conflicts but rather to behold complexity, not necessarily to achieve integration but to be curious about context and our own and others' epistemological commitments, which are formed through messy lived experience over the life course. The goal is to gain not only a synthetic understanding—though this is important—but rather a more capacious understanding that grows out of bringing as much of ourselves as we can to our interactions within a community of learners.

Integrative learning is a contemporary educational reform that helps us to think about what a fecund educational environment might be like. But as Klein pointed out, the idea that there is a cyclical and deeply transformative relationship between experience and learning is certainly not a new one. Indeed, over his long career, Arthur Chickering has often explored how our identities, sense of self, and even our spiritual commitments are transformed by and transform our learning (Chickering and Reisser 1993). David Kolb (1984) situated both experience and reflection as essential components of the learning cycle. And Paulo Freire (2000) saw learning as deeply social and liberating with the potential not only to change lives but also to change human consciousness, social structures, and even entire cultures.

What we mean by *integration* and *integrative* has evolved over recent decades and no doubt will continue to do so. As this chapter makes clear, to observe that the educational community's intellectual commitments change over time does not make what we collectively believe today right or wrong, nor do our strong beliefs of this moment require us to accept a narrative of progress: the story that we are moving inexorably toward more complete understandings, which—according to a reading by Immanuel Wallerstein that we use in one of the courses we describe below—is actually impossible, given that human reality on this planet is moving toward greater complexity, thus greater disorder (Wallerstein, 1999). Rather, at any given time we find some temporary coherence and semblance of sense as a community of learners. We make agreements about what will constitute "partial, provisional" understanding for a time. The goal is not necessarily to achieve clarity or a simple explanation for complex phenomena, but to develop an embodied, holistic sensibility that helps us behold and explore (and live with) complexity, each other, the world, and the very cosmos. This chapter asks these questions: What are the characteristics of this sensibility? How might we know it when we see it and embody it? And how do we help each other develop this sensibility as a long-term, lifewide project?

Our Case Studies

Unlike many case studies presented in the literature we reviewed, the two case studies we want to explore are not ones designed specifically to guide students through the process of undertaking an integrative or interdisciplinary project, nor are they team-taught, theme-focused courses that intentionally address their subjects from different disciplinary perspectives. While our university has—and we both have taught in and supervised—such courses, the particular courses we wish to offer as case studies serve other curricular goals. We want to talk about these courses because the assumptions behind their conceptualization and design involve certain integrative principles and because through these courses we intentionally enact these principles.

In part, our choice of case studies was influenced by what we believe an integrative sensibility is *not*. The process of integrative thinking is not just a mash-up of different ideas or elements gathered from hither and yon, nor is it simply the juxtaposition of different ways of thinking. Nor does integrative thinking predicated on the synthesis of perspectives from multiple disciplinary traditions result in a product, object, or static thing. At the same time, integrative studies—the attempt to contain and institutionalize certain integrative practices—is not a discipline in its own right, though as we've touched on in our brief review of selected literature, our work might fit into a sort of integrative studies tradition. (Let us be clear here that while the concepts are related, integrative thinking, integration, integrative learning, and integrative studies are not interchangeable.) Integrative thinking—and its more formal articulation as an area of study—has no inherent content but is, rather, a process that can be used in any number of areas of inquiry, formal and informal, in the academy, the workplace, and lifewide. That is, integrative thinking is not just a mode of inquiry (though it is that), but perhaps a way of beholding and interacting with the complex, emergent nature of reality; it can even be a way of being and participating in the world (Heron and Reason 1997). As such, we believe that an integrative sensibility is best seen in practice. Since integration is something that one *does*, it is best explored by looking at examples of people attempting to do it. As such, we describe two university courses in which an integrative sensibility suffuses the course design and its enactment.

The first case study is a capstone course in our undergraduate general education program, Senior Seminar; and the second case study, an upper-division undergraduate/graduate gerontology seminar, is the aforementioned Embodiment in Later Life. These two courses are designed to model an engagement with integrative thinking and being, a practice to which we are both deeply committed. One of the problems we encountered while designing these courses was that if integrative thinking is not, as we contend, a set of ideas but rather a practice, how then does one convey and model it to one's students (while also engaging in a close exploration of certain content)? Perhaps the answer is to design learning environments that give learners the real-time, emergent experience of what we are inviting them and each other to learn. While the content of these courses does not explicitly involve the nature of integrative thinking—we may or may not even discuss it, depending on the way discussions unfold in any particular term—these learning environments are designed to give all participants, including each of us as instructors, multiple opportunities to encounter, practice, and demonstrate an integrative process. Our hope is that students will continue to enact an integrative approach lifewide and lifelong. Moreover, our hope is that we will, over time and because of our work with our students and each other, come into more congruence in our own lives with the principles of the integrative approach we teach and enact.

Senior Seminar

Students in Senior Seminar, of course, are academic seniors. They are in the last year of their undergraduate education at Marylhurst, many of them nearing the end of an educational process that has been decades long since they first commenced higher education. As a group they often feel as if they are approaching a watershed moment that has been a long time in the making. They bring with them to the classroom not only their (multi/inter)disciplinary expertise, formed by study in their majors, but also varied family and professional experiences. They may have started a highly successful restaurant or a company manufacturing high-tech navigations systems for recreational marine boaters, or they may have been managers of work groups within Fortune 500 companies. They may be veterans, having served in combat; many have raised families (often as single mothers) and are trying to graduate from college before their own children do; many are currently caregivers to family elders. They may be traditionally aged students with complex adult lives who choose not to participate in a learning environment that assumes they have no other priorities than being a student. They bring an enormous body of experience and personal authority to their learning. They also bring wounds sustained from experiencing crises and traumas: interpersonal violence, serious accidents and illness, loss and betrayal, and profound disappointments. As such, and as seen in the opening example of Velda and her classmates, there are individual-level internal sources of complexity—fear, anxiety, sadness, insecurity, resentment—and external sources of complexity that must be anticipated and acknowledged at least by us as instructors, as these sources of complexity are potential barriers to and opportunities for the integrative learning experiences we hope to design and guide.

Senior Seminar is collaboratively designed and taught by both of us. Our goal in Senior Seminar is to have students reexamine what they think they know and *how* they have come to know what they think they know (as well as try on new ways of thinking). In many ways the course is one in applied epistemology and ethics. Many of the readings and classroom activities in the first half of the eleven-week term are designed to de-discipline students as they prepare to transition to life as educated citizens after their undergraduate educational experience. We explicitly examine how the systems of thought inherent to historically contextualized academic disciplines simultaneously make it possible to think about certain things and condition the ways those things are thought about, both enabling and restraining the production of knowledge, how we know, and what can be known. We take on taken-for-granted concepts and values—for example, objectivity and its antonym, subjectivity—and offer alternative models for and modalities of learning or research in which it is assumed that no one individual nor inquiry paradigm has access to an entirely complete understanding of complex reality (Heron and Reason 1997; Heshusius 1994). All knowledge—including knowledge created through the dominant paradigm of scientific inquiry—is assumed to be in essence partial, provisional, and situated in a cultural and temporal context, a fact we ask students to always be curious about and to interrogate (Wallerstein, 1999). We also offer examples of different scholars and writers who have fundamentally changed their lives in response to situations in which they found themselves acting or living in ways that were not in keeping with their deepest values, by way of illustrating the complexity of individual lives and the challenges involved in living a life of integrity and congruence (Colectivo 2000; Ellsberg 2006; Esgalhado 2000; Isikoff 2008; Ross 2012; Sifry 2011). Sometimes when it feels to us to be authentic and appropriate to do so in service to learning, we may even share our own personal examples of a crisis that brought one of us to the edge of our capacity to cope or make sense of things or of the deep and wide consequences of hiding truths from one's self and others.

We do not work from lecture notes, though sometimes we offer spontaneous explications of stubborn ideas; our primary instructional approach is improvisatory and (meta)dialogical. In fact, the first reading we ask students to muddle through is Gregory Bateson's *Metalogues*—possibly fictional dialogues with his real daughter about the nature of thinking in which the structure of the conversations is a manifestation of the topic (Bateson 1972). We discuss together ahead of each session the overall choreography we each envision and the gestures we want to be sure to make, though we may not know exactly when within the session we will make them (by *gesture*, we mean a question we will pose as a way into a discussion of one of the readings or a small group process to help collaboratively surface some key notions we can then explore as a larger group). In keeping with the collaborative inquiry nature of the seminar, the class sessions in the first half of the term focus on variations on themes, but these themes are open systems, as we want to be able to respond to what we as instructors discover about the interests and areas of expertise our students are bringing to the conversations. In other words, we have a set of big, perennial ideas and questions toward which we want to direct our collaborative inquiry—the contextual nature of belief, knowledge, and truth; ways of knowing; critical thinking and self-reflection; ethical praxis; the tension between individual agency and social structures; the emergent nature of human reality—but exactly how this unfolds week by week and with/in a particular community of learners is unpredictable and always remains to be seen. What this means as well is that students see us negotiate in real time what to do next as we engage in various kinds of discussion and explication about the assigned readings.

We see ourselves as members of the learning community we are fostering, co-learners with everyone else in the room, though we are also explicit from the outset about the fact that we are the instructors of the course, we have an intentional though provisional design for the learning that we hope will be taking place, and we are ultimately responsible for assessing student work (and, alas, for assigning grades). In this way we hope to support each student's agency and sovereignty as an individual and member of the learning community while being honest and upfront about the reality of our roles as instructors. We want to foster opportunities for real, not pseudo, participation and the exercise of freedom but within clear boundaries.

A central learning project for this course is a series of critical reflection essays. These essays provide an opportunity for students not only to mull over and respond to the assigned readings but also to the various waves of group discussions that transpire during each class session. Students write weekly three- to four-page papers (double-spaced, twelve-point, one-inch margins—one must be explicit!) only *after* the class session in which a reading is explored, at the same time they are reading new texts for the following session. We don't want book reports or summaries of important points but rather personal engagements with and responses to the ideas in the assigned readings and/or a development of thoughts that came up in class discussions in response to those readings. These critical reflection essays are in turn commented on by *both* of us as instructors, and we even sometimes comment on each other's comments. We invite students, if they wish, to respond to our comments, to redevelop and deepen their original reflections; we accept as many revisions of critical reflections as students wish to submit. This developmental, ongoing learning project thus enacts a commitment to collaboration, to ongoing dialogue about ideas over time—conversations we feel are essential to integrated learning and being. This practice extends over the term, both for class sessions facilitated by us as instructors and those facilitated by student groups.

A further enactment of our commitment to collaboration takes place at the midpoint of the course when we engage students in an exercise to surface themes they would like to focus on for the sessions taking place during the second half of the term. This is a two-stage process. The first involves open-ended brainstorming—individual brainstorming, followed by group brainstorming—where all ideas are fair game (for example, the psychological implications of alien probing; students will test us to see if we are serious!). In the second, always hair-raising stage, we work together to consider all of the ideas that have been generated, toss out ideas determined to be unviable, and cluster ideas that hang together; by the end of the chaotic process, we agree as a learning community on three or four themes. These themes serve as the organizing principles for subsequent three-hour class sessions designed and facilitated by groups of students who have self-selected the theme on which they want to work. After the groups coalesce around the themes, we devote a week of class time to the groups working together to choose appropriate readings and design learning activities, assisting as necessary to manage group processes: tempering students with a need for order and control; making room for shyer, sometimes brilliant students to have their ideas heard; and encouraging creative thinking about various ways of engaging the learning community in addition to or other than formal lectures or presentations (though almost anything goes). A couple of examples of themes chosen by past Senior Seminar groups include piracy off the horn of Africa as a means of examining how the media constructs the meaning of events as well as an examination of the ways in which prisons serve—or rather, house—inmates with mental health issues (the group facilitating the session on this topic included a former member of the military police, a student who worked as a parole officer, and a seriously mentally ill and formerly homeless student).

Senior Seminar offers a great opportunity to step back from disciplinary commitments and examine the nature not only of the knowledge and skills students have obtained but also of their ways of knowing (and being) as a means of entering a discussion on how, ethically, students want to enact their learning subsequent to completing their undergraduate studies. Such an undergraduate capstone course is a natural point for practicing an integrative perspective, helping students to situate what they have learned as undergraduates within a broader and more complex context, and to gain a deeply embodied understanding of the benefits of integrating different disciplinary perspectives with their own lived experiences as a means of seeking viable paths through complex and seemingly intractable problems.

An integrative approach may seem natural for a capstone general education course. But before we unpack what we mean by *integrative*, we wish to examine another case study—one in which, at least on the surface, the integrative approach may not be immediately obvious.

Embodiment in Later Life

Do human beings have bodies, or are we our bodies? What is the experience of traveling through the human life course with/in a particular body? How do we know that we are aging? At what point in the life course do we become aware of our own aging? Where does age and aging reside within human consciousness, and how is this consciousness experienced in an embodied way? What are the various academic and popular discourses about human aging, and how do these discourses address embodiment? What are the implications of these discourses for lived experience as we travel through the life course? What identity work do we as individuals need to do in order to adapt to, accommodate—and embody—our aging, changing bodies over the life course? (And what on earth does this term *embodiment* mean?) These are some of the questions we explore in Embodiment in Later Life, a core seminar in the gerontology curriculum at Marylhurst University.

This course, first designed and taught by Jennifer in 1998 soon after she joined the Marylhurst faculty, is unique in the higher education gerontology landscape in that it utilizes an alternative framework informed by critical social theory, feminist theory, cultural studies, and aging studies to question the ways in which the field of gerontology has constituted itself historically and even now around the body as well as what happens in and to the body as humans travel through the life course. More typical in gerontology programs are courses that problematize the aging experience as primarily about bodily decline, frailty, disability, and disease. When foregrounded in gerontology courses, the aging body is most often considered an obstacle to be overcome, managed, and taken care of, rather than as an essential aspect of our humanness as we travel through the life course. Embodiment in Later Life challenges the biomedicalization of the aging journey, interrogates the mainstream gerontological discourses on aging (even though designed and taught by a legitimate educational gerontologist), and invites students to enter more fully into their own deep development and learning as a holistic (body/mind/spirit in context), lifewide, and lifelong adventure.

Embodiment in Later Life is a required course for undergraduate students majoring in social sciences with a gerontology concentration, all undergraduate or graduate students pursuing a gerontology certificate, and graduate students in the Master of Arts in Interdisciplinary Studies program focusing on gerontology. But any student is welcome to take the course whether they have prerequisite gerontological experience or knowledge or not; in fact, it is not uncommon for nongerontology students to use the course as an elective or to meet a general education requirement. As such, typically the course is populated by students bringing wildly diverse educational, professional, and personal backgrounds and baseline knowledge regarding the study of human adult development and aging, not to mention experiences and attitudes regarding their own personal aging journeys (as illustrated in our opening tale of Velda and her classmates). This makes for a rich and vibrant learning community but also presents some challenges for creating an environment in which collaborative inquiry can occur in such a way that each individual can contribute to and benefit from what we are up to in our scholarly and personal exploration of aging embodiment.

The seminar is reading-, writing-, and discussion-intensive. The required readings are gathered from multiple disciplines: biomedicine, antiaging medicine, philosophy, social gerontology, disability studies, aging studies, and critical social theory (for example, Moody and Sasser 2012; Olshansky and Carnes 2002; Tulle 2004). There is a core set of readings, some of which wouldn't be considered current from a normative scholarly standpoint (see, for example,

Gadow 1983; Katz 1996; Oberg 1996) that have been used in every iteration of the course because they provide a provocative way into the exploration of aging embodiment. This small collection of essential readings is enhanced each time the course is offered with additional assigned and optional scholarly readings as well as with visual media that are more contemporary or immediate. Each class session involves a combination of contemplation, free writing, and experiential learning activities—and sometimes a special show-and-tell such as a poem, a children's book, or a music video—and small and large group discussions around the questions and ideas addressed in the assigned readings. The order of these activities is unpredictable and varies from session to session, and spontaneous activities erupt in response to the questions and concerns that students bring with them to each session. For the past few years, the on-campus course sessions have been supported by an online course site, so discussion and resource sharing continues between sessions. The virtual extension of our in-person learning community has been a wonderful enhancement to the course and has provided an additional channel via which students can support and mentor each other (and the instructor!).

In addition to the learning activities for each class session, three major learning projects take place throughout the eleven weeks of the term that are designed to provide students a way into the complex and emergent nature of the study and experience of embodied aging. Early on in the course, we commence a collaborative learning project using the supplemental course site Nested Glossary Wiki. The intent of the Nested Glossary Wiki learning project is to provide students with a technique for constructing a system of understanding. It is vital that they not only recognize important gerontological and other disciplinary terms, ideas, and concepts—the components of all theoretical perspectives, philosophical schools of thought, and research methodologies and practice approaches—but also that they contemplate them long enough to be able to rearticulate their meanings in a way that makes sense to them and allows them to communicate their understanding to others. Most importantly, the Nested Glossary Wiki offers students an opportunity to exercise individual agency in terms of deciding which concepts to select, research, and include in the collaborative wiki as well as to participate in a sustained, shared inquiry process in which they learn from and comment upon one another's contributions. The same term can be defined multiple times by different people or redefined by the same person as his or her understanding changes. Often students find terms within definitions that need to be defined, like *matryoshka* dolls nesting inside each other. Examples include the *longevity revolution*, *social construction of aging*, *planned obsolescence*, *embodied agency*, *antiaging medicine*, *frailty*, and *the fountain of youth*. Together, the class community is creating a common learning resource. Students discover that knowledge is produced through exploration, contestation, and critique; is not fixed in time but emergent; happens most fruitfully as a community activity; and that they as learners have a role in knowledge creation.

The second formal assignment, which happens two-thirds of the way through the course, is the styles of embodiment project. For this experiential learning project, students spend some time hanging out at a public location where they can observe a variety of embodied creatures—human and other-than-human—as they move through space, time, and place. Students are asked to engage in a series of contemplative practices as a way to try on different perceptual "lenses" through which to view others and then to narrate via field notes their observations and impressions about the many ways in which the creatures they observe inhabit their bodily selves. Interestingly, this assignment tends to receive the most initial resistance but then often turns out to be among the most surprising and personally relevant learning experience for students.

Finally, at midterm and at the end of the course, students compose moderate-length (six- to eight-page) integrative essays. These essays, which are written in response to a menu of questions supplied by the instructor, offer students an opportunity to contemplate, synthesize, and enact their developing understandings and insights derived from a critical reading of and reflection upon the assigned readings, in-class discussions, and experiential learning adventures. As such, this essaying offers not only a contemplation, critical reflection, and integrative writing opportunity but also another opportunity to practice collaborative inquiry as students share with their classmates the insights they've gathered about their own and others' embodied travels through the life course.

Three Principles for Enacting Integration

We do not pretend that a commitment to a lifewide integrative sensibility is easy to embody and practice. For us, the principles of an integrative sensibility to teaching and learning—and being—we explored in this chapter are not primarily ones that govern ways we seek to understand specific social problems or engage our intellectual and creative work. As can be seen in the examples of the ways we go about designing and implementing integrative learning experiences, these principles ultimately connect to a way into engaging the inherent messy and contingent and often nonsensical nature of human experience. Such an integrative approach does not follow predetermined, predictable patterns. Rather, we are interested in the enactment of a lifewide commitment to a way of being in the world that privileges an intimacy with the chaotic, emergent nature of all of reality. Each interaction, each problem, each group will have many different possible ways it could be engaged, each with different consequences, different losses, and different gains. And each such choice of how to engage results in partial and provisional insights, and we must cultivate a curiosity concerning the consequences of those choices and the reverberations for ourselves and others of our thoughts and actions. The integrative approach requires, in our view, a simultaneous practice of contemplation, critical thinking, and ethical action in the world as sovereign but connected agents. Our actions are at best based on what we understand at any given time to be incomplete, emergent understandings, and a commitment to seeking a more inclusive (dare we say integrative?) embodied consciousness as the basis from which to be present and respond to whatever comes next.

Our first principle, thus, is that *integrative study invites learners into complexity*. In practice, this involves the decompartmentalizing of one's life, of challenging normative conventions and discourses that encourage distance and separation and orderliness and instead trying out more improvisatory ways of being. This is why we teach our courses in a manner similar to the work of jazz musicians: There are themes for any given class session, but the execution depends on current events and the intellectual and personal interests of the collection of people in the room. These improvisations may be events from the world at large or, for example, student dissatisfaction with their lack of involvement in the creation of a new university brand and logo; or for another example, making the most of the opportunity provided by Velda's broken hip and wrist described in the opening paragraph of this essay; or of some students' involvement in the 2011 Occupy encampments. Such improvisations are intended to help all participants make connections between their own personal experiences and the lived complexity of the juicy ideas explored in the course. In addition, like all work that is emergent, integrative study strikes us as slow work, dependent over time on a process of holding in relationship different ways of knowing (see Dreyfuss 2011). The metaphor here is of human relationships, parents and children, siblings, friendships, partnerships and marriages; the transformations that happen in deep relationships, like any deep learning, take time; insights come slowly, often in response to what we experience as sustained conflict, though those apparent conflicts frequently have to do with deeply held and cherished ideas or stories we tell about ourselves and our world; or long-familiar patterns of interacting with others and with ourselves. Thus, what emerges from beholding complexity with an integrative sensibility is not so much a clearer kind of order but rather a more balanced way of engaging with a world that is more complex than we initially imagined (or would let ourselves initially accept).

The underlying belief here is that reality is neither fixed nor finished and that all of our understandings of it, teachers and students alike, are likewise incomplete products of particular temporal and cultural contexts. As such we must be vigilantly curious about what we think we know. The kind of questioning we wish to foster in our teaching is a commitment to a process we also wish to cultivate in ourselves and one that is essential to integrative study. This leads to the conviction that while we may or may not have more information at our fingertips than our co-learners in the room, we are not necessarily any more right about what we think is true. In any discussion, we try to remember to do the following: calm down and breathe so that we can slow time and stay open rather than close up and move our minds to a more capacious space—that is, find a way to shift our thinking so that it is expansive enough to contain and hold together the different, seemingly incommensurable ideas or assumptions by which we are feeling muddled.

Thus, our second principle—*integrative study invites learners to be curious about context and their own and other's epistemologies*—begins with a process of self-understanding. We must cultivate an awareness of our own epistemological commitments and how they shape what we see and hear (and do not see or hear), balanced by a curiosity about the epistemological commitments of others. We must ask ourselves: Where do my strongly held ideas come from? Why do I hold them so strongly? Why do I feel resistance to other ideas? What would happen if I tried on other ideas? In practice, we welcome the expression of all strongly (or tentatively) held ideas and ask that everyone remain curious about what any given set of ideas makes clear and, perhaps more interestingly, the aspect of a phenomenon that available explanations don't seem to explain adequately. We try to model courage to interrogate the different, sometimes conflicting, sometimes frightening ways of constructing meanings about phenomena and how different meanings—on their own, and in synthesis—might inform praxis. We ask students to critically examine the foundations and evidence for their own and others' firmly held beliefs. We ask, if we sincerely believed something is true, what are the implications for how we would act, engage in inquiry, examine a problem, participate in a community, and treat each other? What are the implications for how we conduct ourselves and how we are present? We also invite the participants to engage in reflection and discussion, encouraging them to ground themselves in their own experiences as learners; the reason is that for any learning to be truly meaningful, transformative, and powerful, it must be fundamentally about the project of developing and becoming who we want to be in the world, and each individual must discover and enact this ongoing process on his or her own behalf.

It should be clear by now that another feature of our styles in fostering integrative learning communities is that we prefer to ask questions rather than saying what we believe the answer to any particular questions might be. We prefer that learners develop a habit of questioning. We believe people think better together than in isolation, that a process of dialogue that takes into account different perspectives based on different life experiences will produce ideas or potential solutions to problems more durable over time when they take into account a more complex understanding of reality. This commitment to question-driven, cross-disciplinary, and collaborative inquiry that emphasizes contemplation and critical thinking is the basis of our third and final principle, that *integrative study invites learners into conversation and collaboration.* We favor collaborative learning projects like the group presentations in Senior Seminar or the Nested Glossary Wiki within Embodiment in Later Life. These projects are designed to foster an ongoing scholarly conversation among a community of learners—a community that includes students, instructors, and authors of the assigned readings, and a community in which all members share responsibility and authority. The commitment at the basis of these conversations is to be respectful of relationships—no matter at what point each member of the community may be in their scholarly life or life course.

Enacting integration requires us to practice openness to human experience, even in the face of things we don't understand or things we don't want to have to change about ourselves and our lives. It requires honing our sensitivity to levels of analysis, to the contingent nature of reality, to the force of social structures, and to the importance of historicity—all forms of complexity that we often shy away from or even from which we flee. Sometimes it requires us to practice openness to things that can't be changed in a situation or about others. Enacting integration involves a curiosity about other creatures (human and not human), about the nature of self and other, and about the nature of reality. It involves something ethical, even spiritual, having to do with interconnectedness, how all of our ideas are, and each of us is, part of something larger—families, ecosystems, communities, workplaces, societies, a particular planet, the cosmos—and as such, we have roles and responsibilities to reflect upon and enact with intentionality and care.

Not that we always do. Many times we head off almost mindlessly down what appear to be splendid new paths leading to spectacular new vistas or try something that feels unique with the best of intentions that fails miserably, or engage a problem in a way that feels innovative but has more to do with habit, or perform a role from the standpoint of poorly examined assumptions about the world or ourselves or others. But the integrative impulse is toward an ever bigger mind—no, a bigger self: one that seeks an understanding of why we have suddenly reached the edge of a cliff when the path we have been walking always led somewhere before, or maybe it always led to that cliff and we only went there for the view and now find the view less interesting, the edge of the cliff crumbling, and we see that all along it has never been safe to stand there. Or we see that the only way forward is over the cliff and into the vast and mysterious abyss.

Enacting integration requires a strange and lovely hope about our own and others' capacities for ongoing, lifelong, deep development. It is an improvisatory project that requires courage to live in the midst of the muddle that is complex human reality. It requires that each of us be willing to try stuff, to make mistakes—walk off the edges of cliffs—and perhaps to change in order to live this precious human life with purpose and meaning.

References

Arcario, P., B. Eynon, and J. E. Clark. 2005. "Making Connections: Integrated Learning, Integrated Lives." *Peer Review* 7 (4): 15–17.

Association of American Colleges & Universities. 2002. *Greater Expectations: A New Vision for Learning as a Nation Goes to College.* Washington, DC: Author.

Augsberg, T., and S. Henry. 2009. *The Politics of Interdisciplinary Studies.* Jefferson, NC: McFarland and Company.

Bateson, G. 1972. *Metalogues: Steps to an Ecology of Mind.* Chicago: University of Chicago Press.

Boix-Mansilla, V. 2008. "Integrative Learning: Setting the Stage for a Pedagogy of the Contemporary." *Peer Review* 10 (4): 31.

Chickering, A. W., J. C. Dalton, and L. Stamm. 2005. *Encouraging Authenticity and Spirituality in Higher Education.* San Francisco: Jossey-Bass.

Chickering, A. W., and L. Reisser. 1993. *Education and Identity.* 2nd ed. San Francisco: Jossey-Bass.

Colectivo. 2000. "Critical Psychology or Critique of Psychology?" In *Critical Psychology: Voices for Change*, edited by T. Sloan, 211–22. London: Macmillan.

Czechowski, J. 2003. "An Integrated Approach to Liberal Learning." *Peer Review* 5 (4): 4–7.

Dreyfuss, S. 2011. "Something Essential about Interdisciplinary Thinking." *Issues in Integrative Studies*, 29: 67–83.

Ellsberg, D. 2006. "Notebook: The Next War." *Harpers Magazine* 313 (1877): 7–10.

Esgalhado, B. D. 2000. "The Critical Psychology of Everyday Life." In *Critical Psychology: Voices for Change*, edited by T. Sloan, 223–31). London: Macmillan.

Freire, P. 2000. *Pedagogy of the Oppressed: 30th Anniversary Edition.* New York: Continuum.

Gadow, S. 1983. "Frailty and Strength: The Dialectic in Aging." *Gerontologist* 23 (2): 144–47.

Heron, J., and P. Reason. 1997. "A Participatory Inquiry Paradigm." *Qualitative Inquiry* 3: 274–94.

Heshusius, L. 1994. "Freeing Ourselves from Objectivity: Managing Subjectivity or Turning toward a Participatory Mode of Consciousness?" *Educational Researcher* 23 (3): 15–22.

Himbeault Taylor, S. 2011. "Engendering Habits of Mind and Heart through Integrative Learning." *About Campus* 16 (5): 13–20. doi:10.1002/abc.20076.

Huber M. T., and P. Hutchings. 2004. *Integrative Learning: Mapping the Terrain.* Washington, DC: Association of American Colleges & Universities and the Carnegie Foundation for the Advancement of Teaching.

Isikoff, M. 2008. "The Fed Who Blew the Whistle." *Newsweek* 152 (25): 40–48.

Katz, S. 1996. *Disciplining Old Age: The Formation of Gerontological Knowledge.* Charlottesville: University of Virginia Press.

Klein, J. T. 1990. *Interdisciplinarity: History, Theory, and Practice.* Detroit: Wayne State University Press.

———. 2005. "Integrative Learning and Interdisciplinary Studies." *Peer Review* 7 (4): 8–10.

Kolb, D. A. 1984. *Experiential Education: Experience as the Source of Learning and Development.* Englewood Cliffs, NJ: Prentice Hall.

Kuh, G. D. 2008. *High-Impact Educational Practices: What They Are, Who Has Access to Them, and Why They Matter.* Washington, DC: Association of American Colleges & Universities.

Leonard, J. B. 2012. "Integrated Learning: A Grounded Theory." *Issues in Integrative Studies* 30: 47–74.

Mahoney, S., and J. Schamber. 2011. "Integrated and Deep Learning through a Learning Community: A Process View of Self." *JGE: The Journal of General Education* 60 (4): 234–47.

Moody, H. R., and J. R. Sasser. 2012. *Aging: Concepts and Controversies.* 7th ed. Thousand Oaks: Sage.

Newell, W. H. 2001. "A Theory of Interdisciplinary Studies." *Issues in Integrative Studies* 19: 1–25.

Oberg, P. 1996. "The Absent Body—A Social Gerontological Paradox." *Ageing and Society* 16: 701–19.

Olshansky, S. J., and B. A. Carnes. 2002. *The Quest for Immortality: Science at the Frontiers of Aging*. New York: Norton.

Repko, A. 2011. *Interdisciplinary Research: Process and Theory*. 2nd ed. Thousand Oaks, CA: Sage.

Ross, C. 2012. "A New Politics for a Disorderly World." *The Nation* 294 (9): 24–26.

Sifry, M. L. 2011. "The End of Secrecy." *The Nation* 292 (12): 17–22.

Tulle, E., ed. 2004. *Old age and agency*. Hauppauge, NY: Nova Science Publishers.

Wallerstein, I. 1999. *The End of the World as We Know It: Social Science for the Twenty-First Century*. Minneapolis: University of Minnesota.

Part 2
Scholarly Integration—Application and Practice

Chapter 5

Programming for Integrative Learning

Marcus N. Tanner, PhD, and Charlie Adams, PhD, Texas Tech University

There is a national movement in higher education for nurturing undergraduate students' integrative learning through educational experiences, which combines classroom and out-of-classroom experiences (Czechowski 2003; Newell 1999). The global workplace is actively seeking college graduates who are able to handle multifaceted challenges, solve complex problems, and present ideas in new and uniquely different ways (Huber and Hutchings 2004). As integrative learning becomes a distinguishing mark of a twenty-first century education, curricular, cocurricular, and pedagogical innovations are being used to prepare students to become lifelong learners and to have successful careers.

More and more, businesses and organizations are seeing interdisciplinary collaboration and the ability to synthesize information as highly valued skills in the workplace. Trained specialists from different fields bring unique perspectives to the work environment. These specialists are often used in groups to provide original and creative approaches to situations, problems, and ideas. Interdisciplinary collaboration gives businesses and organizations a competitive advantage because they are able see things from a synthesis of multiple perspectives. Original thought is a cornerstone of business, and integrative learning is an effective means of teaching undergraduate students how to apply their knowledge and skills to their personal lives, education, and careers. This chapter focuses on integrative learning as an effective means to helping undergraduate students.

Integrative Learning

Integrative learning has been defined in a variety of ways. Magdola and King (1992) note that one goal of integrative learning is to provide an equilibrium between an emphasis on thinking processes and attention given to learning specific content. Huber and Hutchings (2004) argue that integrative studies "develops habits of the mind that prepare students to make informed judgments in the conduct of personal, professional, and civic life" (1). The American Association of Colleges & Universities defines *integrative learning* as "an understanding and a disposition that a student builds across the curriculum and co-curriculum, from making simple connections among ideas and experiences to synthesizing and transferring learning to new, complex situations within and beyond the campus" (Liberal Education and America's Promise, 2005, np.). Integrative studies programs help students build this understanding through course design that focuses on "applying knowledge though real-world engagements, or teaching students and communicating with the public" (Huber and Hutchings 2004, 2). Further, it is essential that students develop a wide array of skills and content focuses that enable them to navigate the real world and allow them to operate through multiple lenses. Increasingly, college graduates are expected to operate in a highly technological and global world, which adds complexity to careers that new graduates might seek out. College graduates are now expected to synthesize learning from multiple sources, assimilate experiences, and create valuable links between theory and practice.

The global marketplace is seeking thinkers who can see connections and draw upon their knowledge to make informed decisions in the classroom, the workplace, their personal lives, and their communities. The U.S. Department of Education in 2000 endorsed an interdisciplinary framework that requires schools to use thematic approaches that would help students apply their learning concepts in the real world (Humphreys, 2005). Integrative learning is valuable not only to one's academic experience but for their career and future plans.

Higher Education and Integrative Learning

The Association of American Colleges & Universities (2005) reported that eleven colleges had either developed, improved, or expanded Integrative Learning Project Campuses. Program components included a clear set of communicable goals, learning communities sharing knowledge among students and faculty, electronic student portfolios that track and assess learning across classes for multiple semesters, tiers of courses, and a capstone project. One college specifically noted that the intention of the integrative studies program was to connect professional programs with liberal education cores by expanding faculty and professional involvement in a university forum where faculty and students can clearly communicate and plan for a career (see, for example, Philadelphia University).

In other instances, faculty and students engaged in workshops where they examine various case studies, applying real-world thinking and analytical skills in order to solve complex problems. Buchbinder, Alt, Eskow, Forbes, Hester, Struck, and Taylor (2005) noted that in these workshops, faculty and students collaborated to

> apply self-directed learning and critical thinking skills; analyze the true underlying causes of the problems; apply theoretical knowledge from their disciplines; use creative abilities to synthesize decisions and recommendations; establish methods for evaluation of recommendations; deal with personality conflict and change; [and] demonstrate effective interpersonal and oral communication skills within a team format. (267)

In these instances, teachers were supportive facilitators in a risk-free environment that provided opportunities for people who work together to analyze, apply, and synthesize problems across disciplines (see, e.g., Buchbinder et al. 2005, 267–70).

Integrative studies is a growing field of scholarship that prepares students for the challenges and complexity of the twenty-first century. The Integrative Studies program at Texas Tech University (TTU) was developed using the Association of American Colleges & Universities (AAC&U) Liberal Education and America's Promise (LEAP) initiative and Valid Assessment of Learning in Undergraduate Education (VALUE) rubrics.

LEAP Initiative

"Liberal Education and America's Promise (LEAP) is a national advocacy, campus action, and research initiative that champions the importance of a twenty-first-century liberal education—for individuals and for a nation dependent on economic creativity and democratic vitality" (LEAP 2005) . The economy is changing in the United States, and required workforce characteristics are also being modified. Employers are demanding different skills and knowledge from their college-educated workforce. College graduates are expected to have a broader base of knowledge. They need to possess strong intellectual and serviceable skills to compete successfully in this challenging environment.

The AAC&U through LEAP is helping to transform traditional education in the United States. LEAP helps students achieve a set of essential learning outcomes, no matter their chosen field of study. This is important to students in the University Studies program at TTU (which includes the Integrative Studies program), as they do not have one field of study or major. Rather, these students craft their own degree, incorporating multiple fields of study. The challenge is to allow flexibility while maintaining an overall sense of purpose, providing for rigorous study and connections between their areas of study. The LEAP Essential Learning Outcomes (ELOs) helped to provide such a framework for Integrative Studies and the University Studies program at Texas Tech.

For example, the Integrative Studies program (INTS) utilized the Integrative Learning VALUE Rubric (Rhodes 2010) for measuring student success in the program. In the Foundations course, students are expected to meet the benchmark of the Integrative Learning rubric in each of five categories:

- *Connections to experience*—able to identify connections between life and school
- *Connections to discipline*—present information from more than one field of study or perspective
- *Transfer*—use, in a basic way, skills, abilities, theories or methodologies gained in one situation in a new situation
- *Integrated communication*—fulfill assignments in an appropriate form
- *Reflection and self-assessment*—describe performance through reflection and self-assessment.

In junior-level courses (i.e., 3000, 3301, 3330, and 3350) students should meet milestone 2 or 3 of the rubric. In senior-level courses (4320 and 4350), students should meet the capstone level of the rubric.

Brief History of University Studies and Integrative Studies

The University Studies program at Texas Tech was created in early 2007. University Studies made a number of structural transitions over the past six years. When the degree was first created, it could be described as a multidisciplinary degree. Students took their core curriculum, then chose three areas of concentration that constituted the sixty-plus hours for their major in arts or science in University Studies. Besides a student essay prior to admission to the program, no faculty or staff worked with students to synthesize their areas of concentration. The program had fewer than forty students and in 2010 was transferred from the provost's office to the new University College.

After the transfer, some effort was made to help students choose areas of concentration that made sense, especially in terms of careers and future plans. An advising staff was hired and charged not only with advising students in the program but also helping them create the philosophical connections between the areas of concentration.

In June 2011 University Studies hired its first faculty member and program director for Integrative Studies. Integrative Studies (INTS) was simply a programming idea at the time. The purpose was to teach the skills students would need in order to synthesize their learning across disciplines and apply their learning to their careers and future plans. This required a series of courses, as part of the University Studies degree, that would help students synthesize their areas of study and create connections across the curriculum and beyond the classroom.

Today, the bachelor of arts or science in University Studies (BUS) at TTU has been shifted back to the office of the provost and is unique in that it allows for a flexible, individualized degree while providing structure for integrative learning. Having interdisciplinary programs in the office of the provost is not uncommon in the United States but is usually marked by low, stagnant enrollment. Even with the transition, the BUS program has continued to grow at great speed with almost one thousand students currently enrolled. Students choose three areas of concentration from any college on campus, such as hospitality, personal financial planning, exercise and sports science, organizational leadership, human resource development, psychology, sociology, and so on. Each area must account for eighteen hours, totaling fifty-four hours of the student's minimum 120-hour degree requirement. The three areas of study must logically fit and apply to future studies or a career field. Concentration coursework is delivered primarily by faculty outside of the BUS program, which is a challenge, but one that is being met through INTS programming. Forty-two hours of credit must be taken from the core curriculum. Finally, students are required to take a 12-hour series of INTS courses to complete their degree. All INTS courses are taught by faculty who are part of the University Studies program. These faculty members comprise several full-time University Studies faculty members and part-time faculty members from other colleges and departments on campus.

Integrative Studies Program

The INTS program provides a path of interdisciplinary undergraduate education not previously seen on the TTU campus. The series of INTS courses were designed to help develop students' critical thinking skills by giving them a universal understanding of how to work collaboratively through multiple lenses to solve complex problems, generate new ideas, and evaluate situations from new and multiple perspectives. Integrative thinkers are people who see the importance of lifelong learning as a means to conjoining their experiences into a tapestry of knowledge, information, and perspectives that are always evolving and changing. The result is that integrative knowledge enhances individuals' ability to compete in a complex and multifaceted world because the breadth and depth of their learning provides them with insights, which other forms of education may fail to do.

Faculty challenge students to make connections across their areas of concentration that apply to their careers and future plans. Through the sequence of INTS courses, students are challenged to consider the breadth and depth of their chosen concentration areas, write across the curriculum, make curricular and cocurricular connections, and apply their learning to life beyond the classroom. *Integrative studies* is defined at Texas Tech as a synthesis of study and life, an application of interdisciplinarity to complex problems, providing for a common body of knowledge, recognizing various disciplinary perspectives as well as learning how to synthesize and evaluate those perspectives, and thus empowering people to address meaningful and complex issues in new and unique ways.

Integrative studies is an official minor that any student on the TTU campus may choose as part of a degree; however it is designed specifically for interdisciplinary students in the University Studies program. As of the fall semester of 2012, University Studies students are required to take the following twelve hours of INTS coursework; INTS 2310–Foundations of Integrative Studies, INTS 3300–Perspectives on Integrative Studies, a choice of INTS 3301–Career and Professional Development or INTS 4320–Internship, and INTS 4350–Capstone in Integrative Studies. Two additional courses were designed as electives focused on global perspectives (INTS 3330) and team leadership (INTS 3350). Each course is aligned with the AAC&U's Essential Learning Outcomes from the LEAP program. Many of the assignments in each course are aligned with a specific set of requirements from the Integrative Learning VALUE rubric. At the end of each semester, students are asked to complete a short survey about how prepared they feel at meeting specific criterion of the rubric. In addition, faculty members are required to report the percentage of students in their course who met the minimum required criterion of the rubric categories (connection to experience, connection to disciplines, transfer, etc.).

For example, in INTS 2310, our Foundations course, we are interested in students achieving at least the benchmark performance level described in the integrative learning rubric. Students are asked how prepared they are to meet the minimum level of performance for each of the rubric's five categories.

In the junior-level courses (INTS 3300, 3301, 3330, and 3350), we want students to achieve a milestone set forth in the integrative learning rubric but also want to gauge their achievement in other specific areas. For example, in 3330–Global Perspectives it is important to know whether students are prepared to engage in diverse communities and be involved in solving community challenges, and in 3350–Team Leadership whether students are prepared to work in groups. In 4350–Capstone it is essential to understand whether students achieve the capstone level of the integrative learning rubric as well as several other important areas. In the sections below, information is presented from the three cornerstone courses, INTS 2310, 3300, and 4350. Data is also present that was collected in Fall 2013 concerning the performance level of students in relation to the integrative learning VALUE rubric.

INTS 2310–Foundations

The purpose of INTS 2310 is to introduce students to the foundations of integrative studies. In this course, students learn the developmental process of integrative studies, the fundamentals of integrative research, and the integration of personal, educational, and professional goals. This course is designed to provide students with the essential principles of integrative studies that will serve as a foundation for their future as interdisciplinarians and careers in a professional field of their choice.

Strategically, the Foundations course was the last to be developed. We began with the end in mind, designing and teaching the capstone course first. At the end of the first term, the faculty who taught gathered to provide an informal summative assessment of student learning. The qualitative data were used to design an introductory course to INTS that would provide a foundation for learning and student success. Students desperately needed a solid footing in terms of defining interdisciplinary and integrative study. They needed to understand the process of interdisciplinary research and interdisciplinary integration (Repko 2012). Students required a clear understanding of the Integrative Studies program and its purpose.

In this course, students are introduced to terminology that is important to interdisciplinarity. They are taught the differences between *disciplinary*, *multidisciplinary*, *interdisciplinary*, *integrative*, and *transdisciplinary*. Students reflect on their chosen areas of concentration, their education, their life, and the intersections between those domains. They begin to construct a personal narrative that weaves together the threads of their life, including academic and professional experiences. Many interdisciplinary students at TTU at first find it difficult to understand what makes them interdisciplinary and how to reflect on the connections of the experiences. Bateson's (1994) discussion of the concept of construing continuity-finding connections helps students identify the thread(s) between their seemingly disconnected experiences, whether life, professional, or academic. They learn the basic steps of doing a literature review for an interdisciplinary research project, utilizing Repko's (2012) process of interdisciplinary research. Students end the course by developing the first draft of several portfolio artifacts: a resume, a cover letter, and a personal narrative that includes statements of why they chose their areas of concentration and an explanation of integrative studies. Students leave the course with a preparatory knowledge of what it means to be interdisciplinary and integrative and how these developed skills could be utilized in multiple career fields.

At the end of the course they are asked to complete a survey developed from the integrative learning VALUE rubric. Students at Texas Tech in the Integrative Studies program self-report their own preparedness in achieving the rubric's benchmarks. More than 80 percent of the students feel prepared or very prepared to identify connections between life and academic experiences. Eighty-three percent feel prepared or very prepared to see connections between disciplines, and 87 percent feel prepared or very prepared to make connections across disciplines. Eighty-two percent feel prepared or very prepared to utilize basic skills, abilities, theories, or methodologies in new situations, and 85 percent feel prepared or very prepared to engage in integrated communication. Eighty-six percent feel prepared or very prepared to describe their own performance with general descriptors of success and failure, and 83 percent feel prepared or very prepared to develop their own sense of self.

However, it is not quite enough to say how students felt about their own preparedness to meet the benchmarks of the integrative learning VALUE rubric; some validation through course assignments is needed. Overall, the majority of students in the Fall 2013 course were successful; 76 percent earning a passing grade for the course. Specifically, students completed a literature review map, discussed in Repko (2012) to engage in seeing connections across disciplines in relation to an interdisciplinary research problem; 72 percent of the Fall 2013 students met the benchmark. The personal narrative assignment is used to assess students' ability to identify connections between different domains of life: personal, educational, and professional. It is also used to assess students' performance of integrated communication, reflection, and self-assessment. Seventy-six percent of students in Fall 2013 successfully met the integrative learning benchmark.

INTS 3300–Perspectives of Integrative Studies

The purpose of INTS 3300 is to provide students with an intermediate experience in interdisciplinary research methods and its applications. In this course, students learn to develop important research questions that can be answered using an interdisciplinary approach and are expected to develop an interdisciplinary research proposal during this course. They complete a number of small assignments leading up to the proposal. Students are given an interdisciplinary research problem and asked to develop a specific interdisciplinary research question. As students progress through the course, they conduct a literature review, revise their research question or problem, and consider appropriate methods for collecting data. Their research paper is a culmination of the previous assignments, revised based on instructor feedback and inferences that students might draw based upon their literature review of the problem. Students do not actually collect any data. However, their final project could easily be used to develop hypotheses and conduct an undergraduate research project. Should students choose to go to graduate school, their undergraduate project in this course could be revised into a graduate-level thesis.

Again, at the end of the course students were asked to participate in a survey of their own reflections in terms of their preparedness in meeting milestones 2 or 3 from the integrative learning VALUE rubric. When asked about how prepared they were to make connections to experiences, 78 percent of students fell into milestone 2, and 81 percent of students fell into milestone 3. When asked to reflect on their preparedness to see connections across disciplines and perspectives, 76 percent of students were in milestone 2, while 78 percent were in milestone 3. In terms of transfer—the ability to adapt and apply skills, abilities, theories, or methodologies gained in one situation to new situations—80 percent of students were in milestone 2, and 78 percent were in milestone 3. Students were also asked to reflect on their preparedness to integrate communication. Seventy-six percent of students in milestone 2 felt very prepared to integrate their communication, and 78 percent of students in milestone 3 felt prepared to integrate their communication. When asked about their ability to demonstrate a developing sense of self (reflection and self-assessment), 82 percent of students fell into milestone 2, while 79 percent of students fell into milestone 3.

Faculty also rated the students in each of the five areas of the integrative learning VALUE rubric. When it came to connections to experience, 89 percent were in milestone 2 and 89 percent in milestone 3. Eighty-nine percent of students successfully fell into milestone 2 in terms of connections to disciplines, transfer, and integrated communication. Eighty-eight percent of students were in milestone 2 in terms of reflection and self-assessment. Eighty-nine percent of students successfully fell into milestone 3 in terms of connection to experience. Eighty-six percent of students were in milestone 3 in terms of transfer, connections to disciplines, and reflection and self-assessment. Eighty-five percent of students were in milestone 3 in terms of integrated communication.

INTS 4350–Capstone

The final required course in the series of INTS is the capstone. Students should take this course after they have taken Foundations, Perspectives, and either Career and Professional Development or Internship. The purpose of INTS 4350 is to provide students the opportunity to weave together their personal, academic, and professional experiences to create one cohesive narrative. In this course students have the opportunity to interlace common threads that showcase their education, skills, and abilities. Students are expected to develop an integrated portfolio of their education in preparation for their career and future plans. Bierman, Ciner, Lauer-Gleboc, Rutz, and Savina (2005) suggest that a portfolio helps students transfer their early insights and skills into a participation learning project. The portfolio helps to "unify discourse around student writing at the lower division" (19) while helping students to transfer their knowledge to one another, and between subjects and tasks. Similarly, Flowers and Rhodes (2005) find that an e-portfolio helps to reflect a student's mastery of goals as well as the ability to integrate learning in context. Compiling work samples and creating reflections of students' work occur over the entire series of INTS courses. Flowers and Rhodes (2005) argue that portfolios are "a promising medium for demonstrating what students learn outside the classroom, which contributes helpful information for advising and provides connections to transfer students' co-curricular activities" (23). These portfolios can serve not only as reflective learning devices but also as displays of knowledge when students wish to enter the job market.

Not only do students develop their portfolio, but they write a senior thesis or complete a senior project that is interdisciplinary in nature. At the end of the course, students are expected to showcase their interdisciplinary experience via a video presentation. In designing this course, great care was taken to give students a true capstone experience, one that would end their undergraduate academic career with proficiency to enter the workplace or a graduate program with confidence. Students revisit their self-reflection from the Foundations course. Again, they are asked to write a personal narrative, describing what it means to be an interdisciplinarian, how and why they chose their areas of concentration, and their process of integrating their personal, educational, and life experiences.

Again, at the end of the course we asked students to respond to a survey. The survey asked students to reflect on their preparedness to meet performance level 4–capstone in the integrative learning VALUE rubric. Eighty-six percent of students felt prepared or very prepared to meaningfully synthesize connections among experiences outside of the formal classroom. Ninety-three percent felt prepared or very prepared to draw conclusions by combining perspectives from multiple disciplines. In terms of transfer, 86 percent of students felt prepared or very prepared. Ninety-three percent of students felt prepared or very prepared to engage in integrated communication and envision a future across multiple and diverse contexts.

Overall, 78 percent of the students enrolled in the Fall 2013 course successfully completed it. Although all students must complete a number of assignments in the course, their success in meeting the integrative learning VALUE rubric capstone performance level is assessed using the portfolio, personal narrative, and thesis. The portfolio assignment assesses their connections to experience, integrated communication, and reflection. Forty-five percent of students were successful in meeting the capstone performance level. The personal narrative assignment is used to assess reflection and self-assessment; 65 percent of students were successful. The thesis or project is used to assess all five categories of the rubric; 60 percent of students were successful.

The Integrative Studies program helps students understand more about themselves and their interdisciplinary degree. More than that, it is helping them construct a partnership between their education and their career and future plans. Our overall goal is to help students demonstrate an "application of knowledge, skills, and responsibilities to new settings and complex problems" (Rhodes 2010) across their general and specialized coursework.

This program also helps students prepare for new challenges by teaching them intellectual and practical skills, including inquiry and analysis, critical and creative thinking, written and oral communication, teamwork, and problem solving. In INTS 2310, 75 percent of students feel prepared or very prepared to think critically, 79 percent in INTS 3300, and 86 percent in INTS 4350. Additionally, this program helps students engage in personal and social responsibility by engaging them in ethical reasoning and intercultural awareness. In INTS 2310, 80 percent of students felt prepared or very prepared to engage with diverse communities with values different from those of their own, 73 percent in INTS 3300, and 79 percent in 4350. The program challenges students to become lifelong learners and to become actively involved in diverse communities around the world. Our hope is that these skills will help students achieve personal success, as they define it, and by engaging in complex problem solving, our world may become a better place for all. In INTS 2310, 81 percent felt very prepared or prepared to be involved in solving complex community challenges, while in INTS 3300 and 4350, 76 percent and 93 percent, respectively, felt very prepared or prepared. Additionally, a high percentage of students felt very prepared or prepared to develop skills for lifelong learning: 81 percent in INTS 2310, 80 percent in INTS 3300, and 93 percent in INTS 4350.

The integrative studies curriculum provides students a common body of knowledge for recognizing various disciplinary perspectives, as well as learning how to synthesize and evaluate those perspectives, thus empowering students to address meaningful and complex issues in new and unique ways. Students completing this program will be better educated for addressing the increasingly complex and interdisciplinary challenges of the ever expanding and interwoven world economy and will have enhanced marketability for a wide range of careers. Students will also be better prepared to enter graduate programs related to their interest areas.

Hendra (cited in Augsburg and Henry 2009) discussed the history of the individualized degree at the University Without Walls at UMass-Amherst. He described the flexible and individualized degree as being one of the most "successful innovations of the progressive college movement" (51). Although different than the program at UMass-Amherst, the development of integrative studies allowed program administrators to transform what was a multidisciplinary degree into a unique interdisciplinary/integrative undergraduate experience for students. Because of the flexibility of the University Studies degree, graduates leave Texas Tech University ready for their next steps in life, whether employment in an entry-level position, promotional opportunities, or graduate studies in a variety of disciplines. As the marketplace becomes more and more diverse, employers are increasingly looking for individuals who are comfortable working across a wide array of disciplines and can smoothly transition from one situation or experience to the next. Interdisciplinarity has become more important in the undergraduate curriculum because the need for integration is pervasive. In *Contemporary Understandings of Liberal Education*, Schneider and Shoenberg (1998) write about the need for the capacity to cross boundaries, explore connections, and move in uncharted directions. American higher education is in a period of transformative change, and integration of learning is central to this change. Integrative learning creates awareness of relationships, tensions, and complementarities among ideas, generating links among previously unconnected issues, approaches, sources of knowledge, and contexts of practice.

Although research on job placement for students in integrative studies programs is limited, much has been said about the benefits of integrative studies in terms of training students for the necessary skills in a variety of career pathways. Davies and Devlin (2007) argued as follows:

> Processes need to be in place to allow students to gain enough expertise to recognize the value and need of interdisciplinary study and work. Formal field work programs, on-site experience mentoring arrangements, real "life" work situations, involvement in undergraduate workshops and conferences, and similar mechanisms will likely assist in the creation of such an environment. (7)

An additional strength of the Integrative Studies program is the inclusion of courses that are directly related to potential career paths that students might choose. Students may decide to take a career and professional development course or an internship, although they are highly encouraged to take both.

Teaching from a career and future plans perspective mandates preparing students for the next step in their life, whether a new career or graduate school. The purpose of INTS 3301 is to provide students with the necessary career management skills for workplace success. This course helps students evaluate future career and professional plans. Students taking this course learn how to develop career and professional goals, research career and professional opportunities, and develop and compile artifacts that will be necessary for interviewing for a career or educational placement. They also will be able to identify and describe important steps to making a career or professional transition. This course is designed to be useful to students taking it as an elective or those taking it as part of the series of integrative studies courses.

In this course, students are taught skills they need to do a career search, apply and interview for a job, and know how to accept or decline an offer and how to present their unique interdisciplinary degree to potential employers. Again, students are developing portfolio artifacts in this course—resume, cover letter, generic application, and personal narrative—and learning how to collect other important information they will need in their career search. In the context of learning how to present themselves as interdisciplinarians in a global marketplace, which seeks out this type of college graduate, this course is essential.

Another course that strengthens the career and future plans perspective is the internship course, which provides an opportunity for students to apply to real-world experiences what they are learning in the classroom. The purpose of INTS 4320–Internship is to allow students an opportunity to apply program course material and integrative studies to researching a workplace problem while gaining valuable work experience. The advantage to doing an internship with a research component is that it allows the student an opportunity to apply and showcase interdisciplinary skills to a potential employer. According to the AAC&U and Hart Research Associates (2010), employers (91 percent) are "asking employees to take on more responsibilities and to use a broader set of skills than in the past." Eighty-eight percent of employers say that "the challenges their employees face are more complex than they were in the past." Students in this course are expected to identify a complex interdisciplinary problem at their internship workplace, spend a portion of their internship researching the problem from an interdisciplinary perspective, and present potential solutions to their employer at the end of their internship.

This course has been an invaluable experience for students who have chosen to take it and seriously participated. Because our student population is made of both traditional and nontraditional students, the program needed to consider how to structure the internship. The faculty and administration decided that the course should provide a framework for the internship that included working a certain number of hours during the semester, coursework that needed to be completed, and identifying and researching an interdisciplinary workplace problem. The program did not place students in their internships, and nontraditional students who may have already been working were allowed to continue in their current employment as long as they could identify an interdisciplinary research problem to work on during the semester.

Students have been very successful in this course. One student was working as a barista at a coffee shop near the campus. As a nontraditional student, she was challenged to continue her employment but identify an interdisciplinary workplace problem, research it, and provide potential solutions to the employer. This particular student did just that. At the end of her internship, she was promoted to district manager and put in charge of implementing her solutions to the interdisciplinary workplace problem. Being promoted to district manager meant, for this nontraditional student, a significant increase in pay, benefits, and a title worthy of her work. Another nontraditional student was working for an independent school district. He researched an interdisciplinary workplace problem and presented potential solutions to his employer. The result of his work netted him a promotion and a significant increase in pay. There are many other success stories of how students are using the framework of the internship course in order to create new jobs, receive promotions, or earn permanent jobs with an employer.

If the faculty and administrators of interdisciplinary programs want to help students find jobs or market themselves they need to ensure that students are accurately prepared. Teaching students to vest themselves in all disciplines in which they study is crucial to their long-term success, particularly students taking courses in disciplines that are very different from their first preference. Faculty, staff and administrators of interdisciplinary/integrative programs need to help students choose carefully their pathways for learning and their content in order to help them prepare for the job market. The goal of integrative learning is to get students to make connections between fields and to think critically about the relationships across the content areas. In relation to the job market, students need to become thinkers who can see connections and draw upon their knowledge to make informed decisions in the workplace. Moreover, by implementing relevant programs, faculty and students can make decisions that can enable graduates to find meaningful employment after graduating with an interdisciplinary/integrative degree.

References

American Association of Colleges & Universities and Hart Research Associates. 2010. "Raising the Bar: Employers' Views on College Learning in the Wake of the Economic Downturn." Authors, Washington, DC.

Augsburg, T., and S. Henry, eds. 2009. *The Politics of Interdisciplinary Studies: Essays on Transformations in American Undergraduate Programs.* Jefferson City, NC.

Bateson, M. C. 1994. *Peripheral Visions*: New York: HarperCollins.

Bierman, S., E. Ciner, J. Lauer-Glebov, C, Rutz, and M. Savina, M. 2005. "Integrative Learning: Coherence out of Chaos." *Peer Review* (Summer/Fall): 18–20.

Buchbinder, S. B., Forbes, W., Hester, E., Struck, M., & Dianne Taylor, R. 2005. "Creating learning prisms with an interdisciplinary case study workshop." *Innovative Higher Education,* 29 (4), 257-274.

Czechowski, J. 2003. "An Integrated Approach to Liberal Learning." *Peer Review* 5 (4): 4–7.

Davies, M., and M. Devlin. 2007. "Interdisciplinarity in Higher Education: Implications for Teaching and Learning." Centre for the Study of Higher Education, Melbourne.

Flower, M., and T. Rhodes, T. 2005. "Integrative Learning, E-Portfolios, and the Transfer Student." *Peer Review* 7 (4): 21–23.

Hendra, R. F. 2009. The Devolution of the Individualized Degree at the University Without Walls/University of Massachusetts–Amherst. In T. Augsburg & S. Henry (Eds.), *In The Politics of Interdisciplinary Studies: Essays on Transformations in American Under-*

graduate Programs (pp. 51-65). Jefferson, NC: McFarland & Company, Inc.

Huber, M. T., and P. Hutchings. 2004. *Integrative Learning: Mapping the Terrain*. Washington, DC: Association of American Colleges & Universities.

Humphreys, D. 2005. "Why Integrative Learning? Why Now?'" *Peer Review* 7 (4): 30–31.

Liberal Education and America's Promise (LEAP). 2005. http://www.aacu.org/leap/index.cfm.

Newell, W. H. 1999. "The Promise of Integrative Learning." *About Campus* 4 (2): 17–23.

Repko, A. F. 2012. *Interdisciplinary Research: Process and Theory*. 2nd ed. Thousand Oaks, CA: Sage Publications.

Rhodes, T., ed. 2010. *Assessing Outcomes and Improving Achievement: Tips and Tools for Using Rubrics*. Washington, DC: Association of American Colleges & Universities.

Schneider, C. G., and R. Shoenberg. 1998. Contemporary Understandings of Liberal Education: The Academy in Transition. Association of American Colleges & Universities, Washington, DC.

Chapter 6

Cultivating Integrity: Balancing Autonomy and Discipline in Integrative Programs

P. Sven Arvidson, PhD, Seattle University

If a university program is dedicated to educating the whole person, to maximizing student growth in an integrative way, what should such integration look like and what could integration mean? I believe that ancient Greece can inspire a contemporary response. Reverence for truth, wisdom to admit ignorance, courage to question, and justice for self and others are the virtues that Plato believed a liberally educated person of integrity must have. Here I contextualize these virtues in contemporary higher education, featuring an integrative, interdisciplinary bachelor's degree program at Seattle University. This bachelor of arts in liberal studies has major elements in common with many other integrative and interdisciplinary programs—courses, assignments, and program goals—so significant generalizations are possible about practices and strategies that might connect the integrity of the student and the educational philosophy of integration.

For Plato, self-discipline means leaving the cave of ignorance inspired by the sun of the full truth. It brings with it a kind of virtue, a community feeling of citizenship, motivating the enlightened one to go back into the cave to help others still chained, especially through disciplined conversation. Plato has his teacher Socrates in mind as one who has returned from the heights to educate the youth of Athens. Echoing Plato, many contemporary thinkers would tie education to citizenship, highlighting a necessary balance between autonomy and discipline. Autonomy can be evidenced in a number of ways: the freedom to make choices, individualistic thinking or self-examination, and critical thinking, as Socrates encouraged and university mission statements reiterate today. Discipline can be evidenced through increasing expertise in a body of knowledge and a meticulous embrace of the methodology that produces this knowledge. The balance of autonomy and discipline, gained through education, can contribute to good citizenship. If we were to put modern words in Plato's mouth, he might call one who has been integrally educated a person of *integrity*, and he originated the first university (the Academy in Athens) in order to cultivate integrity.

For us in the twenty-first century, we might simply say that the autonomous, disciplined student is a really good student: a curious, self-motivated, critical thinker who reasons and communicates in a disciplined way, whatever the discipline. We would add, if following Plato, that the autonomous, disciplined student is a really good person: responsible in learning, respectful of others, reverent toward truth, and centered, whole, or consistent. Being a really good student and a really good person—with this we have arrived at the problem of cultivating integrity, a challenge that involves the student and the program together. As educators, how do we identify, arrange, deliver, and encourage the requisite ideas, methods of investigation, historical perspectives, literary sensibilities, and metacognition to cultivate student and program integrity, seen as a balance of autonomy and discipline? This is a problem of organization for development, which is a problem of program curriculum.

To illustrate the curriculum problem, picture the senior synthesis or capstone course in a bachelor of arts in liberal studies program:

A crisp fall day, the first week of senior synthesis class, and Jon and Maria look dumbfounded. "We've never had the opportunity to choose to write a play or a short story as the main assignment in a class." Now I am dumbfounded. Jon and Maria are creative writing majors taking this liberal studies course because English senior synthesis does not align correctly for their prompt graduation. Would they have had an opportunity to write a sustained, creative piece in the English senior synthesis? Week three, Peter wonders aloud about part of the upcoming assignment: "How do I write my own reflection on the school's mission?" adding, "I'm also excited about the personal mission statement we need to write because I've really never been asked to write about myself." This is Peter's last term as a criminal justice major, and like Jon and Maria, he has received permission to take this senior synthesis rather than his own. Remarkably, it seems that no one has asked Peter yet to reflectively tie his academics to his life. These several students, along with the fifteen or so liberal studies majors in the course, are being given the most freedom they will ever have in a required course. They are excited, vaguely confused, or a little terrified. The students presumably think, *If I get so much choice in what to work on and how to express my work, then maybe education isn't what I think it is.*

How did Jon and Maria fare? Jon was ready to expose his personality through his short story but was unprepared for the initiative that autonomy demands. He passed the course after opting for an incomplete. Maria flourished in the creative clearing. If they were both majors in an integrative program, how might they have been "pushed" and "led" into a position of competence and confidence for the senior synthesis project based on maximum autonomy and requiring profound self-discipline?

In the following, I discuss key courses, such as a senior synthesis or capstone, that appear in most well-developed integrative programs leading to a bachelor's degree. First, we look more closely at the concepts of integrity, autonomy, and discipline.

Integrity in Classical and Contemporary Perspective

Plato's *Apology* is required reading in nearly any Introduction to Philosophy course, because Socrates (Plato's teacher) was the first fully dedicated philosopher within a relatively stable democratic society. In the *Apology* Socrates "apologizes" (explains) his life of philosophy in front of the Athenian court, with some five hundred fellow citizens as jurors. And that life is summed up in one word: integrity. With the concept of integrity, we are brought to the contemporary problem of what it is and how can we get it. Integrity is consistency, wholeness. Integrity means achieving an identity that pulls together the various pieces of one's life around a center so that one becomes identified with one's convictions by living them. Integrity is characteristic activity, activity that shows good character. Socrates demonstrated his integrity in various ways, and most are described in the *Apology*. I articulate here four constituent virtues that capture what one can mean by integrity in integrative education: reverence, wisdom, courage, and justice. Philosopher Paul Woodruff defines virtue in a general way that fits this chapter well: "A virtue is a capacity, cultivated by experience and training, to have emotions that make you feel like doing good things" (2001, 62), and "Virtue ethics deals with strengths people develop in communities" (2001, 7). Integrity is not a virtue; it is their embodiment.

Reverence. Socrates has a kind of reverence for truth, following questions wherever they may lead, even unto death. Though he does not have Socrates in mind, English professor Anthony Nuttall (2003) argues that this reverence for truth is a mark of scholarship: "The most obviously moral component in the scholarly ideal . . . [is] an altruistic reverence for truth, in all its possible minuteness and complexity" (194). The reverence for truth, scholarly or Socratic, is an awe for what we do not know and a feeling of respect and trust for each other when faced with human limitation. "If we cannot place a reasonable degree of trust in our scholars, we cannot trust anyone" (Nuttall 2003, 196). To be a scholar or a student in a discipline is to occasionally feel awe for what is transcendent, what somehow exists beyond one's knowledge, and to respect peers who labor in a disciplined way for clarity. As reverent educators, we ask our students in the natural and social sciences to trust that epistemological vagueness will yield to clarity, and in the humanities we also ask them to embrace ambiguity as they search for answers.[1]

Wisdom. In a search for wise citizens, Socrates questions everyone in prominent positions about the truth. As he reports in court, faced with disappointing results, he comes to realize that he is wise to the extent that he admits his ignorance. This "wisdom" is another feature that caring professors assume students have or seek to instill in them. After all, how are they students at all if they are not in some way open and vulnerable to learning?

Courage. Plato's *Phaedo* recounts how Socrates faced his death courageously, staying consistent to his principle that an unexamined life is not worth living. There is a less dramatic sense of courage that we envision in our classrooms. As professors, we try to promote courage against complacency. It is a battle between intellectual contentment and intellectual disquiet, between satisfaction and desire. Students cannot question in a disciplined way unless and until they have opened up to the fact that there is a truth not wholly owned by any one person (reverence for transcendent truth) and that it is a truth they do not yet know (wisdom in admitting ignorance). Disciplined questioning demands courage and encouragement from professors and mentors, if the questioning is to be significant and fruitful. What we try to encourage in students in the classroom and through program planning is the desire to become intellectually vulnerable in the courageous pursuit of truth.[2]

Justice. The *Apology* ends with Socrates beseeching the jury to treat each other and his sons as he has treated them: "Punish my sons, gentlemen, when they grow up; give them this same pain I gave you, if you think they care for money or anything else before virtue. . . . And if you do this, we shall have been justly dealt with by you, both I and my sons" (Plato 1961, *Apology*, pg. 38). Socrates defends himself by saying that his duty is to ask good questions of fellow citizens, the same as he asks of himself. Justice in this context is treating everyone alike, including oneself, or making sure no one is left out. As a component of integrity, justice is opposed to hypocrisy. Justice joins with service, such as in community service or civic engagement.

Integrity demands the virtue of justice, along with the virtues of reverence, wisdom, and courage, because they all align with citizenship or a kind of fellow feeling of responsibility. Reverence fuels the acknowledgment that "we are all in this together," deflating the hubris of tyranny in life or the classroom. Wisdom puts me in the position of wanting to know what you know, rather than arrogantly dismissing your point of view. Courage, linked with intellect, means I not only know what is best for me and others, but will do it. Many argue that cultivating the skills and character needed for democratic and global citizenship is one of the jobs of the university. Martha Nussbaum (1997) claims, "Unlike all other nations, we ask a higher education to contribute a general preparation for citizenship, not just a specialized preparation for a career" (294). W. Robert Connor (1998) laments that the move to vocationalism and away from the liberal arts as "skills of freedom" (7) means that we must argue in a new way for the tie between liberal arts and citizenship.[3]

Autonomy and Discipline in Classical and Contemporary Perspective

Plato's answer to how we can attain integrity—become integrated—is his *Republic*, an ideal society centered on the concept of education. He uses myths, math, metaphors, religions, poetry, and observations of nature to explain the type of education he has in mind, namely philosophical education for leaders. What relevance does his *Republic* have for our modern concepts of autonomy and discipline?

Integrative programs in the liberal arts and sciences are not vocational. Nursing and accounting majors graduate ready for careers in nursing and accounting. A philosophy, history, or English major does not graduate ready for a career in philosophy, history, or English in the same way. Neither do majors in psychology, sociology, liberal studies, theology and religious studies, anthropology, women's studies, Asian studies, international studies, political science, interdisciplinary studies, and so on. Nonetheless, it would seem bizarre for administrators of these arts and sciences programs, their faculty, and their students to act as if vocation has no part in the discussion of what happens in the classroom, in advising and mentoring, and after graduation. Defining an integrative program and cultivating integrity within and through it necessarily involves a stance toward vocation. Plato knew this, as we will see, when he tried to encourage in the general populace, or at least its leadership, the kind of integrity he saw Socrates demonstrate. His way of linking autonomy and discipline to cultivate integrity through education was to discuss the meaning of vocation, especially as it can be displayed in personal and civic justice.

Let us look at an end goal of integrative education as mentioned at the outset—namely, producing really good students who are really good persons and would be responsible citizens.[4] Doesn't this include being productive, finding a place within the community as a teacher, plumber, health-care worker, stay-at-home father, or online marketing specialist? If this goal of nurturing a productive and responsible citizen who is a really good person and lifelong learner is worthwhile, then what do the contributing factors look like earlier in the process? How do we reverse engineer this goal into programs and course assignments? First, let us get clearer on what this goal looks like and how it involves autonomy and discipline.[5]

A personal way to "listen" to Plato's *Republic* is to hear him asking, Is your career a vocation? Vocation is from the Latin *vocationem*, literately *a calling*. When a career is a calling, there is something more to it than bringing home a paycheck and looking forward to not working. Somehow it involves your character, your physical and psychic composition, how you identify yourself in the world, and the way you move through any day. I remember distinctly the insurance salesman who was working our neighborhood door to door in the 1990s. We invited him in, and halfway through the pitch he disowned his work. "I'm just doing this to get through school." To be a vocation, work has to be something more than a means to an end.

One person, one job. In Plato's *Republic*, each person assumes the work that best suits his or her nature. The ruler rules, the soldier enforces, the worker produces and consumes. Justice in the city is when each class of person does his or her job well. Injustice is when each tries to do another's job—the workers try to enforce, or soldiers try to rule. Book 4 of the *Republic* is where Plato crafts his ideal city and works out the one-person, one-job proposal. He links work to vocation; to work is to be called to work. The best fit of our person and our work life involves our idiosyncratic nature as a person.

That I am a professor, or something like it, is my character in some complicated way I cannot understand. Nonetheless, that I am a professor is natural, we might say. It was not natural that the insurance salesman was one. Whatever its source, a calling that becomes a vocation is a kind of economical fit between the person and the world. We call this fit a *career*, which originally meant a *running course* or *track*, and is related to the word *curriculum*, as discussed shortly. The further point about vocation is that Plato believes that settling into this career, finding the fit between our person and the world through work, will bring both a sense of personal identity and the virtue of justice. Said another way, taking up our calling with conviction brings integrity and goodness. In the larger picture, a city or community is just and good to the extent that its citizens find their vocation.

How Do Citizens Find Their Vocation? Education.

In book 4 of the *Republic*, Plato makes a claim that strikes many of my students as at once obvious and odd. In a key passage, the conversation turns to the question of how to get a person into the right career. This question is crucial for justice in the *Republic*, and it is crucial for an average twenty-year-old in the United States. The answer Plato gives is that the rulers must institute and support education, that a right education that makes a person orderly. Many of my students seem let down by this claim, expecting something more mystical or innovative. These students presumably think, *Education? I'm already doing that, and I would hardly call it transforming . . . at least not yet.*

Let us return to the word *curriculum*. It is a Latin cognate that meant a running course or career. So a *curriculum vitae* is literally a "course of one's life." Tying curriculum to career is not a recent invention. In fact, Plato articulates the essential insight about citizenship that most of us have as educators: Between a person and the world there are good and bad fits, flourishing vocations, and misdirected, stunted ones. A good citizen and a good citizenry are possible to the extent that our curriculum, formal or informal, yields to what we call a career. One person, one job suited to his or her nature. Education helps discern the match and maintain the course. The challenge, as Plato might point out, is that the tie between vocation and justice (the last constituent of integrity discussed in the previous section) is difficult to imagine in our time. Part of the reason is that our starting point for the conversation is individualism, born of reformation fire and steeled in a pioneer spirit. For Plato, collectivism is a starting point. Like all the ancient Greek thinkers, Plato's ideal society looks a lot like an ant colony or a beehive. In Plato's worldview, one person, one job would not offend anyone's sense of freedom.

Vocation can mediate justice in the community and in the person. To have a vocation is to have a place in the community; you become a fitting, to use a plumbing term. The one job you do is a job you are naturally talented to do, and it contributes to the well-being and orderliness of your community. Personally, life has meaning because you are meaningfully placed in your activity and effort. You are personally just because, like the ant, you do not see appetitive greediness as good. We discern our vocation in the education of our physical, psychic, and spiritual selves, and our community ensures its goodness in the same education. Hence, personal and civic justice, and the vocation that mediates them, are grounded in the education of the whole person.

The idea of the education of the whole person brings us full circle. Plato's Academy in Athens was the first place the *Republic* was regularly taught, and it is still taught in our modern universities. And like the *Republic*, many of our universities trumpet education of the whole person. For example, the mission statement of my current institution, Seattle University, is a dedication to "educating the whole person, to professional formation, and to empowering leaders for a just and humane world" (www.seattleu.edu/about/mission/). In many ways, in our vocation as professors, we are charged with the responsibility to nurture the link between vocation and justice in our communities.

In short, on our best days, we help students become more fit, to become the fitting that strengthens personal goodness in the context of civic goodness. Guiding students to this fit, whether in thinking critically about an academic journal article in an introductory class, recommending them for jobs or graduate school, or hoping that the classroom lessons in how to research well pay off when it comes time to vote, is a function of life course or career—*curriculum.*

We are working backward from integrity as virtuous character to self-discipline as a way of living and working to integrative curricula that balance autonomy and discipline in a student's career. The following simplified figure summarizes the process of cultivating integrity in integrative programs.

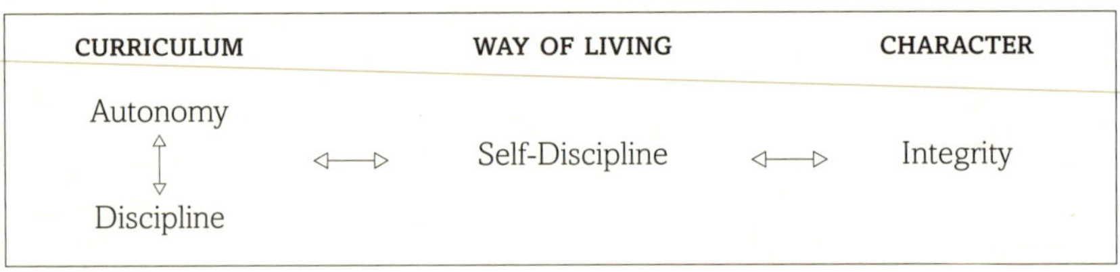

Process of Cultivating Integrity in Integrative Programs

The whole-person result is self-discipline as activity or way of living in light of integrity. What hopefully emerges through the curriculum, discussed in the next section, is a kind of balance between "I am free to choose my work" (autonomy) and "I have to work well" (discipline). This is one of the essential realities of the sphere of work life: I can select or quit my job; I can work well or poorly. Ideally, an integrative curriculum balances autonomy and discipline to encourage self-discipline, and self-discipline as a way of living embodies integrity as descriptive of the student's character. In building courses, curricula, and programs, modern educators express discipline as scholarship, a completeness of intellectual practice and a kind of altruism of the intellect for truth, as Nuttall (2003) puts it, no matter the academic discipline. The question is, *How do we effectively reverse engineer the end goal of being called to a vocation, becoming "fit" or integrated in a community (which implies personal integrity and self-discipline) and create stages leading to this goal through our typical courses and assignments?*

Cultivating Integrity through Coursework in Integrative Programs

Here I examine instructor and program challenges in three key courses that appear in most well-developed programs leading to a bachelor's degree, whether the program is purposefully integrative or interdisciplinary or is a more traditional humanities or social sciences program. These are the introductory, methods, and senior synthesis (or capstone) courses.[6] Examples are from the Seattle University Bachelor of Arts in Liberal Studies program that I direct. Rather than critique apparently nonintegrative programs or curricula, I try to describe what these three courses might look like in programs that aim to cultivate student and program integrity.[7]

Recall that in discussing how higher education might cultivate integrity in integrative programs, we are interpreting Plato's concept of integrity as a curricular balance between autonomy and discipline that yields self-discipline. We saw that self-discipline is a way of living, characterizing a postgraduation life of integrity. In the educational context, constituents of integrity or good character were reverence, wisdom, courage, and justice. Because it is at the apex of the curriculum, the learning goals in senior synthesis ought to be closest to what we expect the student to achieve. Accordingly, I draw connections to educational integrity and the four virtues more explicitly in the senior synthesis than in the methods and introductory course sections. We trace in backward fashion the three significant courses as moments in a student's career, from maximum autonomy (senior synthesis) to maximum discipline (methods) to a mix of both (introduction).

Senior Synthesis or Capstone Course

In theory, the senior synthesis course has one foot in the road beyond the degree and the other foot somehow crossing all the cracks in the sidewalk leading up to that road (synthesis or integration). Beyond the degree, the student is not yet a scholar in the sense that a professor is, even if bound for graduate school. The student may be a working professional nonetheless, but the motivation for completing the degree has not yet flowered in accomplishing it. I think most would agree that the senior deserves and has earned maximum autonomy. If so, in senior synthesis, the problem of integrity—a wholeness or consistency in personal and civic identity anchored in conviction—is not that there is maximum autonomy. The problem is that for integrity to be encouraged, discipline in the face of autonomy must be self-discipline.

I present here practitioner examples of what I mean by drawing on my own senior synthesis teaching experience. The first day of the course, students see the following description of their main assignment in the course, worth 80 percent of the course grade. "The senior synthesis project is assessed as outstanding or academically excellent to the extent that it is equivalent to a *publishable paper project or a project valuable for public aesthetic appreciation*" (Arvidson 2013, 6, emphasis in original). More criteria follow, but they are vague and ambiguous in essential ways, even while they are specific in other ways—vague because they say nothing about the subject matter of the project. To this vagueness, students initially react with joy, anxiety, or feelings in between. The criteria are ambiguous because the criteria imply a confusing array of project forms, from artistic performance to research.

During the first week or so, the autonomy in the course—the openness or clearing a student faces when thinking about his or her legacy project, is misty. For most students, the mist clears, yet never entirely. The freedom they anticipate and experience is manifested in the course's structural elements. For example, students are told that they can change their mind about the content and form of their own project all the way up to the end. They realize that changing late in the game would result in a mediocre project at best.

Free time and free choice are main elements in this autonomy. The syllabus reveals that the course meets about half of the registrar-scheduled days. There is a lot of free time. To play video games? To work on other classes? To produce a sterling senior synthesis project? The decision is up to the student how to use this time, though the professor encourages self-discipline. The syllabus also lists eight general types of projects discussed the first week, yielding lots of possible hybrids: five kinds of papers of at least eight thousand to ten thousand words (research, position, reflective, creative, or professional sphere), creative projects, service learning projects, and scientific projects. These last three also have a reflective written component. The point is that one student can create a graphic novel based on Amazonian lore, while another researches the historical Abraham as the nexus for Judaism, Islam, and Christianity.[8] Neither is the prescribed choice.

Stretching the concept of research and the practice of writing are two more elements that help reinforce maximum autonomy in the course. Research is broadly defined. A student working on "What Is a Congolese Woman in the Twenty-First Century?" might need to interview Congolese women and men as part of her research. A student seeing if a teaching career is a good fit may job shadow his fourth-grade teacher from childhood. A student working on an art installation exploring industrial sounds and silences may need to spend extensive time recording sounds at a working harbor as part of the research. Encouraging students to write how they want to write, rather than how they think they should write according to professor-taught form or style, stretches their writing muscles. In effect, this approach means pushing students to write more creatively. Mimicking formal academic writing, especially from training in a previous methods course, is easier than writing engagingly with flourish.

Asking students, "Why would anyone want to read this?" and working to push them into new ways of writing creates a kind of opening and mistiness that stretches the writing in a productive direction.

How are students led to navigate the mist of autonomy? Discipline in the course as other-imposed structure must lead to self-discipline as self-imposed structure if it is going to significantly contribute to the goals of an integrative education. Examples of discipline in a senior synthesis course are milestones, scheduled mentor meetings, library research help, peer feedback, and a meta-cognitive assignment.

Most courses with larger projects are designed with deadlines. These markers are milestones that show the distance to or from the student's current place in the project and can mark significant events in time. Examples of mile-stones in a senior synthesis course might be proposal, outline, bibliography, required meetings with professor, penultimate draft, senior presentation, and final submission. I believe that making most of these milestones formative rather than summative (except for credit/no credit) means that the milestone is about progress. This puts the professor in a better position to be a mentor. Scheduled mentor meetings can provide insightful guidance and encourage-ment on how to engage the mist just when the student needs it most and in a relatively safe intellectual environment. Research librarians can organize a re-quired session more or less tailored to students' individual projects and offer one-on-one follow-up. Task-oriented, small-group peer feedback motivates students to do their best work. Examples of discussion tasks are "What are your three biggest challenges at this point?" or "How would you explain your project to a seven-year-old?" Students often give high regard to what their peers think about their projects and provide each other with genuinely useful help.

As the capstone in a hopefully integrative career, writing a paper early in the term about education makes sense for students. At religious-affiliated in-stitutions like Seattle University (Jesuit Catholic), the university mission state-ment comes into play in curriculum and policy decisions, and is generally well-known on campus by faculty, staff, and most juniors and seniors. We ask students to assess and critique the mission statement and write about their personal mission. The task of this mission paper is to find and express the nexus between the mission, other assigned readings, and who the individual is as a student and a person. This paper ends with a one-page personal mis-sion statement. The virtue of justice, as social justice, is central to Catholic social teaching so this mission paper requires students to address this component of integrity.[9] The ultimate point, as always in a senior synthesis course, is for students to own their education (self-discipline), to take authority or authorship for it, as they cross the cracks in the sidewalk leading to the road.

Reverence for truth in an integral education accords with the openness or mistiness that senior synthesis students feel because the professor has not authoritatively delivered the topic and form. To choose a project topic because it is comfortable or feels safe is to turn away from something bigger—a transcendent possibility not yet realized. Playing it safe makes the openness feel smaller. Awe for the issue or problem to be addressed is absent. There is little respect for peers' input because so little is at stake, and respect for disciplinary experts working to bring clarity to the topic is shallow. This dimly lit clearing in the student's ultimate course is an opportunity for a genuinely transformative senior project.

Wisdom to admit ignorance comes into play (or not) with the high standard for the project announced in the syllabus. That it must be a "publishable paper project or a project valuable for public aesthetic appreciation" signals right away that the student cannot pretend to have knowledge that he or she does not have, exactly the pose of the poets, politicians, and craftsmen whom Socrates questions in Plato's dialogues. A wise student sees the openness as an opportunity, admitting to something like, "I don't know what it takes to be a nurse after my bachelor's degree, but I'm going to use this free space to find out" (professional sphere project), or "I am not an expert in ethics, but I am willing to learn from the experts and reflect on my own experiences to create an ethics curriculum for ROTC" (creative/research project).

Courage is a mark of good scholarship, whose opposite is toeing the line just to be counted in the lineup. Students in senior synthesis can be emboldened to strike out upon ground that is untrod and unique to their personal identity, which takes intellectual and personal courage. Mentoring by the professor through personal meetings and feedback on milestones, and encouragement by peers through small-group work, can give students courage to question deeply rather than superficially. A looming, end-of-term, formal presentation also means taking a public stand on what has been accomplished, identifying its wider significance and why the topic was chosen. Students are then questioned by their peers and the professor, as in an academic conference. Imagine the bravery needed for sharing in front of your peers your personal doubts about whether law school is the right move for you or publicly discussing the findings and worth of your research on how to start an underage music venue in Seattle. This is courage in the usual sense of overcoming fear of public speaking. But it is also courage to question and be questioned—to be vulnerable or open to questioning. We expect good citizens to be able to make informed decisions and communicate or defend them to others whom they may or may not know.

Justice involves community or fellow feeling. Good classroom learning in many courses is as social as it is intellectual. In senior synthesis in undergraduate programs, students already have a peculiar togetherness because nearly all of them experience the angst of pending graduation. Extended peer discussions in small groups of various sizes can increase a kind of co-responsibility for each other's projects. In-class writing workshops featuring peer critique and formal end-of-term senior presentations where each is the audience for the other can do the same. Thinking of the senior project as a legacy, and referring to it this way in the syllabus and class, aids students in big-picture thinking. In the best scenarios, the senior project becomes a personally historic milestone distinct from previous projects and papers. As a legacy project, many students feel it must have real-world heft and significance. It must be useful to others in a wider community, even if it is, for example, a personal reflection/research paper project on the phenomenon of childhood anxiety. Through peer discussion and formal presentation, this student has educated classmates about the problem and perhaps imagines a wider audience in the future. This imagination is connection or fellow feeling that is prerequisite for justice in the community.

If an academic curriculum is designed to cultivate these four virtues constitutive of integrity—reverence for truth, wisdom to admit ignorance, courage to question, and justice—then it is much more likely that a student's character will be good. The senior synthesis is the course in which this integrity as self-discipline is "tested," since it is largely up to the student to successfully balance autonomy and discipline.

Discipline in a senior synthesis course is different than discipline in a methods course. If a senior synthesis course is to be integrative for the identity of the student as a good student and good person as defined above (achieving an identity that pulls together the various pieces of one's life around a center so that one becomes identified with one's convictions by living them), then narrow disciplinary or interdisciplinary training must take contextual or background status. In this opening of maximum autonomy, students can show self-governance or self-discipline by applying their learning to the issue of their choice, expressed in one of eight manners they choose, or a hybrid form of these. So the sense of discipline as "a rule to follow," which is key in a typical methods course, is less prominent in senior synthesis. What hopefully emerges through the curriculum, as captured and exercised in senior synthesis, is a kind of balance between "I am free to choose my work" (autonomy) and "I have to work well" (discipline)—a balance that we have seen is key to cultivating integrity through education.

Methods Course

Methods courses in integrative and interdisciplinary programs teach students what assumptions and activities disciplinarians and interdisciplinarians use to advance knowledge or resolve problems, often with some level of practical application of the disciplinary skills learned. In the methods course, the rules and their skillful application are a large part of course content. Discipline can be evidenced through increasing expertise in a body of knowledge and a meticulous embrace of the methodology that produces this knowledge.

I use Allen Repko's book *Interdisciplinary Research* (2012) as a prominent example in this section since it is adopted in a number of interdisciplinary and integrative programs.[10] In a workshop on using his textbook at the 2013 Association for Interdisciplinary Studies (formerly the Association for Integrative Studies) meeting, Repko stated that the usual way to use the book is to have all students in the course focus on a particular problem for the term. Students can learn from each other as they build together an interdisciplinary response to the complex issue or problem. To help prepare students for the autonomy component in their future senior synthesis course, our program uses a contrasting approach. Students are required to choose their own problem or issue to research. This requirement dramatically promotes autonomy in a discipline-oriented (i.e., rule-oriented) course and increases chances for "deep learning" (Ramsden 2003; Gibbs 1992). To show how this approach can help balance autonomy and discipline in the three-course sequence and can have its own advantages without losing the advantages of all students working on one theme, I again draw from my own teaching experience.

When there is no mention of the problem to choose, students can choose whatever problem suits them. So twenty students will be working on twenty different projects. This autonomy is more than an introductory course and less than a senior synthesis course. It is less because all students must show that they understand and can apply Repko's interdisciplinary research process to a complex issue or problem that one discipline alone cannot adequately address. Therefore, all students must write research papers, the majority of which have a similar format. Except for this difference, the methods course would be very similar to the senior synthesis course, because the project management milestones described in the senior synthesis course hold here—proposal, bibliography, outline, penultimate draft, and final submission. But the difference is definitive. That students are learning and applying the interdisciplinary research process not only favors discipline over autonomy but also essentially changes the course's performance and learning outcomes. I believe that the continuity and integration of the curriculum are improved if the professor and program can support this freedom of choice in the methods course. Students are better prepared for what they face in senior synthesis.

The most serious problem in interdisciplinary methods courses is the tendency toward shallow research. This problem may be exacerbated by having all students doing individual rather than joint research. Requiring a disciplinary draft as a milestone in constructing the interdisciplinary paper can help expose shallow research earlier in the process or ameliorate it.[11] This disciplinary draft is the main difference in project milestones from the senior synthesis course, and it names the emphasis on discipline in this methods course. Since interdisciplinary insights are the result of integrating disciplinary insights, a disciplinary draft can help the student determine which disciplinary insights are relevant and how to express the disciplinary perspective. In the penultimate draft, students use the achievements in this disciplinary draft to create common ground between the disciplines. At the end of chapter 7, "Developing Adequacy in Relevant Disciplines," Repko writes,

> Adequacy means knowing enough about the discipline to have a basic understanding of how it approaches the problem and how it illuminates and characterizes the problem. . . . The interdisciplinary student has to engage in far more preparatory analysis than does a disciplinary student. As tedious and time consuming as this is, it must be done in order to perform the later STEPS of the interdisciplinary process that involve integration. (2012, 220–21)

Students write a five- to six-page paper, starting with two pages restating the problem to be investigated, followed by two pages on the problem or issue from the perspective of one discipline, and two pages from the other discipline. The paper ends with an initial attempt at stating common ground between disciplinary insights. The professor learns whether the student understands how each discipline approaches the problem, how far he or she is along the research trail, and how well prepared the student is to succeed in the next phase—the penultimate draft.[12] Ignorance is thinking you know how a psychologist or biologist or political scientist thinks without bothering to do the tedious and time-consuming work. Wisdom is a kind of maturity in admitting, "I don't know and I need to find out." That students choose their own topic in line with their interests and passions bodes well for wisdom. To yield deep and significant research, this need to find out must become a personal desire, aligning the tedious work of scholarship more with self-discipline than other-imposed discipline.

Even if each student chooses a distinct project, a methods course can feel like a lockstep journey with arbitrary restraints on personal expression. In addition to the freedom to choose one's own issue or problem, other elements can inject a sense of autonomy and ownership. For example, interspersed with Repko's chapters, students in our methods course read *Imagination First: Unlocking the Power of Possibility* by Eric Liu and Scott Noppe-Brandon (2009). The twenty-eight and one-half exercises are brief, thought-provoking suggestions that ripple the surface of students' minds, sometimes penetrating very deeply into the interdisciplinary project process.[13] A complementary text such as *Imagination First* increases the sense of autonomy by opening up imagination in achieving common ground and interdisciplinary integration, even though the research method of writing is less creative. Elevator speeches, electronic portfolio entries, blogs, or journals can help increase a sense of ownership of the project.

Introductory Course

The introductory course in an integrative program must be a complex mix of autonomy and discipline. One could argue that any introductory course has this quality, but I believe that a future senior synthesis course that gives students maximum autonomy marks a difference. The problem is, how does the curriculum anticipate, preview, and work toward both the maximum autonomy of the senior synthesis course and the deep disciplinary (interdisciplinary) training of the methods course, all in only an introductory course? As first- or second-year students, or as transfers new to the institution, these young men and women are unlikely to be ready for the kind of open mistiness that senior synthesis welcomes them into, nor will they be necessarily appreciative of the rigorous training in interdisciplinarity. Nonetheless, the introductory course can establish clearly marked trailheads.

Ideally, this introductory course would be linked to the project chosen in the methods course. For our program, this means students read *Introduction to Interdisciplinary Studies* (Repko, Szostak, and Buchberger 2014) and accomplish some milestones, such as a project proposal and perhaps a disciplinary draft. Impending autonomy and disciplinary expectations are previewed through the individual choice of topic and the introduction to some steps in the research process. An exercise in autonomy is to require students to choose a text on their own—an "independent text" assignment. The professor leaves open space in the course for students to choose their own text, and all must think about what they want to read. Students are encouraged to ask themselves, *What holes exist in my education at this point that this reading can fill? What do I want to explore that I haven't had the opportunity to research?* This encouragement (courage) to question their own education is also a request to be brave enough to pursue what they feel they must. Without much guidance, students choose texts or challenging novels of appropriate academic worth and length. Not only must students admit ignorance (wisdom) in order to choose a meaningful text, they seem to relish the opportunity to challenge themselves intellectually, the very activity that Plato and Socrates expect of good citizens, especially leaders. Students are delighted to have this freedom, and those who want guidance are put into the situation of discussing their education with the professor, exactly the kind of mentoring they will encounter later when choosing projects in methods and senior synthesis courses.[14] Students are required to give a significant oral presentation and write a paper on the book. If the students are in a semicohort model, moving through the three courses over a few years, they come to know each other's diverse interests in a uniquely public way. This community experience of exercising autonomy together, each in his or her own manner, is a veiled facsimile of the fit that Plato describes in the just community, each working according to calling.

Another way to prepare students for autonomy in future courses is to institute some mechanism in the introductory course for metacognition, a skill further developed through the methods and senior synthesis courses. Metacognition is directly tied to Socrates's most famous claim found in the *Apology* (38a): the unexamined life is not worth living. (Plato, *Apology* 1961, p. 26) I use an electronic portfolio to create a template with instructions that allow for personal expression and style; the main site function is for students to reflect on their current or previous coursework in the e-portfolio (Arvidson 2012). The rubric asks for reflection on challenges and accomplishments—not just description. The site also has sections on educational goals and the resume. In short, students in the introductory course are asked to start a kind of record of thinking about the thinking they are being asked to perform in college. They are asked to take a semipublic stand on their education, to start taking responsibility for it. The metacognition demanded in the senior synthesis course through the mission paper assignment is anticipated by having a similar assignment in this introductory course. I also bring in seniors or alumni to the introductory course for a day to let students discuss what lies ahead in the major, previewing and personifying the self-discipline that will be expected.

On the discipline side, as an alternative to starting a methods-type project, students can spend a week or so learning about integrative interdisciplinary research. They can be taught one style of citation (e.g., APA or MLA) and how to research generally. It is useful for the discipline side of the equation to have students read and write on big-picture thinkers from each division of knowledge: humanities, social sciences, and natural sciences.[15] In a paper assignment, students are asked to take a stand on the relationship between sciences and humanities and how it is important for human welfare—an issue of social justice for most students. Students preview the road ahead by considering in this course the divisions of knowledge and disciplines that will inform their upcoming methods coursework, and they are given this space to take a position and defend it. Hopefully this experience helps guide them into sound investigative choices in the methods and senior synthesis courses.

Challenges for Integrative Interdisciplinary Programs

An integrative program is not the same as an interdisciplinary program. I would claim that interdisciplinarity must be a critical moment in the whole curriculum, but if the whole is about cultivating integrity through balancing autonomy and discipline, interdisciplinarity is not equivalent to the whole. Teaching an interdisciplinary method or process, such as Allen Repko's, is worthwhile for integrative programs. It gives a program an easily assessed measure of rigor, for example, by using the methods course project as an embedded assessment of a research program learning outcome. It contributes positively to program identity and narrative and helps recruit and retain students who seek the challenge of interdisciplinary scholarship. For majors in integrative programs, such as many liberal studies or similar programs, it encourages them to talk and think clearly about what it is they do when they do research, whereas the nature of research seems more obvious to majors in sociology, philosophy, economics, and history.

However, in an integrative program, students are able to pursue their interests in ways not restricted to the interdisciplinary research process as Repko describes it. Undergraduate students can even build on previous work through the three courses discussed above, as graduate students often do in their coursework.[16] For example, Sean Simpson, an ROTC participant and recent graduate from our liberal studies program, developed the theme of military ethics from theory to practice. In the introductory course, he chose a book on war and morality for the independent text (James Toner, *Morals under the Gun*, 2005); in the methods course, he used insights from psychology and philosophy to find common ground and integration concerning military ethics training content; and in the senior synthesis course, he applied the concepts by constructing a curriculum for moral training for ROTC that he also presented to his commanding officers. The senior synthesis product was informed by and built upon the introductory and methods courses, but it could not be produced following only an interdisciplinary research process. Another recent graduate, Djamba Okonda, originally from the Democratic Republic of Congo, chose to build in each course a thematic exploration of how to help oppressed peoples. In the introductory course, she chose for her independent text a book about helping less privileged people in another country (Tracy Kidder, *Mountains beyond Mountains*, 2004); in the methods course, she examined the political oppression of the Congolese by their own government using political science and psychology; and she wrote a reflective senior synthesis project on how Congolese women are kept voiceless and powerless by religious dogma and polygamy.

For Sean and Djamba, the methods course featuring the interdisciplinary research process was a necessary precursor for the senior synthesis project—but not sufficient. More creativity and a wider range of expression were needed. Each had to bring more of who they are, more of their whole person, into the project and expand the possible modes of expression. It is pertinent in the context of the discussion of vocation and fit that Sean is now in U.S. Air Force pilot training (as an officer/leader) and Djamba is in the master of nursing program at the University of Rochester (New York).

There are significant and constant challenges internal to integrative programs that try to balance autonomy and discipline. Autonomy in coursework for fifteen or thirty students means a lot of work for the professor. In an introductory course, there are as many independent texts as there are students. In the methods and senior synthesis courses, each project is distinct. It is a challenge to keep up with students' developing ideas. Another challenge, implied in the examples of Sean and Djamba, is program cohesion and continuity. The intense training in interdisciplinary methodology, how to research and write interdisciplinarily, is not necessarily repeated in the senior synthesis course unless the student chooses to express the senior project that way. This is a problem of program unity that needs to be discussed in a transparent way with majors. I describe it to students as an hourglass, where the wide bottom is the introductory course, the tight middle is the methods course, and the wide top is senior synthesis. It is also a challenge to integrate the interdisciplinary method with other program requirements for community service. For example, it is a stretch to directly relate our required upper-level course Leadership for Community Engagement, an intense service-learning course, with the interdisciplinary research process of the methods course. That is why the wider narrative of an integrative program can be more appropriate and compelling.[17]

One way to achieve more cohesion and continuity (integrity) in a program with distinct internal goals—for example, interdisciplinarity, community engagement, and metacognition—is to make sure that the introductory, methods, and senior synthesis courses and any others originating from program faculty are project-centered or project-based. A project-centered curriculum was assumed throughout the previous section. Project-centered learning is a teaching and learning model that engages students in complex tasks that include planning and design, problem solving, decision making, creating artifacts, and communicating results (Mergendoller, Markham, Ravitz, and Larmer 2006, 583). The sustained nature of project-centered learning encourages reflection over a longer course of time than traditional assignments, and such reflection has been shown to transform student experience into retained knowledge (Bransford, Brown, and Cocking 2000). There are liabilities to project-centered learning, however. Students who are not reasonably self-motivated will not do well. If it is a group project, this type of learning is susceptible to the same problems as any learning strategy that uses collaboration. Since there are multiple possible products or solutions in one project assignment, the instructor must be comfortable with uncertainty in what the final outcome might be (Arvidson 2008, 95–96).

Conclusion

This chapter has asked what integrity in integrative programs might look like and how it can be cultivated in the student and the program, using Seattle University's bachelor of arts in liberal studies as an example. Drawing from ancient and contemporary sources, *integrity* was defined as consistency and wholeness; it means achieving an identity that pulls together the various pieces of one's life around a center so that one becomes identified with one's convictions by living them. The constituents of educational integrity were described as reverence for truth, wisdom to admit ignorance, courage to question, and the search for justice rather than hypocrisy. A curriculum that balances autonomy and discipline, balancing freedom of choice and doing one's work well, can help cultivate integrity through self-discipline. The whole-person result hoped for in integrative programs is self-discipline as a way of living a life of integrity. As students transition from the sidewalk of classes to the road of vocation, a well-balanced, integrative education can help them find their place or fit in the community.

Finding this fitting has moral implications, as Plato, Nussbaum, Connor, and others argue when they link liberal education to citizenship. After graduation, the academic interplay between autonomy and discipline becomes real in the "real world." In the academic setting, introductory courses can establish autonomy and discipline trailheads. Methods courses can convey the skill of disciplinary and interdisciplinary research while encouraging significant autonomy and ownership of education in preparation for senior synthesis. And senior synthesis or capstone courses as the culmination of an integrative education can have maximum autonomy as a way to encourage discipline to become self-discipline. Students can be prepared to approach the high clearing of senior synthesis with confidence and competence, and rest atop it both exhilarated and exhausted, before reentering the cave.

References

Arvidson, P. S. 2008. *Teaching Nonmajors: Advice for Liberal Arts Professors.* Albany: State University of New York Press.

Arvidson, P. S. 2012. "E-Portfolios in a Liberal Studies Program: An Experiment in Sustainability." In *Teaching Sustainability and Teaching Sustainably*, edited by K. Bartels and K. Parker, 161–77. Sterling, VA: Stylus Publications.

Arvidson, P. S. 2013. Syllabus LBST 301: Methods of Interdisciplinary Research. Seattle: Seattle University, unpublished.

———. 2013. Syllabus LBST 490: Senior Synthesis. Seattle: Seattle University, unpublished.

Bransford, J., A. Brown, and R. Cocking, eds. 2000. *How People Learn: Brain, Mind, Experience, and School.* Washington DC: National Academy Press.

Connor, W. R. 1998. Liberal Arts Education in the Twenty-First Century. [Presentation]. Keynote Address at Kenan Center Quality Assurance Conference, May 19–20, 1998, Chapel Hill, NC. http://www.hunter.cuny.edu.

Gardner, H. 2008. *Five Minds for the Future*. Boston: Harvard Business School Press.

Gibbs, G. 1992. *Improving the Quality of Student Learning*. Bristol, UK: Technical and Educational Services.

Heidegger, M. 1962. *Being and Time*. Translated by J. Macquarrie and E. Robinson. New York: Harper and Row.

Liu, E., and S. Noppe-Brandon. 2009. "Imagination First: Unlocking the Power of Possibility." San Francisco: Jossey-Bass.

Mergendoller, J., T. Markham, J. Ravitz, and J. Larmer. 2006. "Pervasive Management of Project-Based Learning." In *Handbook of Classroom Management: Research, Practice, and Contemporary Issues*, edited by C. M. Evertson and C. S. Weinstein, 538–615. Mahwah, NJ: Lawrence Erlbaum Associates.

Nussbaum, M. C. 1997. *Cultivating Humanity: A Classical Defense of Reform in Liberal Education*. Cambridge, MA: Harvard University Press.

———. 2010. *Not for Profit: Why Democracy Needs the Humanities*. Princeton, NJ: Princeton University Press.

Nuttall, A. 2003. *Dead from the Waist Down: Scholars and Scholarship in Literature and the Popular Imagination*. New Haven, CT: Yale University Press.

Plato. 1961. "Apology." In *The Collected Dialogues of Plato*, edited by E. Hamilton and H. Cairns, 3–26. Princeton, NJ: Princeton University Press.

———. "Republic." In *The Collected Dialogues of Plato*, edited by E. Hamilton and H. Cairns, 575–84. Princeton, NJ: Princeton University Press.

Ramsden, P. 2003. *Learning and Teaching in Higher Education* Abingdon, UK: Routledge.

Repko, A. F. 2012. *Interdisciplinary Research: Process and Theory*. Thousand Oaks, CA: Sage Publications.

Repko, A. F., R. Szostak, and M. P. Buchberger, M. P. 2014. *Introduction to Interdisciplinary Studies*. Thousand Oaks, CA: Sage Publications.

Task Force on General Education. 2007. *The Harvard Report of the Task Force on General Education*. http://www.generaleducation.fas.harvard. edu/icb/icb.do?keyword=k37826&tabgroupid=icb.tabgroup116510.

Wilson, E. O. 1997. *Consilience: The Unity of Knowledge*. New York: Vintage.

Woodruff, P. 2001. *Reverence: Renewing a Forgotten Virtue*. New York: Oxford University Press.

Chapter 7

Mary Parker Follett: Creativity, Power, and Diversity in the Integrative Process

Judy D. Whipps, PhD, Grand Valley State University

The models of integrative problem solving developed by Mary Parker Follett (1868–1933) add historical depth and community-based insight to the current conversation about integration and synthesis. Although she all but disappeared from our intellectual history during the twentieth century, the emergence of interdisciplinary fields of work such as leadership studies and mediation practice has allowed Follett's work to find a new vitality. In 2011 the International Leadership Association granted Follett the Lifetime Achievement Award, and she is acknowledged as a foundational thinker in negotiation theory and mediation (Mansbridge 1998; Cohen 1971). Follett's work is also being used as a resource for feminist and pragmatist philosophy (Banerjee 2008; Pratt 2011) and is being utilized once again in management theory and practice (Drucker 1995).

Using Follett's biography to demonstrate the historical continuity that has led to contemporary discussions of integration, this chapter compares Follett's understanding of the process of integration to those of contemporary interdisciplinary scholars. Given that Follett's model of integration grew primarily out of her community work, and later in her work with businesses, she stressed the importance of action for genuine integration and thus provides a source for integrating theory and practice around contemporary issues. Her work can be usefully compared to the methods of contemporary academic interdisciplinary research, but it also can be a guide for building community relationships in a variety of settings. As described in this chapter, integration is creative process and can be a methodology for innovative interdisciplinary problem solving.

Follett's work is particularly useful in her analysis of power, a topic often ignored in discussions of interdisciplinary integration. Yet as anyone who does interdisciplinary work knows, integration and interdisciplinarity are often complicated by issues of contested power. Follett's analysis of power concludes that working in a *power-with* rather than *power-over* environment is essential for integration.

Biography and Education

Mary Follett was raised in a somewhat chaotic home environment in Boston, where as the eldest child she frequently was in a position of responsibility. Her father was injured and suffered emotionally as a result of his service in the Civil War. His subsequent alcoholism and her mother's recurring invalidism meant that the family often relied on Mary to care for her mother as well as her younger brother. Yet Follett was a serious student and passed the rigorous entrance exams to Boston's Thayer Academy at age eleven, two years earlier than the usual required age of thirteen. At Thayer, Follett had the good fortune to study with Anna Boynton Thompson, who became a role model and later an intellectual friend. Follett completed Thayer's challenging academic program in three years. Her father's death when she was seventeen required her to spend more time at home caring for her mother and younger brother, so Follett continued her studies with the Society to Encourage Studies at Home. In 1888 she enrolled for courses at the Harvard Annex for Women (later Radcliffe). At Harvard she studied with political historian Albert Bushnell Hart, and she began to write her first book on the history of the Speaker of the U.S. House. In the summer of 1890 Follett was invited by Anna Boynton Thompson to spend a year at Newnham College in Cambridge, England, primarily studying history, economics, and political philosophy. She later returned to Boston, finished her coursework at Radcliffe, and continued to work on her research in what, according to her mentor, could have been PhD work. While at Radcliffe she was influenced by the pragmatist philosophies of William James and the idealism of Josiah Royce, both dominant figures in American philosophy at the time. While continuing her studies she supported herself by teaching political science in high school and later by doing legal research for a Boston attorney who represented corporate interests taking over public transit. Here she saw the interconnecting interests of various aspects of the community (businesses as well as community members). Her first book on political theory, *The Speaker of the House of Representatives*, was published in 1896. When Radcliffe received permission to award degrees in 1898, Follett graduated summa cum laude.

In the early 1900s Follett turned her primary energy to community work, at first starting a debating club for boys and men, which grew into a community center in the troubled Roxbury neighborhood of Boston. In 1903 she secured permission from the School Committee to use the Dearborn School for her new Roxbury Industrial League. Included in the work of this league were activities to prepare young people for self-government (Tonn 2003).The success of this program resulted in the creation of neighborhood social centers that met at the Boston schools during after-school hours. As a leader of this movement, Follett worked to secure permanent funding for the centers, work that involved cultivating relationships with politicians and community members, fund raising, creating publicity materials, defending programs in print, and recruiting leaders to take over programs. As one of her contemporaries said, she was the "heart and brain" for the School Centers movement (Tonn 2003, 233). In 1908 Follett became chairperson of the Women's Municipal League's Committee on Extended Use of School Buildings, and in 1917 Follett was elected vice president of the National Community Center Association.

Connected to her work with the neighborhood centers, Follett created a privately funded Placement Bureau in 1913. At that time, many teens left school at age fourteen or earlier to find work in the factories. When possible, the bureau's workers attempted to convince the teens to stay in school. When that was not possible, the bureau's charge was to "find permanent positions, not stray jobs, to sacrifice no child to industry, and to fit each child as wisely and as well as we knew how" (Tonn 2003, 221). The bureau's intent was to find or, if possible, create an environment where the teens would continue their education through on-the-job training. Bureau employees investigated job conditions and sanitation, worked with employers in some instances to raise wages, and did extensive follow-up work with the adolescents and companies to protect the workers. They provided a service to the employers in terms of finding the right employees and also worked to ensure job satisfaction for the teens. In this work, Follett developed relationships with employers as well as an intimate understanding of the conditions of the workers' lives, which was useful in her later organizational consulting work. As a mark of its success, the Placement Bureau was eventually transitioned into a department in the school system, the Department of Vocational Guidance, in 1917. The former Placement Bureau's director, Susan Ginn, was the new director of the department, and Follett became a member of the advisory council. In her memoir, Ginn said of Follett that she was "a woman of rare vision and foresight" who had exercised a "powerful influence in developing the policies" of vocational guidance programs. As Ginn said, "Whenever [Follett] spoke she commanded attention and respect" (Tonn 2003, 224).

Follett continued her writing during this active period from 1900 to 1917, but nearly all of her publications concern the use of schools, adult education and recreation, or the Placement Bureau. As the Placement Bureau was being incorporated into the school system, Follett turned her attention to more theoretical work, crafting a vision of a political process based on local community groups, which was published in her second book, *The New State: Group Organization, the Solution of Popular Government* (1918). Here she proposed a radical vision of democracy that integrates diverse opinions of local communities and brings those voices to the larger state-level decision-making process. *The New State* tapped into the progressive hope—what she later called the "exultant feeling"—that politics and democracy would be reinvented after the war,[1] and thus is a book of hope and passion. The book was received and reviewed positively in the popular press as well as in academic journals in philosophy, sociology, and political science (Tonn 2003).

After the publication of *The New State*, Follett turned her attention to group studies. She had over a decade of experience working with committees, groups, and political figures as she secured funding and space for her school-based community centers, but she sought out more direct experience in group problem solving. She got this experience when she was appointed to the Massachusetts Minimum Wage Board, where she participated in negotiations that established minimum wages in industries that employed women and young workers. This experience allowed her practical experience in group processes as she continued to study and write. Follett's 1924 book *Creative Experience* resulted from her continued study and experience with groups. This book goes into more detail about the methodology of integration, issues of power, and ways to develop the individual capacity for integration.

The publication of *Creative Experience* resulted in Follett being "flooded with letters" from businessmen, asking for consultations as well as invitations to give public lectures (Tonn 2003, 388). She was invited to give four talks on business administration to the Executive Conference Group in New York, and soon she became part of a rich dialogue in the developing field of management. In business Follett found concrete group processes to study, and by 1926 she had dedicated herself to applying her theories of integration to the work of business management and organizational leadership. She became a well-known lecturer for business groups, giving talks in New York, Boston, and England. In management she was able to combine her theoretical work in political history, philosophy, and psychology, along with her extensive community work, to create new conditions of an integrated workplace. As historian James Hoopes later said of her, "No one has better described the corporate job than as an experience of being integrated into a larger whole" (2003, 121).

Follett's ideas changed the global dialogue on employer–employee relations. For example, according to Japanese management professor Tokihiko Enomoto, Follett's work had a direct influence on Japanese management theory, which was then later incorporated into U.S. management theory and practice. In his 1995 "Commentary on 'The Individual and the Group,'"[2] Enomoto says that Follett had a significant impact on Japanese industrial practices starting in the 1950s. Management theorists were first substantially influenced by the work of Chester Barnard's "principle of cooperation as the basis for effective organization" (Enomoto 1995, 241) leading to what is termed the *Barnard revolution*. In studying Barnard, Japanese scholars found that he "had read and annotated Follett's works." This led to Japanese management scholars studying Follett in her own right, and she became "highly prized in Japanese management circles" (Enomoto 1995, 243). In 1986 Enomoto and colleagues established the Mary Parker Follett Association of Japan.

Follett's work also influenced social work practice (Cohen 1971) and established the principles of mediation and conflict resolution.[3] Her work has been and is being studied in a wide range of disciplines. Interestingly, she has been called a "prophet of management," and a "prophet of chaos and complexity" (Mendenhall, Macomber, and Cutright 2000) As this chapter demonstrates, in that her integrative methods resonate with today's integrative and interdisciplinary thinkers, she could also be considered a prophet of integrative studies.

Integration as the Basis of Human Nature

Follett's theory of integration begins with her understanding of what it means to be human: She sees the individual as ontologically integrated with community. As she says, "The group and the individual come into existence simultaneously" (Follett 1918, 127). From her earliest work she rejected the "dualism" of individualism, of seeing oneself in opposition to the state or separated from others. Instead she claimed that a person "is ideally free only so far as he is interpermeated by every other human being; he gains his freedom through a perfect and complete relationship" (69).

This understanding of the nature of the self as integrated is foundational for all of Follett's work. We necessarily become something new when encountering difference since integration means change in the individuals and in the situation. She used words like *interpenetration* and *interweaving* as synonyms for integration, rather than words like *adjustment*, which too often implies change on only one side. As she says, "I never react to you but to you-plus-me. . . . I can never influence you because you have already influenced me; that is, in the very process of meeting . . . we both become something different" (Follett, 1924/1951, 62–63). She termed this phenomenon of continual change in the individual and in the situation *circular response*. She worked to understand, use, and expand the integrative process as a methodology for social change—as the foundation of an improved democratic community, a basis for human interactions, and useful for problem solving. For Follett, integration is a primary value, a source of human good.

Integration Requires Creativity

Integration results in something new that was not there before, and so is a fundamentally creative process, an idea that Follett developed in *Creative Experience*. The best problem-solving work abandons "either-or" thinking, where one side wins the argument and rejects compromise because it does not produce anything new. Both of these approaches merely keep us in old ways and sow the seeds for further conflict (Follett 1924/1951, p.160). Instead, Follett called for a full discussion that looks at all of the factors and creates multiple alternatives by combining and recombining different elements. Only then can a new possibility be created, one that works for all sides. This dialogue process is essential—rushing to a vote does not allow new innovations to be developed, so Follett said to "curb those who wish to vote the moment two alternatives appear in the discussion . . . We do not get full participation unless we avoid either-or situations" (1927/1973, 185–86). Instead, the integrative process is successful when the dialogue uncovers a new resolution or creates a third way, an option that was not apparent before the discussion started. In *Creative Experience* Follett gave the example of someone trying to decide to go to New York by boat or train; a third option would be to discover that one could get a ride on an airplane instead, or, as one of her colleagues pointed out, the third creative option would be to *invent* the airplane. In integration "the best way out is always when someone invents something new" (1924/1951, 157). How, then, do we get to this third way, this creative new solution? The first step is to carefully consider and analyze the different opinions that people bring to the table.

Integration Requires Listening

Careful and mindful listening and paying attention to the words and their underlying symbols and meanings begin the process of integration. Listening is a skill that Follett personally cultivated and one that she had an opportunity to develop in her community work. As Lieutenant Colonel Lyndall Urwick, a European business colleague and friend, wrote about her in a 1970 letter to Avrum Cohen:

> [Follett had] a combination of complete intellectual integrity and a deep respect for people as people. . . . She was interested, vitally interested, in them and their experience, as individuals. . . . *Their* experience was important because it was part of the general human experience. So no-one ever felt that she was inquisitive or personal, only immensely interested. I don't think I've ever talked to anyone as freely as I did to Mary Follett. (Cohen 1971, 179)

Without listening and being open to others' ideas, integration is not possible since, as Follett said, "You cannot integrate differences until you know what they are" (1927/1973, 186). Part of the activity of careful listening to people's demands involves breaking up a *whole* or the overall request, work that requires analysis and differentiation. This analysis helps all parties clarify what various sides want from the outcome they advocate, including what it means symbolically to them. Follett said to be careful to look beyond empty moralistic terms such as *altruism* or *self-sacrifice* to the concrete particulars of the demands. In her own work, careful listening and being open to other perspectives allowed Follett to bring the views of multiple disciplines to her work. As her friend Richard Cabot wrote about her in 1934 shortly after her death, "Biologists, psychologists, and sociologists found their views so well stated that each group might almost think that she was one of their tribe." He went on to say that Follett used these different views "sympathetically . . . in the development of her own ideas" (qtd. in Cohen 1971, 34).[4]

Over time, Follett learned that self-sacrifice or being submissive to others' views does not add to the creative process. Earlier in her career, in 1913, she said that democracy required "the subordination of the individual to the well-being of all" (Tonn 2003, 238). She radically changed her mind about this when she wrote *The New State*. Here she called compromise an "antiquated notion," which is "on the same plane as fighting." Instead, she said, "The individual is not to facilitate agreement by courteously (!) waiving his own point of view. That is just a way of shirking." She continued, "I must not subordinate myself" (Follett 1918, 26). In 1924 she pointed out that compromise is merely suppression of one's views and could ultimately lead to a backlash (Follett, 1924/1951, 164). In the same way, being open to careful listening to diverse views does not mean the type of "open-mindedness" where people willingly and easily abandon their own thinking. Instead, Follett wanted people to respect their own viewpoint and keep "a firm upholding of it until you are convinced. Mushy people are no more good at [integration] than are stubborn people" (1925b/1940/1995, 85).[5]

Integration Requires Action

Integration results from action together with others in an attempt to find a resolution to a vexing issue or problem. A decision must be made, and a course of action must begin; the process is not a matter of theory. As Follett said, "Genuine integration occurs in the sphere of activities, and not of ideas or wills" (1924/1951, 150). In terms of integrative problem solving, she said that when people come together with the need to take action, theoretical oppositions are often laid aside in order to move forward toward the necessary action. Action is also necessary for an individual or a society to integrate, change, or grow. As Follett said, "Behavior must be changed through experience. . . . It cannot be changed by the impact of ideas" (1924/1951, 200). She understood that repeated action leads to new habits of behavior, which leads to social change.

Intentionally providing opportunities for groups to act together leads to the type of understanding that can produce further trust and integrative problem solving. This extends even to the level of international relations; as Follett said, "The aim [of international conferences] should not be intellectual agreement alone, but to provide opportunities for actual agreement through the activities of the nations involved" (1924/1951, 150–51).

The fact that Follett's integrative method is action- and goal-oriented sets it apart from some concepts of interdisciplinarity, which may set differing disciplines side by side for the purpose of theoretical understanding rather than action. Integration will result in a decision, a plan of action, an activity co-created by the group; it solves a problem through a new and creative resolution.

Integration Requires Difference

Follett's integration requires a deep commitment to difference and diversity, because out of differences emerge the possibilities of newness that she was seeking. As she said, "All diversity wisely handled may lead to . . . 'something new'" (1924/1951, 162). She was not expecting differences to be erased in the process of integration but rather to be accentuated and understood in integration. "We seek a richly diversified experience where every difference strengthens and reinforces the other" (Follett 1924/1951, 202). Integration may result in growth on the part of the individual and more cohesiveness in the group as a result of hearing and acknowledging differences, but the diverse perspectives should remain in place.

Follett was clear that integration most emphatically does *not* require assimilating differences. She said in 1918 that "differences must be integrated, not annihilated, nor absorbed." In a footnote to this point she listed the "bad" words that should *not* be equated with integration: "fuse, melt, amalgamate, assimilate, weld, dissolve, absorb, reconcile (if used in the Hegelian sense), etc." (1918, 39). She would have rejected the U.S. "melting pot" analogy because she saw difference as the "hope of democracy" (1918, 159). She extended that perspective to international relations, saying, "War can never cease until we see the value of differences, that they are to be maintained not blotted out. . . . Tolerance is intolerable" (1918, 344).

Because differences and even conflicts are sources of innovation, Follett worked to find, highlight, and acknowledge difference rather than to evade or suppress it. It is interesting that Follett did not talk about finding common ground as an essential element in integration, but rather she urged listening to find the "frankest and fullest kind of recognition of our differences" (1918, 345). Yet, her letters show clearly that when she wrote to those who may have disagreed with her, she attempted to hear and acknowledge their differences, but she also stressed the places where they may find agreement as a starting place for further discussion.

Power in the Integrative Process

Power is "the central problem" of social relations, according to Follett (1924/1951, xii), and she addressed this issue in many of her writings. Her work in this area is innovative and groundbreaking, yet power remains the area that reviewers questioned in her day and still today.[6]

Power in itself is positive; it enables us to act in the world, and Follett wanted to find ways to develop and grow power—especially the power that comes out of integration and leads to growth. In the introduction to *Creative Experience*, she termed this genuine power of creating with others *co-active*, which she contrasted with *coercive* power, the latter being, according to Follett, "the curse of the universe" (1924/1951, xiii). She later renamed these two types of power as *power-with* and *power-over*. Power-with, "the only actual power," dismantles expert or economic hierarchies and puts the authority in the group to resolve the problem. Power-with is a slow process, which "takes time and education and training to develop" (1924/1951, 188).

Integration through power-with opens the space for a path to action and real change. "An interweaving experience produces social ends *and* power," according to Follett (1924/1951, 192). It decentralizes authority by acknowledging how workers can and do influence leaders. In contrast, power-over environments clearly can impede integration by repressing difference and thereby suppressing creativity.

Yet Follett's description of power seems in some ways naïve, particularly since she does not address the interlocking systems of power that result in race-class-gender discrimination. Given her work, it seems odd that Follett does not address how these preexisting oppressions skew the integrative process of dialogue. However, this seeming lapse may be due partly to the direction in which her work moved after *Creative Experience*. If Follett had continued her political/social/philosophical work, she would have likely further developed her power analysis in social relations. However, after 1924 nearly all of her work was written for a business or organizational management audience. She worked to convince managers of the efficacy of stepping away from exercising power over their employees; she wanted to convince them to create a more progressive democratic workplace. This was essential work in the 1920s and '30s, and it consumed all of Follett's limited energy.[7]

It was left to others to use Follett's power analysis by extending it to other situations. For example, even though Follett herself did not call herself a feminist, later feminists have found her power distinctions useful. Political theorist Jane Mansbridge noted that "one of her central insights on democracy and conflict, an idea [Follett] called 'power-with,' has become a working part of feminist theory" (Mansbridge 1998, xvii). Mansbridge notes that Dorothy Emmett, the first woman president of the prestigious Aristotelian Society, used and cited Follett's theory of power, and Mansbridge goes on to describe how early feminist thinkers used Follett's power-with distinction, often without citing her.[8]

Integration Requires Reflection and Self-Knowledge

In 1925 at a meeting of the Bureau of Personnel Administration, Follett succinctly described the process of integration and conflict resolution in an essay titled "Creative Conflict." In this essay we see once again that conflict and difference are essential in the creative integrative process but also that the process requires self-knowledge and reflection. Integration begins with honesty: one has to desire genuinely to find a resolution to the issue. Then it is necessary to "put your cards on the table, face the real issue, uncover the conflict, bring the whole thing into the open" (Follett 1925b/1950/1995, 75). This requires knowing oneself; a person has to address "the conflicts which the individual has within himself," as well as understand the conflicts arising in the negotiation (75). The work of integration is thoughtful work, involving "the examination of symbols, that is a careful scrutiny of the language used to see what it really means" (78).

A person who goes into a conflict situation must understand that the conflict is not one individual (or opinion) versus another. One must recognize that she or he has partially created the situation to which she or he is responding, something Follett called circular response. As she said, "I can never fight you, I am always fighting you plus me. . . . I respond not only to you, but to the relation between you and me" (Follett 1926). , 81). It is a hermeneutical approach to dialogue. What she did not acknowledge is that this type of honesty requires trust; perhaps that trust is addressed partially in the very first agreement that both sides must "genuinely desire agreement" (Follett 1925b/1940/1995, 74). Yet this is heady work—thoughtful, intensively reflective, and usually slow—the type of work that is seen more often in humanities types of settings. One wonders at the positive response that Follett got from the group of business managers. What we know is that she was asked back again and again to speak to this group and to other managerial development meetings.

Comparison with Models of Interdisciplinary Integration

Given her interest in integration, it is not surprising that Follett also addressed interdisciplinarity. She was invited to the School for Citizenship and Public Affairs at Syracuse University on multiple occasions to give lectures and talk with the faculty. In a 1926 summer institute she spoke with faculty and students about the need to unify the social sciences (Tonn 2003, 421). In this talk she critiqued the fracturing of social problems into issues of economics, psychology, and ethics, pointing out that the solution often requires all of these fields. Follett also was involved in a yearlong faculty seminar at Harvard, organized by her friend Richard Cabot, which had as one of its aims to create a cross-disciplinary dialogue among the social sciences (Tonn 2003, 437).

In many ways, contemporary interdisciplinary thinkers echo the work of Follett, although it seems unlikely that many would have read her work. Interdisciplinary teaching and research is currently a hot topic, although the meaning of the term *interdisciplinary* varies in its many contexts. At its basic level interdisciplinarity means looking at a topic from multiple disciplines for the purpose of deeper understanding. However, integration goes a step further; it necessarily brings together the pieces that critical analysis has taken apart and moves it into the larger world. As Follett understood, integration requires action, but academic work typically does not involve students taking action. For the theorists discussed herein, the work of integration is also larger than interdisciplinarity; it synthesizes perspectives from outside the academy as well.[9] For example, Huber, Hutchins, and Gale (2005) broadly define *integration* as "connecting skills and knowledge from multiple sources and experiences; applying theory to practice in various settings; utilizing diverse and even contradictory points of view; and, understanding issues and positions contextually" (2005, 4).[10] Klein agrees that *integration* is a broad term for perspectives and action that "bridges numerous divides" (2005, 8) and may include the disciplines but also can address issues that arise from "cultures, subcultures, or life experiences" (2005, 9). Klein contrasts this with interdisciplinary perspectives, which, she cites Newell as saying, "come solely from the disciplines, though today they may also come from interdisciplinary fields and paradigms" (2005, 9). In his later 2010 article, Newell distinguishes interdisciplinarity as distinct from but analogous to integration, but he goes on to say that both interdisciplinary work and integrative skills are essential. It is clear from the literature that the skills of integration and synthesis underlie all true interdisciplinary work.

In his influential college textbook *Interdisciplinary Research*, Repko (2008) builds on the work of Newell, Klein, and other contemporary theorists to describe the steps necessary in the integrative interdisciplinary process in a way that resonates with Follett's. The first step for all of these theorists is identifying the actual conflicts. For Follett this includes identifying the various components of the conflicts, including such things as understanding the symbols behind the language. For Repko, identifying the conflicts requires understanding the basic assumptions and methodologies in each discipline, an activity that can be surprising for people who assume that most academics start at the same foundational principles. Newell also recommends closely examining the competing perspectives, suggesting that the researcher "find what is useful in each of the perspectives you dislike and what is problematic in each one you like" (2010, 11).

As we have seen, Follett was adamant in her opposition to compromise and wanted instead to look for the innovative solution. Repko and Newell agree. Interdisciplinary integration is the process of creating something new—as Repko (2008) says, "the activity of critically evaluating and creatively combining ideas and knowledge to form a new whole or cognitive advancement" (116). This "new whole" does not grow out of an either/or mentality but instead utilizes a both/and approach that requires an openness to create common ground, or as Newell puts it, "embrac[ing] contradiction, asking in what sense a situation can be 'both'" (2010, 9). Follett talks about the new whole as that which is always in process, as a "whole a-making" (by which she meant that both the person and the situation are in process). This creative process for Follett involved innovative thinking, "to not let one's thinking stay within the boundaries of two alternatives which are mutually exclusive" (1925b/1940/1995, 70).

For Newell, Repko, and Follett, the creative process of integration means embracing difference and searching for variations and contradictions, or as Newell says, "valuing diversity" (2010, 9). Follett was more explicit about transformation of the person as well as the individual in the process of integration; she understood that individual growth is part of the integrative process, but this idea is inherent in other models as well. All of these writers on integration point out that intentional education is required in order to create the personal and professional capacity for integration.

The model of integration that Newell (2010) describes in his article "Educating for a Complex World: Integrative Learning and Interdisciplinary Studies" can be seen as deeply dialogical, requiring active listening, creative inventiveness, and a willingness to embrace contradiction. Going into the conversation, he says that we should "assume every perspective that has stood the test of time has a kernel of truth to it" (11). This establishes a condition of respect where one can begin to find commonalities between concepts and goals. Finding common ground is also an essential step in Repko's (2008) process of interdisciplinary integration. However, it is clear from Repko's and Follett's writing that in prioritizing diversity, it is essential to avoid prematurely assuming common ground without first clearly understanding the divergences.

Shared Understandings and One Point of Departure

As we have seen, there are important similarities between these thinkers and Follett, particularly in four areas: (1) understanding integration as a problem-based active process, directed at resolving a perplexity; (2) embracing diversity: pluralism, multiple perspectives, differences, and contradictions; and (3) utilizing creativity to avoid either/or situations and compromise in favor of something new. A fourth similarity, as we will see, is that all of these thinkers also advocate for intentional education in integrative thinking.

One of the things that Follett brought to the discussion of integration that may be missing in the other models is an analysis of power. Issues of power are often identifiable in community cultural hegemonies or business structural hierarchies, and per Follett, this must be put on the table in integrative problem solving. However, structural and disciplinary hierarchies are present in academic work as well, and they must be addressed. Therefore, Follett's analysis of power is also important in interdisciplinary work. Newell hints at this when he says that in constructing a solution to an issue, one should "seek an understanding that is responsive to each of the contributing perspectives but is not dominated by any one of them" (2010, 11). As anyone who works in interdisciplinary fields knows, power is entrenched in the long-established disciplines. The disciplines are well-funded, have established faculty lines, and even have particular theoretical and historical perspectives, which many sometimes claim cannot be utilized by others. I know of several examples when heads of departments have instructed interdisciplinarians that even certain terms are off-limits and may not be utilized.[11] Follett understood the necessity of acknowledging these power inequalities, being aware of undue influence of certain leaders and their manipulation of others. The process of integration builds a power-with setting prior to and throughout the problem-solving activity. This process is also absolutely essential when academics work with community partners around problem solving. And as Follett reminds us, establishing this power-with environment can be a long and slow process requiring self-reflection and listening. As she said of power-with work, "It takes time and education and training to develop; it cannot be got by revolution, it involves a process and a slow process" (Follett 1924/1951, 188).

Educating for Integration

Academia has done a poor job of preparing our students for integrative work. As Huber and Hutchins noted, "Developing such a synthesizing, creative cast of mind has long been a goal of liberal education, albeit one that students have been expected, more often than not, to pick up for themselves" Huber et al. 2005, 4). Follett too understood that the integrative process requires intentionally reflective education and training as well as a certain predilection for integrative work. A "high order of intelligence, keen perception and discrimination, more than all, a brilliant inventiveness" (Follett 1925b/1940/1995, 82) are needed, along with a rich imagination and freedom from manipulations of those who may be in positions of domination. She knew that for those who wanted the thrill of the battle and conquest, integration can seem like "a tamer affair" (82). Yet, information is rigorous in that it requires a heightened sense of self-reflection, understanding the ways that "my behavior is helping to develop the situation to which I am responding" (1925b, 81) and the ability to engage in active problem solving based on self-reflection and shared power. This could be achieved through engagement with their communities or through a case study pedagogy whereby students could learn cooperative problem solving.

In 1928 Syracuse University asked Follett to address the faculty regarding leadership and the teacher-student relationship. In the paper she wrote for this talk she proposed that "beyond what can be taught directly through the subject, the class itself may be a training ground in joint thinking" (Follett

1928/1973, 314). In the process of learning to think jointly, she said that "our purposes, our interests, desires, satisfactions often take on new aspects when compared with others" and that this process "liberates us from the purely personal" and increases one's "spiritual energy and vision" (315). In education, according to Follett, the role of teacher is a meaning-making activity, a "joint search for meanings" between the teacher and the students (319). But then the students must be able to translate that into action, to use their experiences and understandings to find ways to live effectively and harmoniously with others. Education that integrates personal meaning and community life results in a process of growth, "the realization of our creative function" in which we come to "the realization of our responsibility in a universe which is being created anew at every instant" (312). These are high goals indeed for any educational process, requiring depth of reflection and active engagement with others.

In education, Follett had the same message that she had embodied in all of her life work, be it in business, community activism, or political life. Holding the truth of oneself as essentially integrated with others, there are methods we can use to enhance integration, thereby improving our lives, our communities, and our workplaces. Integration necessitates stepping away from hierarchical power structures and instead listening carefully and being willing to experiment with others to find new solutions.

References

Banerjee, A. 2008. "Follett's Pragmatist Ontology of Relations: Potentials for a Feminist Perspective on Violence." *Journal of Speculative Philosophy* 22 (1): 3–11.

Cohen, A. L. 1971. *Mary Parker Follett: Spokesman for Democracy, Philosopher for Social Group Work, 1918–1933.* Ann Arbor: UMI Dissertation Services.

Drucker, P. 1995. "Introduction: Mary Parker Follett: Prophet of Management." In *Mary Parker Follett, Prophet of Management: A Celebration of Writings from the 1920s*, edited by P. Graham, 1–9. Cambridge, MA: Harvard Business School Press.

Enomoto, T. 1995. Commentary on "The Individual in the Group." In *Mary Parker Follett, Prophet of Management: A Celebration of Writings from the 1920s*, edited by P. Graham, 240–45. Boston: Harvard Business School Press.

Follett, M. P. 1918. *The New State: Group Organization, the Solution of Popular Government.* New York: Longmans, Green and Co.

———. 1924/1951. *Creative Experience.* New York: Peter Smith.

———. 1925a/1949/1987. *Freedom and Co-ordination: Lectures in Business Organization.* New York: Garland Publishing.

———. 1925b/1940/1995. "Constructive Conflict." In *Mary Parker Follett, Prophet of Management: A Celebration of Writings from the 1920s*, edited by P. Graham, 67–95. Boston: Harvard Business School Press.

———. 1926. "The Influence of Employee Representation in a Remodeling of the Accepted Type of Business Manager." In *Dynamic Administration: The Collected Papers of Mary Follett Parker*, edited by Henry C. Metcalf and L. Urwick, 167–82. New York: Harper Brothers.

———. 1927/1973. "The Psychology of Consent and Participation." In *Dynamic Administration: The Collected Papers of Mary Parker Follett*, 2nd ed., edited by H. C. Metcalf and L. Urwick, 211–92. New York: Harper and Brothers.

———. 1928/1973. "The Teacher-Student Relationship." In *Dynamic Administration: The Collected Papers of Mary Parker Follett*, 2nd ed., edited by H. C. Metcalf and L. Urwick, 95–116. New York: Hippocrene Books.

Graham, P., ed. 1995. *Mary Parker Follett—Prophet of Management: A Celebration of Writings from the 1920s.* Boston: Harvard Business School Press.

Hoopes, J. 2003. *False Prophets: The Gurus Who Created Modern Management and Why Their Ideas Are Bad for Business*. New York: Basic Books.

Huber, M. T., P. Hutchins, and R. Gale. 2005. "Integrative Learning for Liberal Education." *Peer Review* 7 (4): 4–7.

Klein, J. 2005. "Integrative Learning and Interdisciplinary Studies." *Peer Review* 7 (4): 8–10.

Mansbridge, J. 1998. "Foreword." In *The New State: Group Organization, the Solution to Popular Government* (reprint), xvii–xxviii. University Park: Pennsylvania State University Press.

Mattson, K. 1998. *Creating a Democratic Public.* University Park: Pennsylvania State University Press.

Mendenhall, M. E., James H. M., and Cutright, M. Mary Parker Follett: prophet of chaos and complexity. *Journal of Management History* 6, no. 4 (2000): 191-204.

Newell, W. 2010. Educating for a complex world: Integrative learning and interdisciplinary studies. *Liberal Education* 96 (4): 6–11.

Pratt, S. 2011. "American Power: Mary Parker Follett and Michel Foucault." *Foucault Studies* 11 (February): 76–91.

Repko, A. F. 2008. *Interdisciplinary Research: Process and Theory*. Thousand Oaks, CA: Sage.

Rowe, S. C. 2009. "Access to a Vision." In *Reflection and Engagement*. 4th ed., edited by J. D. Whipps et al., 382–92. Acton, MA: Copley.

Tonn, J. C. 2003. *Mary P. Follett: Creating Democracy, Transforming Management*. New Haven, CT: Yale University Press.

Whipps, J. 2012. "Feminist-Pragmatist Democratic Practice and Contemporary Sustainability Movements: Mary Parker Follett, Jane Addams, Emily Greene Balch, and Vandana Shiva." In *Contemporary Feminist Pragmatism*, edited by M. Hamington and Bardwell-Jones, 115–27. New York: Routledge.

Chapter 8

Participation, Commitment, and Dynamics: Lessons from an Integrative Graduate Education Program

Elizabeth Lowham, PhD, California Polytechnic State University, and Annalisa Schilla, PhD, California Air Resources Board

The belief that synthesized knowledge is required to solve the complex issues that face society has become pervasive. As a result, integrative and interdisciplinary education[1] and collaboration have become buzz phrases in both academic and nonacademic circles. A growing number of graduate-level programs exist that seek to train integrative scholars and researchers. Many of these programs seek to augment students' traditional graduate education with an integrative curricula and approach separate from their disciplinary education. Participation in such programs can be challenging for students and faculty as they seek to find acceptance for their work in the mainstream of their discipline and as they attempt to integrate their discipline and approach with others from different fields.

Integrative research, *both* formal and informal, has a long history. Accounts differ, however, as to when federally funded interdisciplinary research in the United States truly began. Wolfle (1981) argued that the first interdisciplinary, mission-oriented project began in 1830 when the government provided money to the Franklin Institute for the study of steam boiler explosions.[2] Other researchers pointed to the Lewis and Clark exploration of the Upper Missouri River in 1803 (Klein 1990). In both of these cases, the interdisciplinary research was problem- or mission-oriented; the research was instrumental in purpose. In other contexts and in the more modern interpretation, interdisciplinary research is often a search for unification of knowledge by way of conceptual integration.

Perhaps most remarkable about the long history of interdisciplinary research in the United States is that, despite considerable funding, support with nearly religious fervor, and much practice, interdisciplinary research and education often fell short of genuine integration; the results were stymied "by disciplinary chauvinism and the psychological, social, and epistemological problems of working across disciplines" (Klein 1990, 35). As Frodeman, Mitcham, and Sacks (2001) note, interdisciplinary research also has tended to produce new fields of specialization rather than any general understanding.

Part of the failure of interdisciplinarity might be related to the abundant confusion over its meaning. The term *interdisciplinary* took a place in the *Dictionary of Diseased English* in 1977 (Klein 1990), prompting arguments about whether the term had any actual, real meaning. The problem is not that interdisciplinary has *no* meaning but simply that it has so many meanings (Wolfle 1981), often ones that conflict with each other (Klein 1996; Salter and Hearn, 1996). These variations in definitions can make assessment and learning difficult. By providing a participant-level view on integrative graduate education in an attempt to understand the failures and success as well as the promise and pitfalls of such programs, this chapter presents a case study of the integrative processes and outcomes of one of the National Science Foundation's Integrative Graduate Education and Research Training (IGERT) programs. The case study presents a unique view on integrative studies—that of the participants—as they attend to both their disciplinary degree programs and the integrative nature of these types of add-on programs. Based on participation in one IGERT cohort, participant observation of another cohort, scholarly research into interdisciplinarity and integration, and interviews with other IGERT participants, this chapter discusses the challenges and rewards of such graduate training. The chapter concludes with lessons and techniques for improving interdisciplinary and integrative graduate education programs with a particular focus on the integration of multiple disciplines. We believe that these insights into the practice of graduate integrative studies will help future leaders and participants build more successful integrative programs.

Case Study: Carbon, Climate, and Society Initiative

The Carbon, Climate, and Society Initiative (CCSI) was one of nineteen initial proposals funded by the NSF's IGERT program. The NSF granted faculty at the University of Colorado $2.6 million to train budding researchers and graduate students to more effectively solve real-world problems, hoping to create scholars "with multidisciplinary backgrounds and the technological and professional skills needed for future career demands" (Office of News Services 2000). CCSI was funded for a total of six years and encompassed two separate cohorts of graduate students (Cohorts 1 and 2). At its inception, CCSI was unique among IGERTs for the broad range of disciplines it endeavored to bring together, including (but not limited to) geologists, political scientists, chemists, economists, engineers, biologists, and journalists.

The CCSI principal investigators (PIs) argued that there are essentially two types of problems related to graduate education and research on climate change. The first type relates directly to the general understanding of climate change. Within this set of problems, the core PIs[3] argued that "humans have been far more adept at causing environmental change than at understanding the impacts of those changes" (CCSI IGERT Abstract) and further that one of the causes of our inability to address environmental problems is a lack of integration between understandings of human and natural systems (J. White, personal communication, 2003). This lack of cohesion between the natural and social dimensions was a fairly common critique and characterization of research in the area of climate change at the time, yet it also revealed a second problem related to climate education. The core PIs argued that the disconnect between human and natural systems extended further into graduate education and training than most academics (and perhaps practitioners) appreciated.

> Our current disciplinary-based graduate educational structure does not effectively meet that need [to integrate]. Students are not learning how to cross disciplinary boundaries, particularly across the social and natural sciences, and how to work effectively in teams. Neither are they taught how to effectively communicate with the press and the public in order to make their research findings more broadly known and accepted. (CCSI IGERT Abstract)

This problem, the PIs argued, extended back to the difference in underlying paradigms of natural and social scientists. They believed that traditionally trained natural scientists used a scientific method that the public did not appropriately understand, that social scientists could and should not use a reductionist approach to studying human systems, and that there was not an effective method for presenting the current state of knowledge to the public in meaningful ways (White 2003).

The PIs argued that education—of students, faculty, administrators, and the university community—was crucial to bridging the gap between humans and natural systems. NSF IGERT funding provided not only the necessary financial support but also the legitimacy required to implement and experiment with science and graduate education to improve the training of graduate students in the hopes of improving future climate research.

The challenge then became one of implementation. Given the problematic nature of climate change research and education, one of the main challenges was to develop and implement a project that fully realized the skills of the team and integrated participants' skills and knowledge in unique ways. The general model for CCSI was to fund students for two years. During the first year, students learned together about climate change, typically in a seminar-style setting. Over the summer, students would participate in a short-term internship. The PIs preferred that the internships be outside students' discipline, but there was no formalized method for ensuring this arrangement. Examples of the mini-internships undertaken included a journalism student who traveled to Botswana to "work on" water chemistry with one of the students in environmental engineering, an ice core student who went to Copenhagen to learn some advanced techniques for interpreting ice core data, and a geoscientist who took a journalist and a political scientist to Iceland to study and write about climate change in the Arctic. In the second year, students would undertake a bigger collaborative project related to climate change. Each cohort had a different second-year project.

Cohort 1 (Fall 2001–Summer 2003)

Cohort 1 of CCSI included fifteen students (eight males, seven females) composed of one economist, two political scientists, two journalists, three biologists, five geoscientists, and two environmental engineers.[4] Eighteen faculty members from these same disciplines were attached in varying degrees to the program. Participating faculty nominated students from their discipline to participate in the program who the faculty felt were interested in climate change.

In the second year, Cohort 1 was responsible for developing and implementing a team research project. Subgroups within the cohort had conducted Colorado- and climate-relevant background research in the first year, with the understanding that this background research would directly inform the second-year research project. As a group of students, Cohort 1 was unable to develop a cohesive research direction during the second year (a breakdown discussed in depth later). The final report contains some very interesting pieces of research but remained unfinished in large part due to the cohort's dysfunctional team dynamics, in spite of a last-ditch effort in the spring of 2002 to salvage the cohort's efforts by bringing in a facilitator. In the fall of 2003 CCSI hosted a retreat in Aspen to review and provide some closure for Cohort 1. The retreat was also meant to provide Cohort 2 with an initial team-building opportunity that Cohort 1 had lacked and to guide Cohort 2 away from some of the problems that Cohort 1 encountered.

Cohort 2 (Fall 2003–Spring 2006)

Cohort 2 also included representation from a broad set of majors. Among the twelve students (three males, nine females), there were four environmental studies students—all of whom emphasized policy[5]—one environmental engineer, three journalists, one geoscientist, two biologists, and one business student. The selection process for participants in Cohort 2 was more focused and directed. Rather than simply having participating faculty nominate who they considered their best students, PIs took an active role ensuring that students had the desire to participate on an interdisciplinary project and that at least some of the students had relevant experience and expertise working with and leading groups.

Cohort 2 also was allowed to struggle with defining its second-year project, with the initial belief that they could complete that project in the second year. As with Cohort 1, faculty guidance ultimately was required to determine the project, which was to prepare an interdisciplinary course for undergraduates covering the many aspects of climate change. In the end, participation of Cohort 2 was extended to a third year so that the students also taught the course; thus, Cohort 2 dedicated three semesters to course development and one semester to teaching the course.[6]

Challenges of Interdisciplinary Graduate Education

Over the course of CCSI, each cohort faced its own set of challenges and rewards. In the following section, we highlight some of the major problems of collaboration and interdisciplinarity as well as problems that exist at the intersection of collaborative and interdisciplinary education. We first review these challenges as they exist in the literature and then as they existed for the students. This analysis is based on our participation, observation, and interviews with CCSI participants.

Challenges of Collaboration

In many ways, internal dynamics are one of the most critical components of integrative graduate education and research. Such dynamics can govern the development of shared visions as well as serve as a valuable indicator of personal satisfaction and evaluation of the project. Most of these challenges are related to the dynamics of any group of people working together, regardless of their disciplinary background.

Common language, meaning, and communication. Interdisciplinary teams typically undertake complex problems. As Senge (1990) notes, "Without a shared language for dealing with complexity, team learning is limited" (268). The ideal situation occurs when a research group develops a common vocabulary bolstered by a common understanding, across the group, of what the terms mean.[7] This language is not a disciplinary language but, rather, a compilation of important disciplinary concepts—as well as, if required, the creation of unique terms that focus around the problem the group has undertaken (Gilbert 1998; Lightsom 2002; Pickett, Burch, and Grove 1999; Senge 1990). The development of such a language takes time and trust among the group members (Lightsom 2002; Monroe 2002).

Communication in an interdisciplinary research group is a difficult and ongoing task. Initially, researchers must pay close attention to group communication (Lightsom, 2002). Once the group has started to implement its research agenda and has begun developing a common language, the group must continue to encourage and improve their communication with each other. Many groups suffer through a stage when there is the *illusion of agreement* across disciplinary boundaries (Robinson 1996). In these instances, individuals may use the same words (e.g., *problem*) but hold drastically different meanings attached to those words (e.g., causes and implications attached to the problem). Thus, while individuals appear to agree, their communication may not be deep enough or open enough to accommodate or elucidate the important differences between their areas of agreement. Therefore, the structure of the project ought to encourage open, honest, free, and continuous communication throughout the project lifetime (Lightsom, 2002).

For the most part, both cohorts successfully created their own interdisciplinary language and style of communication. These languages included general terms underpinning research in climate change (*teleconnections* and *IPCC*, for example). Thus, much of each cohort's integrated language was shared not only across cohorts but also with the community of scholars engaged in climate change research. This part of the shared language connected each participant to a broader community of scholars focused on climate change. Additionally, each cohort had a layer of communication and language that was unique; included in this layer were inside jokes and commentary based on their own shared experiences. This part of the shared communication connected members to one another, helping build group identity and cohesion. Examples of this type of communication included Cohort 1's use of the word *problem*, a term that initially caused some miscommunication because it meant something very different to the natural scientists than to the social scientists but eventually became a joke for everyone in the cohort. Other examples of this type of communication in Cohort 1 included references to shared experiences, such as the roles that various students adopted in a mock senate testimony or in a skit at a retreat. Note that when the authors participated in the third year of Cohort 2, we lacked this layer of communication that connected us to the group. While we could (and attempted to) learn as much of this layer of communication as we could, our integration into the group was potentially limited by the lack of shared meaning and experience.

Challenges of Interdisciplinarity

Some of the challenges faced in interdisciplinary graduate education are focused largely around the integration of the disciplines involved, and may be unrelated to the dynamics of a group tackling an interdisciplinary project. In other words, an individual researcher trying to do interdisciplinary research might face certain problems, even if the researcher is working alone. These challenges of interdisciplinarity can be magnified within a group working on an interdisciplinary problem.

Disciplinary balance. Gaff and Wilson (1977) note that faculty members from different disciplines vary according to educational values, teaching orientations, and lifestyles, implying "that there are fundamental differences between professors, and that the differences extend beyond subject matter into the realm of values and ideology and are associated with fields of specialization" (187). These differences are more likely than not to be more broadly applicable. Thus, the way a researcher (or group of researchers) chooses to deal with differences in pedagogy, methodology, values, and so on is a fairly important piece of the interdisciplinary question. Another critical piece is that included disciplines or disciplinary representatives do not feel stigmatized within the project because of these differences.

Certainly, Cohort 1 struggled to manage successfully the real or perceived differences among the involved disciplines. Some of these differences were, for example, related to workflow and work location. The social scientists and journalists had much more flexibility in the location and timing of their work; they were, for the most part, not working in labs or sharing equipment as the natural scientists were. This created some tension over perceptions of the shared balance of workload. Further, during the second year of Cohort 1, the group split into two separate research groups. One of the common reasons that several students in Cohort 1 gave for the division centered largely on substantive differences that were ill-managed and stigmatization. This division was at least partly related to the fact that each participant, for the most part, was undergoing training in the pedagogy, methods, and values of their own disciplines while trying to maintain and build an identity in the context of the interdisciplinary group. For example, one student reported, "I felt a constant tension between my disciplinary training in early graduate school and my participation in this program. One of the other participants from my own field derided my efforts to tackle aspects of the interdisciplinary project that extended beyond our shared disciplinary training."

Cohort 2 had fewer issues with disciplinary differences, which may partly be due to the fact that several of the participants in Cohort 2 came from the newly created environmental studies graduate program. Thus, for these individuals, their disciplinary and interdisciplinary identities were not in conflict. Further, the PIs had learned from their experience in Cohort 1 that disciplinary expertise did not necessarily equate to strong interdisciplinary skills; PIs selected graduate students for Cohort 2 using more specific behavioral, intellectual, and skill criteria.

Evaluation. One of the bigger-picture professional questions facing interdisciplinary and integrative research is the existence of appropriate criteria for evaluating whether an interdisciplinary group has been successful in the integration and production of knowledge. Further, these criteria should be able to measure *quality* and *impact* despite differences in definitions and formulations of productivity across disciplines. Klein (1996) argues that the "criteria for judgment constitute the least understood aspect of interdisciplinarity, in part because the issue has been the least studied and in part because the multiplicity of tasks seems to militate against a single standard" (210).

The traditional disciplinary criteria of citations are not generally applicable to interdisciplinary study, largely because interdisciplinary projects have fewer citations, and further, such projects generate citations that are coauthorships outside of mainstream disciplinary journals (Klein 1990; Monroe 2002). Additionally, there are no accurate methods of measuring the impact of an interdisciplinary project on individual learning, the direction of future individual research, and the future participation and behavior in other interdisciplinary projects (Klein 1990). There is, thus, a problem of "yardsticks" and "perspectives" (Hackett 2000, 258).

Funding agencies rarely detail criteria of what is implied or required by the term *interdisciplinary*—and by corollary, *integration*—or to provide steps on how to achieve it (Weingart 2002), thereby complicating the evaluation of successful interdisciplinarity and integration. However, proponents argue that interdisciplinary programs should be evaluated by their ability to integrate successfully and produce knowledge (Klein 1996). This measure has two components: The project should create (1) meaningful and credible science[8] that is (2) different from what researchers could have produced independently or additively.

The success of the projects undertaken in the CCSI program is debatable. In both cohorts, many participants questioned whether they had created something that was greater than the sum of its parts or that was greater than any individual or disciplinary group could have created. Thus, participants in both cohorts were uncertain still whether their second-year project met the second component of success.

Evaluation of the first component—meaningful and credible science—is complicated by the variations in the personal objectives of participants. It seems likely, based on interviews, observations, and experiences, that the meaningful and credible science was assumed as a common standard across all participants, though, to our knowledge, neither cohort discussed the standards for meaningfulness or credibility beyond traditional academic standards. The result of this assumed common standard was that participants tended to evaluate CCSI and the final project based on personal learning and professional goals rather than the credibility of the research produced.

So CCSI may not fare well if success is measured by the creation of products that signify new, meaningful, and credible science. However, CCSI participants had many of their own definitions for successful interdisciplinary research. Because of the lack of a common definition of or criteria for integration, each student developed her or his own definition of success. For many, success was related to their intellectual development, through the growth of their understanding of themselves and their own discipline and its relationship to other disciplines. One participant noted that success would occur when the skills of each disciplinarian were utilized directly in the same project. Others noted that researchers should be able to place their own research in relation to others, with specific emphasis on where and how different disciplines define problems. Thus, for many participants, a key evaluative criterion was based on their individual needs, goals, and productivity.

For some (but not all) CCSI participants, the individual focus extended into producing joint answers or a collaborative approach to a problem. For others, success in interdisciplinary graduate education was largely related to a continued desire to participate (and gain relevant skills) in interdisciplinary research that extended past their graduate careers and into their future work. Interestingly, although CCSI extended the period of time in graduate school for many participants, more than half of the participants have continued active work on interdisciplinary research teams and projects after graduation. One participant reported, "CCSI provided me with the background necessary to tackle interdisciplinary problems in my postgraduate career. It was the experience that I found myself constantly referencing during job interviews."

This value for and continued work on interdisciplinary research—a sign that integration has occurred—is perhaps one of the most valuable and tangible successes of the CCSI program. This measure of long-term success could be assessed only through longitudinal studies of the participants and would not be known or attributable at program completion.

Challenges at the Intersection of Interdisciplinary and Collaborative Research

In many ways, the relationships between knowledge integration, institutions, teamwork, and interdisciplinarity are paradoxical. Academics appear to excel at the task of knowledge integration, even when that knowledge is from another discipline. For example, political scientists have integrated (borrowed from) parts of many other disciplines, including evolutionary biology, economics, and psychology. Part of the reason for this apparent excellence is a combination of the search for explanation as well as the search to make an individual theoretical contribution within a discipline. Yet something about combining the tasks of knowledge integration and of working with people seems to stymie even the most well-intentioned individuals. Here, at the intersection of interdisciplinary and collaborative research, we find most of the difficulties of interdisciplinary graduate education.

Shared understandings. Nearly all the literature on interdisciplinarity indicates that participants ought to come to a shared understanding of what they want to create or are trying to accomplish (Gilbert 1998; Katzenbach and Smith 1993; Lightsom 2002; Pickett, Burch, and Grove 1999; Senge 1990; Stone 1969). When participants on an interdisciplinary project take the time to develop a shared understanding of their collective purpose and goals, participants can act as individuals who are motivated to work toward the shared understanding; that is, they can expand their concept of research and knowledge production to encompass that of the group and their fellow teammates (Lightsom 2002).

The shared understanding can, and most likely will, be multifaceted. In other words, a shared understanding of the project does not imply that no conflict exists over that understanding or that different participants have the same conception of the project.[9] The implication here is that conflict is expected and can be extremely healthy. In fact, conflict can propel the group forward. This conflict, however, ought to be balanced by the shared belief in a common, uniting purpose or in shaping a common purpose as well as by a healthy respect for other viewpoints. A shared understanding in interdisciplinary graduate education should include some agreement on goals or outcomes, on research agenda and methods, and on a framework for resolving these conflicts.

Initially, participants and partners in interdisciplinary projects likely have different desired outcomes from the project.[10] Klein (1996) and Salter and Hearn (1996) argue that a distinction exists between instrumental and epistemological (synoptic) interdisciplinary ends. Instrumentalism uses interdisciplinarity and integration as instruments of problem solving, while synoptic ends search for the one uniting body of knowledge.[11] This distinction is a challenge because it is likely that disciplines as well as individual participants are not likely to view the end goals similarly. Each interdisciplinary project must define for itself where the appropriate balance between knowledge and action lies. The distinction and balance between knowledge and action also speak to the idea that an interdisciplinary group should have a shared understanding of its audience.

Proponents also argued that another hallmark of successful interdisciplinary groups is the identification of a common problem or a set of common problems (Gilbert 1998; Lightsom 2002; Pickett, Burch, and Grove 1999). Ideally, the group initially should have worked together to identify and define the problem and research questions they planned to undertake together.[12] The common research agenda can help set the tone and aspiration for the group (Katzenbach and Smith 1993) and serve as a way for individuals to understand and respect their own and others' roles, methodologies, and epistemologies within the group. The common questions also help individual researchers set aside their own disciplinary interests for the interests and needs of the team (Lightsom 2002).

While each CCSI cohort faced its own dilemmas in defining a shared understanding, perhaps the most obvious example of the importance of shared understandings and the difficulties of achieving them occurred during Cohort 1's second year. During the first year, the PIs divided Cohort 1 into three subgroups to study topics that related to both climate change and Colorado: urbanization, energy, and agriculture. As subgroups, students were tasked with identifying the major components of these sectors that related to climate change. Intriguingly, all three groups independently reached the conclusion that, although relevant to climate change, these sectors faced environmental challenges that were perceived to be much more immediate than climate change.

This subtle shift in focus away from climate change was also pervasive during Cohort 1's second year. As a team of students, Cohort 1 was supposed to develop and implement its own research project. However, Cohort 1 could not settle on a single research direction or on whether there should be an internal leadership structure. Eventually, after letting Cohort 1 attempt to resolve these issues on its own, the main PIs intervened and selected both a leader and a topic: developing a plan for the mitigation of climate change causes in Colorado. The faculty's response was partly related to their belief that Cohort 1 should have a more specific climate change focus. For Cohort 1, this faculty intervention illustrated the confusion between faculty and students, and among students themselves, as to the goal of the CCSI program. For example, some students (and related faculty) believed the goal of the project was to identify how climate change concerns could (or should) be integrated into these sectors across Colorado, while others believed the goal was to identify how climate-sensitive sectors in Colorado were affected by climate change and to investigate how the state and communities could and should respond. Substantial disagreement remains among participants in Cohort 1 about the definition of the ultimate goal of the project.

The intervention of the faculty and the resulting perception of a change of course was the most obvious symptom indicating that Cohort 1 had run into significant problems. Several students felt that this intervention was unnecessary and incorrect. As a remedy, the student participants elected two other subleaders to form a type of executive council. As far as the newly selected topic, the group was divided—almost neatly in half—as to whether mitigation or adaptation was the appropriate focus when studying climate change in Colorado. In response, the cohort essentially split in two; one half, including one of the elected leaders and the appointed leader, took on mitigation of emissions in Colorado. The other half, including the other elected leader, took on issues of adaptation to possible climate changes in Colorado. Despite this split, the cohort was somewhat united in the desire to produce a single, cohesive report and potential book about climate change in Colorado. Thus, students observed the direct consequences of the inability to develop a shared understanding: Cohort 1 literally divided in two, and participants were ultimately unable to produce the planned outcome of a report on the current impacts and policies regarding climate change in Colorado.

Leadership and accountability. Perhaps the most daunting problem across both cohorts was the search for and continual refinement of methods of leading and ensuring accountability. Each cohort developed a unique leadership structure. In Cohort 1, leadership was initially haphazard, followed by a mix of mandated leadership and then to democratically elected leadership. In Cohort 2, leadership, at least during the first two years, occurred largely through a rotation whereby each member held the reins for a month. Perhaps most interesting from the standpoint of graduate education is that when it came time to actually produce a product, both leadership schemes fell short. That is, the structure of the leadership likely was not driving results. For example, while Cohort 2 was producing the final project, no one on the project actually could remember whose turn it was to lead, and no one wanted to take leadership responsibility for the outcome of the project.

Rather, we feel that the driving force behind the creation of products or outputs was largely the accountability of participants to each other and to the project. In Cohort 1, this feeling of accountability varied widely. Some participants felt accountable to each other and to the idea that, as students, participants were being paid to produce an outcome. Our interviews revealed that others did not. This variation in accountability made it difficult for any leadership, including from the PIs themselves, to prompt sincere participation or research. In Cohort 2, there was far less variation in the level of accountability across participants (though there was still some). One of the easiest ways to identify this increased level of accountability is through primary group orientation (Klein 1990). Cohort 2 was far more likely to refer to each other as *we* as opposed to *you* or *I*. Cohort 1, especially after the division in the second year, was far more likely to use *I* and *you* to refer to the group. This grammatical difference indicated a more important shift in orientation and group commitment to a common task and shared understanding.

The greater accountability in Cohort 2 may stem from the more careful selection of participants, more focus on internal dynamics, and so forth. More accountability made it somewhat easier for Cohort 2 to produce an outcome, as did the scope and formalization of the product. That is, the nature of a scheduled course on climate change was perhaps a more tangible product than an unstructured report. However, as we discussed previously, participants in Cohort 2 still questioned whether their final project (the climate change course) was different or more innovative from an interdisciplinary perspective than what any one of them would have taught alone.

Conclusion

Given that the goals of the IGERT program are largely to train graduate students in interdisciplinary education, there is little doubt that CCSI was a success. Each cohort received training and experience with other disciplines beyond their traditional disciplinary colleagues. At some point in the IGERT experience, each student was asked to step outside the traditional disciplinary comfort zone and engage with other disciplines (though there was variation in the engagement with other disciplines). Further, more than half of CCSI participants across both cohorts still are actively involved in projects, research, or teaching that involves other disciplines, which alone indicates that interdisciplinary graduate education can be successful. However, it also highlights that project leaders need to think carefully about and define what they are trying to achieve with interdisciplinary graduate education, which is particularly true if, as Hackett (2000) argues, the burden of developing evaluative criteria continues to fall to proposal writers.

The variation in experiences across cohorts and individuals reveals some important lessons for those of us who wish to continue interdisciplinary education and research. These lessons are particularly important if we are undertaking projects with a substantial variation in disciplines.

Who Participates (and Why They Participate) Makes a Difference

Almost universally, across both cohorts, participants came to believe that who participates and why they participate matters in integrative graduate education. Our experiences indicate that it is incredibly difficult to orchestrate interdisciplinarity or integration. Several of our colleagues from both cohorts believe that on these types of projects, the question/project must determine participation—not the other way around. Thus, the research should drive participation. If it does not, the probability of problems related to insincere commitment to the project and people increases. Cohort 1, for example, developed problems of commitment to CCSI with roughly one-third of participants. In a group of fourteen, the lack of commitment from four or five people made it incredibly difficult for the remaining members to work together and to include the noncommitted.

The lesson stemming from this experience for graduate education is twofold. First, not every graduate student is prepared for or is a good fit for interdisciplinary research. Project leaders and faculty need to select participants carefully and with intention. Second, it is probably better, at least in the initial development of interdisciplinary skills and research, to allow the research problem to narrow the list of potential candidates to be selected as participants. This strategy increases the probability of sincere commitment to the project, which should increase the probability that conflict is constructive rather than destructive. Once participants build relationships with other participants, some of this commitment hopefully will transform into commitment to the other participants, particularly if there are early victories and successes. In this case, people may begin to seek out additional research problems that extend past the project. However, our experiences indicate that the first step ought to be developing a research problem.

Group Dynamics and Team Building Need Constant Care

The approach that "we are all smart people; we should simply be able to get together and do this" does not work. This sentiment is particularly true for graduate education. Given the inherent difficulties of interdisciplinary research, it is highly unlikely that any group of graduate students who are simultaneously being indoctrinated into their own disciplines will be able to produce successful interdisciplinary work. Rather, PIs (or other sponsors) and participants themselves should be aware and constantly tend to the internal group dynamics.

One of the most startling observations for us was that an individual's perception of the internal dynamics of the group was directly related to their perception of the success or failure of the group. What was perhaps startling about this observation was that it was difficult to separate perceptions about the cohort from the productivity of the cohort in both positive and negative aspects. Additionally, given the academy's focus on outputs and outcomes, this relationship between feelings and outputs is particularly interesting.

The lesson from this observation simply is that individuals who are planning to lead or participate in interdisciplinary projects, especially when they include graduate students, ought to be not only aware of and careful of group dynamics but also value (and show value for) those dynamics. Participants, faculty, and students should be aware that group dynamics are important and value them as important. We also tentatively offer that such groups might benefit greatly from regular facilitation by an individual trained in collaboration. Certainly, this option is not viable for every interdisciplinary project. However, we feel that regular work with (or including on the project) someone who can facilitate well may help avoid some of the regular problems with group dynamics.

Faculty Commitment

Interdisciplinary graduate education requires a significant and active commitment by faculty, which at first seems quite obvious. However, faculty members need to be aware of how large the undertaking is and of some of the nonobvious constraints that may impede the project. For example, when Cohort 1 ended, the main PIs identified the need for co-teaching the courses associated with CCSI. The main PIs came to believe that they were not modeling good interdisciplinary behaviors for the graduate students involved on the project. However, even with the legitimacy of a large NSF grant, faculty faced institutional barriers of allocating teaching credit and the perceptions of other faculty in their home departments regarding the value of the project. In other words, even though PIs did identify the need for co-teaching, there were substantial institutional barriers that prevented faculty members from implementing a co-taught course. Further, there is some evidence that the perceptions of what constituted or defined *co-teaching* varied substantially among faculty.

In both cohorts, the students in the program were at some point required to step outside of their disciplinary comfort zone and to think in terms of other disciplines. As a result, they were forced to develop skills they previously had not exercised. This is revolutionary in graduate education and harkens back to a fundamental question about research that integrates across disciplines: Is it really interdisciplinarity that we strive for, where we must ultimately step out of our own field and learn to ask research questions in an entirely new way? Or do we really seek better efficiency at multidisciplinary research, where we provide only our own expertise to the team? This question surely has more than one answer. However, as science and society face increasingly complex challenges, problem-driven research certainly will be forced to undergo more than one revolution, one of which likely will be a greater emphasis on interdisciplinary and integrative work. Programs such as IGERT are an important part of that process.

References

Cameron, W. B. 1965. "The Hydra-Headed Curriculum: The Proliferation of Interdisciplinary Studies." *Journal of Higher Education*, 36 (6): 307–12.

CCSI IGERT Abstract. http://www.igert.org/projects/207.

Frodeman, R., C. Mitcham, and A. B. Sacks, 2001. "Questioning Interdisciplinarity." *Science, Technology, and Society Newsletter* 126/127: 1–5.

Gaff, J. G., and R. C. Wilson. 1977. "Faculty Cultures and Interdisciplinary Studies." *Journal of Higher Education*, 42 (3): 186–201.

Gibbons, M., C. Limoges, H. Nowotny, S. Schwartzman, P. Scott, and M. Trow. 1994. *The New Production of Knowledge: The Dynamics of Science and Research in Contemporary Societies*. Thousand Oaks, CA: Sage.

Gilbert, L. 1998. "Disciplinary Breadth and Interdisciplinary Knowledge Production." *Knowledge, Technology, and Policy* 11: 4–15.

Hackett, E. J. 2000. "Interdisciplinary Research Initiatives at the U.S. National Science Foundation." In *Practising Interdisciplinarity*, edited by P. Weingart and N. Stehr, 25–42. Toronto: University of Toronto Press.

Katzenbach, J. R., and D. K. Smith. 1993. *The Wisdom of Teams: Creating the High-Performance Organization*. Boston: Harvard Business School Press.

Klein, J. T. 1990. *Interdisciplinarity: History, Theory, and Practice*. Detroit: Wayne State University Press.

———. 1996. *Crossing Boundaries: Knowledge, Disciplinarities, and Interdisciplinarities*. Charlottesville: University of Virginia Press.

———. 2005. Integrative Learning and Interdisciplinary Studies. *Peer Review*, Summer/Fall: 8–10.

Lattuca, L. R. 2001. *Creating Interdisciplinarity: Interdisciplinary Research and Teaching among College and University Faculty*. Nashville: Vanderbilt University Press.

Lightsom, F. 2002. "Preliminary Suggestions for Success in Interdisciplinary Teamwork." *New Directions Institute.* http://sciencepolicy.colorado.edu/newdirections.

Monroe, K. R. 2002. "Interdisciplinary Work and Search for Shared Scientific Standards." *PS: Political Science and Politics* 35(2): 20305.

Office of News Services. 2000. "CU-Boulder Awarded $2.6 Million from NSF for Carbon, Climate and Society Study." Press release, Regents of the University of Colorado, Boulder, CO. http://dirwww.colorado.edu/news/r/ 5115f1039ffadf82c97f90715ff514d6.html.

Pickett, S. T. A., W. R. Burch, Jr. and J. M. Grove. 1999. "Interdisciplinary Research: Maintaining the Constructive Impulse in a Culture of Criticism." *Ecosystems*, 2: 302–7.

Robinson, J. B. 1996. "Falling between Schools: Some Thoughts on the Theory and Practice of Interdisciplinarity. In *Outside the Lines: Issues in Interdisciplinary Research*, edited by L. Salter and A. Hearn, 85–92. Montreal: McGill-Queen's University Press.

Salter, L., and A. Hearn, eds. 1996. *Outside the Lines: Issues in Interdisciplinary Research.* Montreal: McGill-Queen's University Press.

Senge, P. M. 1990. *The Fifth Discipline: The Art and Practice of the Learning Organization.* New York: Currency-Doubleday.

Stone, A. R. 1969. "The Interdisciplinary Research Team." *Journal of Applied Behavioral Science* 5 (3): 351–65.

Weingart, P. 2002. "Interdisciplinarity: The Paradoxical Discourse." In *Practising Interdisciplinarity*, edited by P. Weingart and N. Stehr, 25–42. Toronto: University of Toronto Press.

White, J. Personal communication, 2003.

Winthrop, H. 1966. "Specialists and Generalists: An Argument for Abolishing Artificial Boundary Lines in Scholarship and research." *Journal of Higher Education*, 37(4): 193–201.

Wolfle, D. L. 1981. "Interdisciplinary Research as a Form of Research." *SRA: Journal of the Society of Research Administrators* 13: 5–7.

Chapter 9

The Taxonomy of Significant Learning in a Math, Music, and Art Course

Heather Pinson, PhD, and Monica VanDieren, PhD, Robert Morris University

Under a restructuring of the Robert Morris University Honors Program, we were tasked with designing and co-teaching the program's first integrated learning seminar, which was intended to establish several shared components of math and music that apply learning in a real-world context. This seminar would serve junior- and senior-level honors students who had varied mathematical and musical backgrounds. Because we could assume the students had no prior experience with music theory or upper-level mathematics, we decided to include examples of literature and art as accessible visual aids to introduce abstract mathematical and musical concepts. We narrowed our focus to twentieth-century developments in math, music, and art, since this time period addressed a gap in coverage in our university curriculum, related to our own personal research interests, and provided a framework for classroom discussion on current restructuring of these disciplines. During our course development, the challenge was to create a significant learning experience worthy of upper-level honors credit without alienating students who had math anxiety or limited musical experience. Therefore, Fink's taxonomy was an essential guide through the design process.

What Is Fink's Taxonomy?

In *Creating Significant Learning Experiences: An Integrated Approach to Designing College Courses,* L. Dee Fink (2003) proposes a taxonomy of learning to guide course development and implementation. Fink identifies six taxa of learning (foundational knowledge, application, integration, human dimension, caring, and learning how to learn) that, as a whole, provide a road map for learning-centered education.

The idea of applying a classification of educational objectives to curriculum development is not new. Fink (2003) recalls Benjamin Bloom's framework for formulating course objectives based on six kinds of learning: eval-

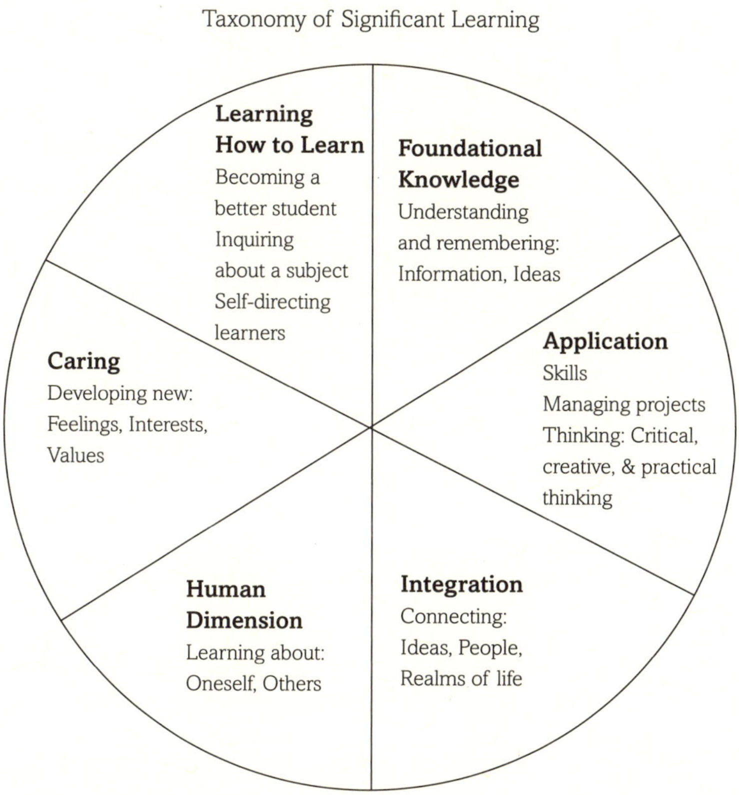

Fink's Taxonomy of Significant Learning (Fink 2003, 30)

uation, synthesis, analysis, application, comprehension, and knowledge (i.e., information recall). Fink's integrated taxonomy differs from Bloom's hierarchical taxonomy since achievement in any one of Fink's six taxa can improve the other areas. Furthermore, Fink's taxonomy captures objectives (such as lifelong learning skills) that do not emerge in Bloom's cognitive domain (Fink 2003). Since its introduction, Fink's taxonomy has been applied successfully to undergraduate course design in many subjects, including music theory, art history, Spanish, and psychology. It also has been used to design courses in subjects such as accounting and science in which the taxa of human dimension and caring are not typically taught (Fink and Fink 2009).

Applying Fink's Taxonomy to Designing an Integrated Honors Course

While many courses have been created or redesigned using Fink's taxonomy, few (if any) of the documented cases are integrated or constructed within an honors program. The definition and composition of honors courses vary from one university to the next; however, the general purpose of honors resides in its distinction from more mainstream university courses through accelerated learning and exploratory curriculum design. Fink's taxa of significant learning appear implicitly in both of these aspects. In honors courses, students are asked "to assume a larger proportion of the burden of teaching themselves than in equivalent courses elsewhere in the curriculum" (Schuman 2005, 33). The taxon of learning how to learn can help instructors prepare students for this new responsibility. Honors curriculum is often challenging, innovative, intellectually rigorous, enriching, and enhanced (Mullins 2005, 19). In other words, the students are presented with a significant learning experience through the application and integration of foundational knowledge:

> The dialog with self is central to any meaningful honors experience and requires a shift from the familiar high school preoccupation with book knowledge to one that includes self-knowledge and a willingness to develop new skills requiring both self-reflection and risk-taking. (Slavin and Mares 2008, 196)

Self-reflection and self-knowledge are key not only for learning how to learn but also for developing the human and caring dimensions of learning. Furthermore, gaining confidence with risk taking and exploring uncharted territory without a guide is critical for lifelong learning outside of the classroom.

Fink's taxonomy is appropriate for designing courses with the goal of integration as a means to move beyond disciplinary and interdisciplinary practices. Integrative learning, including the construction of multidisciplinary and interdisciplinary themes for course organization, "is an increasingly powerful component of the overall honors curriculum" (Braid 2008, 33). Because students and faculty in honors programs hail from many departments, each with their own disciplinary language, the students and faculty must develop a common investigative language as they explore new territory (Brai 2008, 32). "In the drive to help students develop integrative habits of mind, it is important to remember that the effectiveness of curricular innovations depends on the pedagogies that support them" (Huber, Hutchings, Gale, Miller, and Breen 2007, para. 9). These pedagogies address the idea that the changing world creates problems that an isolated discipline cannot solve (Huber et al. 2007, para. 10). These problems require one to look beyond foundational knowledge and to consider the application, human dimension, integration of knowledge, and application into real-world scenarios. Integrative pedagogies also provide "multiple opportunities for structured reflection to help students take a more intentional approach to their own learning" (Huber et al. 2007, para. 10). As students reflect on their intentional learning, they will enhance their ability to learn how to learn and care for the material.

When designing a course, Fink (2003) suggests first to identify course goals associated with each of the taxon and then design classroom activities and assessments for these learning objectives. When preparing for our course, we determined the best approach was to organize the semester around four broad themes, allowing room for students to interject their own examples and select their own topics for the final project. Our learning objectives were selected and mapped onto Fink's taxonomy, and the activities for these objectives represented the three components of active learning: (1) gather information, (2) engage the student with this information, and (3) encourage reflection of the material and the learning process. Fink (2003) proposes student involvement in the thematic organization of the course as a pedagogical practice in order to accomplish significant learning. Therefore, we solicited student involvement in the selection of the material and assessment mechanisms since "it does not just call for a one-way flow of information into the minds of students; rather it insists that students act upon the information and construct ways of organizing it. This is essential in order to stimulate cognitive development" (Hursh, Haas, and Moore 1983, 48).

Themes in Mathematics, Music, and Art

Once we limited our time frame for the course to the twentieth century, we spent several months researching the interconnection between mathematics, music, and art. We did not find a syllabus, a single text, or an approach to the integration of such diverse disciplines that satisfied us. On one extreme, we encountered some connections comprising discipline-specific jargon and advanced skills that were not suitable for our shared interdisciplinary course. But even more often, we found examples in popular texts that were superfluous or, borrowing a phrase from Newell and Green (1982), "academic froth" (23). For instance, a geometric sculpture may have substantial artistic content; however, the mathematics involved is nominal. Conversely, the mathematical analysis of waves is rich and developed, but it does not contribute much to the understanding or compositional structure of music, which in this case is treated as a passive object of study. We also struggled with keeping the material relevant and easy to digest by any college student, even one in honors.

Newell and Green (1982) suggest that truly integrated content must originate from questions with a scope beyond the reach of a single discipline. Embracing Newell and Green's strategy to find questions that recurred throughout our initial research ultimately led us to the identification of four themes: symmetry, the finite and infinite, searching for self and truth, and improvisation as a part of the creative process (see Figure 9.2).

Questions Guiding the Selection of Four Integrated Themes.

Recurring Questions in Our Initial Research	Newell and Green–Style Focused Question	Course Theme
Why do certain structures keep reappearing in each discipline? How are abstract properties utilized in each subject?	What makes a piece of music or mathematics beautiful?	Symmetry
What ideas inspire mathematicians and musicians? What mysteries motivate the work of mathematicians and musicians?	How can we comprehend infinity in a finite world?	The Finite and Infinite
Math and music are more than arithmetic and sound. But what are they?	How do advances in each of the disciplines contribute to the understanding of the discipline and the practitioner himself or herself?	Searching for Truth and Self
Why are certain mathematicians and artists remembered for their contributions while others are not? What stages of development are found in each discipline?	How do pioneers make creative leaps and overcome obstacles in their work?	Improvisation as a Part of the Creative Process

During our research, we found that *symmetry* appeared often in the interdisciplinary math, music, and art expositions, but most sources only superficially covered the mathematical treatment of symmetry, focused on purely visual instances, and skimmed over any musical correlation. While such examples as M. C. Escher's tessellations serve as an accessible introduction to symmetry, they do not demonstrate the integration of math with art. In fact, Escher (1989) was not trained in mathematics and did not formally appeal to mathematics to create his work. As an integrated course, our goal was to demonstrate intentional and significant interactions between all three areas.

We found that the recent work of Dmitri Tymoczko (2011), for example, best represented this scholastic endeavor through the application of symmetric group actions (neo-Riemannian transformations *P*, *L*, and *R*) to the analysis of chord progressions. Not only is the mathematical content of symmetric group theory substantial and only covered in a senior-level math course at our university, but also the music theory required to understand this application is a highly developed field in its own right and also is not taught in traditional music theory classrooms. Furthermore, Tymoczko's contemporary integrated work demonstrates to the students that mathematics and music are living fields with new advancements and creations made daily.

Our discussions of disciplinary milestones of the twentieth century—such as the work of mathematician Paul Cohen, composer Harry Patch, and painter René Magritte—led us to consider the finite and the infinite. Tracing the mathematical treatment of infinity from Zeno's paradox to the twentieth-century works of Paul Cohen, Saharon Shelah, and W. Hugh Woodin, we introduce the students to the dilemma of formalizing a concept that conflicts with Euclid's axiom: the whole is bigger than the part. While mathematicians grapple with this long-standing axiom, musicians are breaking out of the traditional confines of the finite chromatic and diatonic theories through their experimentation in atonal composition, as seen with Arnold Schoenberg's "Emancipation of the Dissonance." Other twentieth-century composers such as John Cage, Max Neuhaus, and Brian Eno dabble with infinite sound. Appropriately, the surrealistic artwork of René Margritte explores finite and infinite space, harkening back to Ambrogio Lorenzetti's *The Annunciation* as well as countless other examples of perspective and infinite space in the visual arts.

Contemplating the question, "What is infinity?" often brings to the surface paradoxes and ambiguities, some of which originate from the object or thing referring or reflecting back on itself, often called *self-reference*. For example, the statement, "This is not a true statement," is paradoxical because it counterintuitively can neither be considered true nor false, and M. C. Escher's lithograph *Drawing Hands* seemingly has no beginning or end. Self-referential paradoxes are not only entertaining puzzles, but they also arise in twentieth-century mathematics, music, and art as pioneers question the conventional definition of their fields, demonstrate new possibilities, and redefine themselves. For instance, Kurt Gödel explores the consequences of using mathematics to describe itself in his incompleteness and completeness theorems. Gertrude Stein, in *The Autobiography of Alice B. Toklas*, pushes the conventions of autobiography as she portrays herself through the voice of another. Paul Lansky's *Notjustmoreidlechatter* blurs the line between speech and music, which begs the question, "What is music?" These examples inspired our theme of searching for self and truth.

Finally, through a similar creative process, artists, musicians, and mathematicians redefine the boundaries of their disciplines and produce works that challenge the conventional definitions. Their work is not done in isolation but could be viewed as conversations with the history and tradition of their field, with themselves, with others in their field, with a broader audience, and with formal models in their field. These conversations are what Paul Berliner (1994) defines as "improvisation," which is obviously tied to the musical style of jazz but equally can be applied to other artistic styles and mathematics. So, in our course, we emphasize a culture of musical and mathematical improvisation by demonstrating composers and mathematicians practicing their trades, borrowing from each other, importing ideas into new contexts or pieces, repeating their signature styles or arguments, and eventually creating new pieces of music or innovative theorems. In essence, as a mathematician proves a new theorem or a composer writes a new piece of music, he or she is synthesizing or integrating what has been done before—but doing so in a new way. Thus, although not explicitly named, integration serves as the motif for our course.

Mapping Learning Activities and Objectives to Fink's Taxonomy

After we determined our course material and four themes, our next step was to apply Fink's taxonomy directly to our course development and implementation with the purpose of creating the most efficient integrated learning opportunity for our students. Figure 9.3 outlines how Fink's taxa influenced our course structure and objectives.

Classifying Learning Objectives under Fink's Taxonomy.

Taxonomy	Learning Objective
Foundational Knowledge	· Read symbols in mathematics and music. · Know the definitions of the circle of fifths, cardinality, and symmetric group. · Be able to recall the names of mathematicians, musicians, and artists and to connect these people with their works. · Have a conceptual understanding of how works of math, art, and music relate to one another.
Application	· Use symbols in mathematics and music as a form of communication. · Analyze chord progressions using PLR theory.
Integration	· Identify course themes in different contexts. · Consider a theory/object from multiple perspectives. · Work with students and professor to understand a subject.
Human Dimension	· Gain personal confidence in the knowledge of the subject matter. · Adopt student self-awareness and observed motivation. · Develop empathy toward other students. · Increase awareness of collaborative and social influence on historical accomplishments.
Caring	· Determine how the creative process emerges in the student's major or future career. · Gain a deeper appreciation of mathematics, music, and art.
Learning How to Learn	· Question assumptions and conventions in mathematics, music, and art. · Define and redefine problems in mathematics, music, and art. · Be familiar with resources in mathematics, music, and art. · Be able to set a learning agenda.

Although in Figure 9.3 and in the discussion below we separate objectives by the taxa, many of the objectives and class activities overlap with two or more of the taxa. Of course, this overlap is exactly what Fink wanted in the relational layout of his taxonomy of significant learning. An example of cross-taxa cataloguing occurs when considering the learning objective currently located in Figure 3 under the *caring* taxa: Determine how the creative process emerges in the student's major or future career. This objective could be classified under all six taxa since it relies on a formal understanding of the components of the creative process (foundational knowledge, learning how to learn, and application), and it integrates this process with a student's career interest (integration, human dimension, and caring).

Foundational Knowledge

Foundational knowledge extends beyond memorizing terms and concepts by incorporating conceptual understanding of the subjects (Fink 2003). Even in an interdisciplinary course, discipline-specific knowledge and terminology must be understood in order to communicate ideas precisely. Traditionally, students can rely on a textbook as a reference as they gain fluency in the discourse of the discipline. However, in our class, since the themes and material that we selected do not appear in a single textbook, we take special care to introduce students to the generation of ideas in the three disciplines over time through reading assignments and lecture material structured chronologically around the four themes. Without a single reference, we employed interactive classroom activities to facilitate acquisition of the new vocabulary and concepts as an example of integrated learning. A few of these activities are provided below.

We orchestrated one class meeting around the major and minor chord constructions by having twelve students form a circle, representing the space from one half-step to another on the scale, and assigning one chromatic note to each student. Then, we instructed a student to play his or her assigned note on the piano and then toss the ball to the next person in the chromatic scale. Transitioning from C to C# would involve one student tossing the ball up one half-step to his or her neighbor. In this manner, the students spell out a triad or a few measures of any melodic phrase by first examining a pattern of notes or scales and then imitating that relationship with the ball. This tactic also was applied to more complex musical structures such as the circle of fifths or the twelve-tone matrix.

Since some content for the course required upper-level mathematical concepts that were new to most of the students, we used hands-on activities in class to practice communicating mathematics. In an activity designed to learn groups of symmetries of geometric objects, students used paper models of cubes, triangles, and rectangles to generate the group multiplication tables, inventing their own notation and descriptions for the symmetries. Since the students had little to no experience with the abstract concepts of bijections, multiple dimensions, and proofs, we used not only the classic Hilbert Hotel metaphor but also a physical model to understand the proof that a three-dimensional lattice (N×N×N) has the same cardinality as the natural numbers (N). For many students, it is difficult to comprehend the concept of N×N×N, much less a bijection (i.e., one-to-one correspondence) between N×N×N and N. So we asked students to create a three-dimensional lattice using Play-Doh and toothpicks, which helped them visualize N×N×N and ultimately describe a bijection between their infinite sculpture and the natural numbers. Our students with limited mathematical background appreciated this transformative approach; one student reported, "Visualization and incorporation of additional material contributed the most to my learning" (anonymous student response to the end of the course survey, May 2011).

To assist with student understanding outside of class, we created an extensive Blackboard shell that stores PowerPoint files, mp3s, YouTube clips, assigned readings, and website links. In addition, throughout the semester, we established a routine vocabulary quiz compiled by the students, which empowered the students to become responsible for their own comprehension of the material and to identify other resources outside of the classroom. The students chose any unfamiliar term from the assigned readings and PowerPoint files and researched the term, putting the definition into their own words. In this manner, students gained conceptual understanding of the assigned subject matter, which established a functional platform for the next stages of learning to occur.

Application

Fink subcategorizes the application taxa into developing particular skills, learning how to manage complex projects, and developing the ability to engage in various kinds of thinking, which includes critical, creative, and practical thinking—or what Robert Sternberg, as cited in Fink, called a "triarchic" view of thinking (Fink 2003, 38–39). Our math, music, and art course allowed several opportunities to address all three forms of thinking within the application taxa.

During an introductory lesson on basic mathematical terms such as *axioms*, *theorems*, and *proofs*, students explored logical relations, conjectures, and proofs on their own using the cards in the game Set. For instance, a student may be given a system of axioms such as, "Every red card is adjacent to a purple card, and no purple card is an oval." The students are then tasked with applying their practical thinking to logical connectives and quantifiers to produce a collection of cards in which their axioms are all true. This activity also allows students to make their own conjectures and to either prove or disprove propositions under the assumption of their given axioms.

During a lesson on symmetry, we encountered examples of students' critical and creative thinking. After learning about the three types of symmetric patterns such as rosette patterns, frieze patterns, and wallpaper patterns, the students were encouraged to take a picture on their smartphone of a symmetrical pattern found on the school's premises and identify which specific pattern it was. This pattern could be naturally occurring, found in the architecture of school buildings, or seen on material objects belonging to the students. We then compared pictures and analyzed the various repeating patterns. Most of the student images consisted of wallpaper patterns typical of materials found in the upholstery, brick, and carpet of the surrounding buildings. A future adaptation of this particular assignment will be for the students to not only identify which symmetrical construction this was but also to replicate on paper the isometry of the plane that preserves the pattern. This exercise provides a direct link from course material to the application of this material in everyday life, thus exemplifying integrated learning.

One of two major assessments for the course required students to work together to conceive, plan, and execute a project that tied together at least two themes of the course. While this assessment is a prime example of integration and is further described in the section below, this activity also had students managing a complex project, a skill Fink classifies as *application*.

Integration

As an interdisciplinary component to the course, we deem our thematic approach as both a primary learning tool to organize complex topics and a concise method for students to consider each theme from multiple perspectives. While much of the teaching of mathematics and music is conveyed to the students in lectures, discussions, and readings, we make an effort to encourage our students to conduct their own investigation of the material. As a beginning exercise, we define symmetry and provide many examples in art and mathematics; then we charge the students with finding their own use of symmetry in music. Their diverse collection of examples, including rhyming patterns in lyrics, symmetries in chord structures, and mirror images in melody lines, incites class discussion on what is considered as musical symmetry. This small assignment prepares the students for a more complex integration project later in the course.

Our vision of integration also included the students' ability to synthesize concepts and collaborate on theme-based assignments. In a semester-long project, students are encouraged to integrate concepts from the course (or concepts of their own) in at least two of the disciplines and present their findings to the class. Student presentations have included an application of mathematical transformations to create new arrangements of music, musical demonstrations on the difference between just temperament and equal temperament, and a neo-Riemannian analysis of John Williams's music that was coupled with a graphically animated *tonnez—thundering boom*. Venturing out of their comfort zones, three actuarial science majors performed their arrangement of Pachelbel's *Canon in D*, which they based on various mathematical transformations.

Team teaching is a pedagogical tool we use to facilitate integration because team teaching shifts the emphasis from one primary teacher as the "owner" or possessor of knowledge to a shared instructional leadership opportunity where the teachers become students and the class functions a little more democratically. Functioning more as a laboratory instead of a typical classroom, we often place the chairs of the room into a circle, allowing for the subject of that particular lesson to be "in the center" instead of the teacher. This stratagem often is found in seminar-style classes that allow for greater opportunities of integrated learning to occur.

Human Dimension

One of the most interesting discoveries pertaining to human dimension is the students' reaction to the team-teaching model. They empathize with our daily struggle to translate complex jargon into bite-size segments during regular ninety-minute sessions. In addition, we as professors perform the role of the student-as-learner by sitting in the classroom and asking questions along with the rest of the class. According to the students, they take greater interest when they witness our efforts to understand the other professor's topic and our supportive reactions to one another when learning and reacting to new materials not commonly found in our own discipline. If we understand clearly each other's material as professors, so do the students. When we struggle to understand, so do they.

We help students identify obstacles that others, as well as themselves, experience when tackling new material—only to realize that pioneers in mathematics, music, and art also rely on one another for support through the creative process. This consideration is one of many reasons for selecting the historical, graphic novel *Logicomix: An Epic Search for Truth* by Apostolos Doxiadis and Christos H. Papadimitriou as a required text for our course as opposed to third-person textbooks that "emphasize the material outcomes of important discoveries rather than the human process that led to these discoveries" and omit the false starts and collaborations (Myers and Haynes 2002, 180). *Logicomix* describes the struggles, successes, and collaborations of Bertrand Russell and traces the development of the digital computer back to theoretical work on abstract mathematical problems. It demonstrates that mathematics is not done in isolation but builds upon the work of others. We supplement this text with more traditional reading assignments from scholarly sources, but we also assign firsthand accounts of artists, musicians, and scientists describing their collaborations and approaches to their craft from the collections *The Creative Process: Reflections on the Invention in the Arts and Sciences* edited by Brewster Ghiselin and *Spark: How Creativity Works* by Jule Burstein and Kurt Andersen.

Obtaining an awareness of the development of historical accomplishments helps students with their own collaborations. They work together on class projects and assignments and attend field trips, which strengthens learning as a unit rather than as individuals. "College students frequently report that learning about themselves and about others is among the most significant experiences they have during college" (Fink 2003, 44). Students have been able to relate to other students, learn about themselves and about others in the class, and obtain the freedom to explore their own interests in self-directed projects.

In one project, students worked in teams to design, execute, and present a creative presentation that related to at least one of the course themes. For example, two students coming from different majors worked together to present a found-sound musical recording based on applied learning from class. One student sought and recorded the found sounds heard in everyday life, such as a car alarm or a train going over train tracks, transferring each individual sound digitally into a waveform audio file. The other student manipulated and organized these sounds into tones to compose a musical piece that not only demonstrated chord progressions using PLR theory and a twelve-tone chromatic scale but also was aurally pleasing.

In the other major project, students chose from selected readings that broached two or more disciplines and were asked to analyze in a four-page written paper the creative process found in each trade and postulate what the creative process means to their own major. One student highlighted this final project and integration in his evaluation of the course: "The final [creative process project] also seemed very fitting, while still interesting. As I was writing it, I was making all the connections from the semester. I will not look at art or music the same way" (anonymous student response to the end-of-course survey, May 2011). Testing the boundaries of the assignment, another student wrote his entire paper as a four-page poem. This excerpt of his poem summarizes beautifully the human dimension of this class:

> But most of all, know your past
> Know the creators and the concepts that last
> Know that all math, all music, all art
> Has spawned from a mind, a soul, and a heart.
>
> Willing to go where others refused
> Willing to give a chance the ideas that others abused
> Willing to fail for the sake of success
> For failure is part of the creative process. (Travis Loncar, HNRS 3923–Math, Music and Art final project, May 2011)

Caring

Regarding Fink's caring initiative, our students gain a deeper appreciation of math, music, and art through live musical performances and class field trips. In a previous semester teaching this class, students demonstrated their enthusiasm for the material by sharing with fellow honors students who were not part of the class. Not only did our students invite fellow honors students to attend our class trip to the M. C. Escher exhibit at the Akron Museum of Art, but two students also took the initiative to organize a preshow presentation of Escher's influence on the movie *Inception* for an honors movie night.

At our invitation, composer-musician Nathan Bartlett gave both a lecture and live performance in three dimensions on his five-octave Malletech Imperial Grand marimba with electronics, a powerful Linux-based custom computer, and an eight-channel cube of loudspeakers (plus subwoofer). "With the audience positioned in the center of the loudspeaker cube, an elaborate three-dimensional sound environment can be projected into the audience space, totally immersing the listeners in the music," creating a kinetic audio sculpture in the form of a "three-dimensional soundfield" (Bartlett 2012). Using a combination of Midi interface and variations on pitch and volume, Bartlett designed a method of composition rivaling the engineering studios of the most austere audiophiles. He spent a great deal of time with our students to demonstrate the computations to control each speaker's output, making it "appear" as if sound is heard above, behind, beneath, next to, or in front of the listener. This experience, along with the Akron field trip, was the most memorable to our students, mostly because they were able to experience math, music, and art in person.

Learning How to Learn

Finally, the ultimate success for any teacher is inspiring students to become lifelong learners. The presumed ending of a course transpires once student grades are turned in; however, it is not the exchange of knowledge that ceases to exist but the format with which the knowledge was conceived. Through team teaching, first-person reading assignments, guest discussions, and student involvement in course design, students not only enhance the skills for lifelong learning but also acquire the motivation and curiosity to continue to ask questions about the interactions between mathematics, music, and art.

Through team teaching, we model lifelong learning skills to the students as they witness us take on the role of student or learner in the classroom when the other professor is presenting. On a daily basis, students see us—the "experts"—struggle with our own understanding, question our assumptions, research new topics, and navigate cognitive dissonance. Because most of the course content does not appear in a seminal source but instead is collected by the instructors from several sources, students see what it takes to assemble, organize, and integrate new knowledge. Additionally, students witness lifelong learning occurring in a collaborative, supportive environment of peers with similar interests and varied expertise.

Another aspect of lifelong learning related to this integrated course is that the subjects presented are not final but are living and evolving. Often when students learn mathematics or classical music in school, they are exposed only to work from over two hundred years ago. By reading narrative accounts of twentieth-century artists and mathematicians—many of whom are still living—students see that these disciplines are advancing, and the students may become motivated to continue to learn after the semester ends.

In order to be a successful lifelong learner, one must develop the ability and confidence to set goals and overcome obstacles. Through a discussion on the creative process, guest composer Nathaniel Bartlett demonstrated the obstacles he faced as he followed his plan to develop a new musical instrument, style, and notation. After reflecting on our course, one student connected the creative process with her struggles in writing:

> I have noticed that I am more successful when I make an attempt to keep the big-picture in mind. Most times when I have run into trouble or lost my creative "mojo," I can attribute it to getting caught up in the details and missing the big picture. (anonymous student response to the end-of-course survey, May 2011)

Lifelong learning is tied to student motivation. "Motivation to learn is an internal, naturally occurring capacity of human beings that is enhanced and nurtured by supportive relationships, opportunities for personal choice and responsibility for learning, and personally relevant and meaningful tasks" (McCombs 1991, 120). Because some of the students began the semester with low motivation or even an anxiety about one of the subjects in our interdisciplinary course, we intentionally selected content that would break preconceptions about mathematics and music. For instance, formulas and arithmetic are kept at a minimum, and students learned more music theory than musical performance. Furthermore, students are involved in the course design. Assessments are not high-stakes exams written by the instructors but are quizzes composed of questions proposed by the students themselves, emphasizing the responsibility of the student in his or her education. Many of the assignments in the class involve student choice for subject matter or approach. Having students submit ideas for quiz questions and propose project topics not only provides them with opportunities to reflect on their learning and learn how to learn, but it also helps foster trust between the students and the faculty and shifts the focus from teaching to learning (Myers and Haynes 2002).

While we did not measure student motivation, there is some evidence of increased interest in math, music, and art. Many times class discussions continued in the hallway after class periods ended; even after the semester ended, several students emailed or posted to the class Facebook page YouTube videos, online articles, and comics that they found connected to our class. The final comment on one course evaluation read as follows: "There is just so much to talk about with this subject. It always seemed as if we ran over and had more to talk about or were rushed. However, I would feel ripped off if we didn't cover as much as possible" (anonymous student response to the end of the course survey, May 2011).

As architects of the HNRS–3900 Math, Music, and Art honors course, we sought to provide enough exposure to course themes to evoke continual discoveries after the course ends and enough engagement in the skills to ensure fluency required for effective lifelong learning, even for those students who may not have pursued further education or involvement in mathematics, music, and art.

Conclusion

In designing an integrated course, there are three main challenges: (1) to construct and organized content in a manner that breaches several disciplines, (2) to identify learning objectives that not only incorporate these disciplines but also provide a framework for holistic and engaged learning, and (3) to construct applied learning activities to support these objectives in a real-world context. We sought a sound pedagogical framework to navigate these challenges. L. Dee Fink's taxonomy of significant learning provided a natural framework for us. Furthermore, Fink's taxonomy is general enough to apply to any honors or integrated class, and we encourage other instructors to consider Fink's taxonomy as a guide to developing new integrated courses.

The success of the course can be attributed to both our exhaustive research in uncovering connections between math, music, and art and the incorporation of Fink's taxonomy. The success is predicated by attentive and patient honors students who are able to acquire highly conceptual and abstract ideas despite various levels of mathematical and musical training. We are unsure if such a course as this would have the same results on a freshman or sophomore level, but we would be eager to find out. Of course, the level of success for any such college program is incumbent upon the amount of resources available for field trips, guest speakers, and musical performances; yet, these activities, while highlights of the course, are used as supplemental excursions to support the greater experience of significant learning.

While our course achieved many of the goals, including the integration of three disparate subjects, we have identified a few key areas of improvement, some of which we employed in the second offering of the course in Spring 2013. Several of the students expressed difficulties organizing the material chronologically since it was presented thematically throughout the semester and because there was no textbook that adequately covered our interdisciplinary objectives. At the onset of the Spring 2013 class, we provided a timeline of the material that was color-coded by theme, which helped the students navigate the content. By creating this timeline, we also had the opportunity to reflect on and refine our selection of examples. Another area of improvement concerns the creative project. Although some students met or exceeded our expectations of designing, implementing, and reflecting on a well-researched creative project that ties together several of the course themes, other students struggled. To address this in the future, we plan to provide students with examples of previous projects, clarify our expectations for each project or presentation, and offer students better feedback. Finally, while we have intentionally created opportunities for the students to contribute to the design and direction of the course, most of the delivery of course content remains slanted toward a one-way flow of information from lectures and readings to the students. In the future, we hope to have students assist in the delivery of some content. Balancing out the demands between meeting and assessing learning outcomes and student involvement in the synthesis and selection of course content is a challenge that we will face every time we teach this or any integrated course.

References

Bartlett, Nathaniel. 2012, March 3. nathanielbartlett.com.

Berliner, P. 1994. *Thinking in Jazz: The Infinite Art of Improvisation*. Chicago: University of Chicago Press.

Braid, B. 2008. "Engagement in Learning, Liberal Education, and Honors." In *Inspiring Exemplary Teaching and Learning: Perspectives on Teaching Academically Talented College Students*, edited by L. Clark and J. Zubizarreta, 3136). Lincoln, NE: NCHC. Council.

Escher, M. C. 1989. *Escher on Escher: Exploring the Infinite*. New York: Abrams.

Fink, A., and L. Fink. 2009. "Lessons We Can Learn from the Voices of Experience." *New Directions for Teaching and Learning, 2009* (119): 105–13.

Fink, L. D. 2003. *Creating Significant Learning Experiences: An Integrated Approach to Designing College Courses*. San Francisco: Jossey-Bass.

Huber, M. T., P. Hutchings, R. Gale, R. Miller, and M. Breen. 2007. "Leading Initiatives for Integrative Learning." *Liberal Education* 93(2): 46–51. http://www.aacu.org/ liberaleducation/le-sp07/featurefour.cfm.

Hursh, B., P. Haas, and M. Moore. 1983. "An Interdisciplinary Model to Implement General Education." *Journal of Higher Education* 54(1): 42–59.

McCombs, B. L. 1991. "Motivation and Life-Long Learning." *Educational Psychologist* 26: 117–27.

Mullins, D. W. 2005. "What Is Honors?" *Journal of the National Collegiate Honors Council.* Fall/Winter: 19–22.

Myers, C. and C. Haynes. 2002. "Transforming Undergraduate Science through Interdisciplinary Inquiry." In *Innovations in Interdisciplinary Teaching*, edited by C. Haynes (179–97). Westport, CT: American Council on Education Oryx Press.

Newell, W. H., and W. J. Green. 1982. "Defining and Teaching Interdisciplinary Studies." *Improving College and University Teaching* 30(1): 23–30.

Schuman, S. 2005. "Teaching Honors." *Journal of the NCHC*, 31–33.

Slavin, C., and C. Mares. 2008. "Honors Curriculum Development in the Real World." In *Inspiring Exemplary Teaching and Learning: Perspectives on Teaching Academically Talented College Students*, edited by L. Clark and J. Zubizarreta (195–203). National Collegiate Honors Council. Lincoln, NE: NCHC.

Tymoczko, D. 2011. *A Geometry of Music: Harmony and Counterpoint in the Extended Musical Practice*. New York: Oxford University Press.

Chapter 10

Digital Interdisciplinarity, or Using E-Portfolios to Encourage Interdisciplinary Thinking in a General Education Program

Natalie McKnight, PhD, Boston University

We first began using e-portfolios at the College of General Studies, Boston University, because we were looking for a tool for assessment. We wanted, as many colleges and universities do, to gauge the impact of our program, but in the four years since we began using them, we repeatedly have found that e-portfolios can play a much richer and more varied role by encouraging students and faculty to reflect on learning and by facilitating the integration of courses.[1] Like students who take a course because it's required, only to discover that they really love the subject and plan to study more in the area, many faculty and staff at the College of General Studies embarked on our e-portfolios project somewhat reluctantly, realizing that we needed some means to gauge the effectiveness of our general education college but not particularly eager to master new technology or work through the fine points of establishing an e-portfolio assessment project. Many of us now recognize how much e-portfolios have strengthened the interdisciplinarity of our curriculum and encouraged students to reflect on and thereby extend their learning. At the same time, they give us a tremendous archive of student work. In addition, e-portfolios have helped us gather quantitative and qualitative data that demonstrate that students make significant progress in critical thinking, writing, and other competencies in their two years in our interdisciplinary program.

The contribution of e-portfolios to reflection is a serious matter. Much has been written about the importance of reflection in learning. Asking students to reflect on what they've learned and their own progress seems like it should be an obvious part of any undergraduate curriculum, but it hasn't been a part of most general education programs until recently. As Carol Rodgers (2002) states,

> The function of reflection is to make meaning: to formulate the "relationships and continuities" among the elements of an experience, between

> that experience and other experiences, between that experience and the knowledge that one carries, and between that knowledge and the knowledge produced by thinkers other than oneself. (848)

Asking students to reflect on their learning takes that learning one step further, helping students integrate their coursework and become more conscious and articulate about what they know. Using a rubric helps students focus their reflections on particular competency areas tied to the goals of their program and also leads them to become more intentional in their learning. Knowing that their courses are designed to improve their critical thinking and perspective taking, their writing skills, and their ability to find and use sources makes students more conscious about the development of these skills as they progress through their undergraduate years. Getting students to reflect on their growth in these competency areas encourages them to focus on their learning and intellectual progress and not just on their accumulation of credit hours. Moreover, analyzing what they have learned in reflection assignments at certain points throughout their undergraduate careers will enable them to be more articulate in interviews for internships, jobs, and graduate schools.

Students' e-portfolios aid reflection and integration of coursework by providing them with an archive that can pull much of their academic activity together in one site.[2] At our college, we ask all our students to set up one e-portfolio with sections for each of the general education classes they take with us, and we encourage them to create sections for their electives as well. We ask students to post their work for every class in the appropriate sections so that they can access it later and see their own progress. Students post short reading reflections, major papers, lab reports, and group projects all on one site, which they control. We also ask students to set up a tab for "Interdisciplinary Reflections" under which they can explore formally and informally the connections among their courses throughout their two years with us.

We assign a self-reflection project at the end of students' freshman year and again at the end of their sophomore year, using a rubric we composed, based on models from the American Association of Colleges & Universities (2012). The rubric designates four levels of competency, from a rating of 1, which is "no mastery," to a rating of 4, which is "excellent"; the rubric specifies seven competency/skills areas: written and oral communication; gathering, analyzing, and documenting information; awareness of specific historical, literary, and cultural contexts; rhetorical and aesthetic conventions; critical thinking and perspective taking, integrative and applied learning; and quantitative methods (see Figure 10.1).

CGS Assessment Rubric.

	Level 4—Excellent	Level 3—Competent	Level 2—Developing	Level 1—No mastery
Written and Oral Communication	Demonstrates detailed attention to and successful execution of a wide range of conventions particular to a specific discipline and/or writing task (including organization, content, presentation, formatting, and stylistic choices); uses graceful language that skillfully communicates meaning to readers with clarity and fluency and is virtually error-free	Demonstrates consistent use of important conventions particular to a specific discipline and/or writing task; uses straightforward language that generally conveys meaning to readers. The language in the portfolio has few errors.	Follows expectations appropriate to a specific discipline and/or writing task for basic organization, content, and presentation; uses language that generally conveys meaning, although there may be problems with clarity and the writing may include some errors.	Attempts to use a consistent system for basic organization and presentation; uses language that sometimes impedes meaning or clarity; contains errors in usage.
Gathering, Analyzing, and Documenting Information	Synthesizes in-depth information from a range of high-quality, credible, relevant sources that are appropriate for the discipline and genre to develop ideas, and documents these sources fully using MLA or Chicago style.	Consistently presents in-depth information from credible, relevant sources appropriate to the discipline and genre to support ideas; documents sources with few errors or exceptions using MLA or Chicago style.	Demonstrates an attempt to use credible and/or relevant sources to support ideas and to document these sources properly using MLA or Chicago style.	Minimally attempts to use sources to support ideas in the writing; these sources may not be correctly documented using an acceptable style manual and/or may not be fully relevant to the task at hand.

Awareness of Specific Historical, Literary, and Cultural Contexts	Uses appropriate, relevant, and compelling content and sufficient detail to illustrate mastery of the subject, including historical, literary, and cultural contexts.	Uses appropriate, relevant, and compelling content to explore ideas within the context of the discipline(s) but many not yet provide sufficient detail or illustrate mastery of historical, literary, and cultural contexts.	Uses appropriate and relevant content to develop and explore ideas through most of the work; does not display a consistently clear or adequately detailed understanding of historical, literary, and cultural contexts.	May use appropriate and relevant content to develop simple ideas in some parts of the work.
Rhetorical and Aesthetic Conventions	Demonstrates a thorough understanding of context, audience, and purpose; makes skillful rhetorical choices and shows deep appreciation for literary and aesthetic conventions and their effects.	Demonstrates adequate consideration of context, audience, and purpose; understands rhetorical effects and shows appreciation for literary and aesthetic conventions and their effects.	Demonstrates some awareness of context, audience, and purpose; can identify rhetorical strategies and shows some appreciation for literary and aesthetic techniques and conventions.	Demonstrates minimal attention to context, purpose, and audience; may not be aware of rhetorical effects of one's own work or of rhetorical strategies and literary techniques in works analyzed.
Critical Thinking and Perspective Taking	Questions are examined from a range of viewpoints, taking into account the complexities of an issue; conclusions and related outcomes are logical and reflect the student's informed evaluation and ability to place evidence and perspectives discussed in priority order.	Specific position takes into account the complexities of an issue and acknowledges other viewpoints; conclusion is logically tied to a range of information.	Information is presented with some interpretation or evaluation but not enough to develop a coherent analysis or synthesis; acknowledges different sides of an issue but may be more aware of others' assumptions than one's own (or vice versa).	Specific position is stated but is simplistic and obvious; conclusion is inconsistently tied to some of the information discussed; information from sources is presented without interpretation or evaluation.

	Level 4—Excellent	Level 3—Competent	Level 2—Developing	Level 1—No mastery
Integrative and Applied Learning	Makes insightful connections across disciplines and perspectives; draws conclusions by combining examples, facts, theories, or methodologies from more than one field of study to arrive at a sophisticated interdisciplinary understanding.	Makes connections across disciplines and perspectives by independently combining examples, facts, theories, or methodologies from more than one field of study.	When prompted, connects examples, facts, or theories across disciplines and perspectives; may not show a strong understanding of how methodologies differ across fields of study or could be applied in a new situation.	When prompted, presents examples, facts, or theories representing different disciplines and perspectives; shows a limited interdisciplinary understanding.
Quantitative Methods	Uses quantitative analysis of data as the basis for deep and thoughtful judgments, drawing insightful and carefully qualified conclusions from this work.	Uses the quantitative analysis of data as the basis for competent judgments, drawing reasonable and appropriately qualified conclusions from this work.	Uses the quantitative analysis of data for basic judgments, drawing plausible conclusions from this work.	Uses the quantitative analysis of data for tentative judgments; hesitates to draw conclusions from this work.

In the reflection assignment at the end of the year, students are asked to look back over their freshman year and assess their growth in these competency areas while making specific references to work posted on their e-portfolios. Their reflections can take the form of written essays, or they can be done as videos; the projects are assigned in their rhetoric classes but must refer to work in their other classes as well. We ask students to submit a similar reflection at the end of their sophomore year as part of their capstone project (described below).

Could students have done such reflections before we had e-portfolios? Of course. However, for some reason we never asked them to do so. The emphasis on reflection within the e-portfolio community inspired us to make reflection an integral part of our program. Moreover, e-portfolios make successful, detailed reflections much more likely because the work has been preserved digitally in one site where students can move back and forth between materials from different courses with ease (and, in many cases, have already begun exploring connections among courses in joint projects and informal interdisciplinary reflections). E-portfolios certainly are a better system for preserving work than a bunch of dog-eared notebooks that students may or may not keep. Preserving work in the cloud definitely is better than preserving it in a moldy basement. More importantly, electronic portfolios enable students to upload videos and pictures and link to sites related to their curricular and extracurricular interests—capacities that make e-portfolios an infinitely richer, more engaging, and more fluid record of students' lives than the paper trails of the past. Plus, letting students know that we want to preserve their work far into the future validates their work and them as learners.

The electronic archive is also something that faculty and administrators can use as a basis for research into the effectiveness of their programs. This is something we simply were never able to do before at the College of General Studies. Up until our adoption of e-portfolios, if a parent or representative from an accrediting agency or the Department of Education had visited our college and asked to see the work students had done in our program, we would have had to report that we did not keep any. It is an odd but understandable reality that colleges and universities, in general, do not keep records of what students have done while working on their degrees. Of course, from the standpoint of storage, it would have been impossible to archive hard copies of students' essays, reflections, labs, videos, and so on over the years. Whole buildings would need to be built to house such materials. But *not* having a record of undergraduate work is a little bit like being a construction company that can only show blueprints of projects and no completed buildings. However, now we have a rich archive that not only showcases students' products and processes but also demonstrates the progress students make over their first two years of college.

While e-portfolios encourage reflection and provide a rich archive of undergraduate work, they also strengthen many high-impact educational practices that were already part of our college. The AAC&U has advocated ten high-impact practices in education, among which are "capstone courses and projects," "undergraduate research," "collaborative assignments and projects," "writing intensive courses," "learning communities," and "common intellectual experiences" (2009; Kuh 2008); all of these practices are integral to our general education program, which can be seen most clearly in our college's sophomore-year capstone project. And the use of e-portfolios enhances all of these high-impact practices. At the end of their sophomore year, students in our college work together in groups of five or six on a capstone project that involves writing a fifty-page research proposal that offers a viable solution to a real-world problem.[3] Students have written on subjects such as ending hunger in Boston; preventing deforestation in Chiapas, Mexico; and disposing of electronic waste safely. Capstone projects are advocated by the AAC&U because, if they are well-designed, they help students pull together their learning from a series of courses. Our project asks students to draw from courses in rhetoric, humanities, natural science, and social science that they take during their freshman and sophomore years. But of course, the project, being a group-written research paper, also involves intensive writing, undergraduate research, learning communities, and common intellectual experiences, thereby addressing five of the ten high-impact practices targeted by the AAC&U. Sometimes it also includes a sixth high-impact practice—service and community-based learning—if the project involves a local issue (the hunger in Boston project certainly had a community service aspect).

The capstone project has been in place for thirty-five years, and we have utilized e-portfolios with it only for the last three years. However, already we can see the positive difference they make. First, the capstone is a group-written project, but the final grade students get for it is composed of a grade for the paper plus an individual grade for participation in the project and in the oral defense. The individual grade has always been difficult to assess, though. We tend to gauge it by the individual's contributions to meetings with the professors over the course of the project and his or her comments in the defense. But the process can disadvantage unfairly students who are hesitant to speak up. Sometimes the students who contribute the most to the research and writing of the paper are the quietest of the groups, so their contributions may not be noticed. We ask each member of the group to grade the other members on their participation, but sometimes the students' perceptions of each other's work are contradictory, leaving us uncertain about what an individual's participation grade should be. Since we've begun using e-portfolios, we have asked students to post not only the completed project on their sites but also a log of all the work they do individually each week on the paper—the sources they have read, the experts they've interviewed, the drafts they've written (they have to post all the drafts they write, whether the drafts make it to the final "cut" of the completed capstone project or not). Being able to see the individual's contribution to the group project has been tremendously helpful—and helpful long before we actually have to assign grades. If we have concerns about a student while the group is still researching and drafting, we can check the student's e-portfolio; if we do not see any work there (or very little), we know to intervene. If students in a group are divided about a particular member's participation—some saying the member was a great contributor, some saying the opposite—we can check the person's drafts and logs so that we can make a more informed decision.

E-portfolios also facilitate collaboration and strengthen the function of the learning community during the capstone project. Students in a group can give each other access to their portfolios, which means that sharing notes, annotated bibliographies, and drafts is much easier. The different sections of the project, usually each written by a different member, become more cohesive when students have immediate access to each other's latest sources and drafts. They truly become research collaborators through their use of e-portfolios, not just individuals writing separate sections that must then be stitched together in the final days of the project. Their e-portfolios facilitate their research, drafting, and discussions, thereby encouraging a rich and constant exchange of ideas that helps them to see more clearly how their close collaboration can lead to a viable solution to a real-world problem.

In addition to encouraging reflection and strengthening the capstone project, e-portfolios also have helped us gauge the effectiveness of our interdisciplinary program. Grades, graduation rates, and anecdotes from alumni and professors all have indicated for decades that our college provides an effective general education to freshmen and sophomores, but these factors really do not demonstrate intellectual progress or the development of essential skills. Using the rubric described previously, our Assessment Committee during the summer of 2012 assessed 106 student e-portfolios, each with two years' worth of formal and informal assignments.[4] Our work was funded by a generous grant from the Davis Educational Foundation, which allowed us to offer stipends to faculty doing the assessments. The results of our assessment show that, on average, our students improve in each skills area of our rubric by at least 0.5 points (on a four-point scale). In other words, students improve at least half a competency level in every area. In general, students scored in the lower 2s in their first term (about 2.2) and in the upper 2s by the end of their fourth term (2.8 to 2.9 on average), meaning that they began at the lower end of the "developing" category and ended at the higher end of "developing" (see Figure 10.2).

Assessment Score Sheet: Averages 2012.

	Term 1	Term 2	Term 3	Term 4	+/– Change
Written & oral communication	2.23	2.50	2.63	2.83	.60: +27%
Gathering, Analyzing, and Documenting Information	2.27	2.56	2.67	2.93	.67: +29.5%
Awareness of Specific Historical, Literary, and Cultural Contexts	2.27	2.46	2.75	2.89	.62: +27%
Rhetorical and Aesthetic Conventions	2.30	2.50	2.61	2.80	.51: +22%
Critical Thinking and Perspective Taking	2.34	2.49	2.66	2.92	.58: +25%
Integrative and Applied Learning	2.23	2.41	2.67	2.90	.67: +30%
Quantitative Methods	2.00	1.54	2.40	2.55	.55: +27.5%

Skill Levels: 1—No mastery; 2—Developing; 3—Competent; 4—Excellent

For instance, in the area of written communication, students averaged 2.23 in the first term and 2.83 in the fourth term, resulting in an increase of .60; in the area of critical thinking and perspective taking, students averaged 2.34 in the first term and 2.92 in the fourth term, resulting in an increase of .58. We are pleased to see that we have evidence of significant progress in all skills areas—progress much greater than what is reported in the much-discussed *Academically Adrift* by Richard Arum and Josipa Roksa. Arum and Roksa (2011) collected data from thousands of students in twenty-four four-year colleges who took the CLA (Collegiate Learning Assessment) test in their first term and again at the end of their fourth term (the same points we are focusing on in our project). In their study, in the important areas of written communication and critical thinking, students showed only a "seven percentile point gain, meaning that an average-scoring student in the fall of 2005 would score seven percentile points higher in the spring of 2007" (35).[5] By contrast, our students show a 27 percent gain in written communication and a gain of 25 percent in critical thinking and perspective taking. Students seem to make the greatest progress—30 percent—in the area of integrative and applied learning, which is perhaps not surprising since we stress interdisciplinary connections throughout our program.

We are pleased with these results, but we would like to see even greater improvement in the future. Therefore, we now are discussing the assessment averages within our assessment committee and with our divisions to see how we might increase our students' improvement in all skills areas. One relatively simple fix became clear to us right away: We need to improve student and faculty buy-in to e-portfolios. In our analysis of e-portfolios over the summer, we found that some faculty obviously encouraged students to post their work on e-portfolios more than others. Some e-portfolios were unusable to us because they had so few artifacts posted. Others had a sufficient amount posted—but not much in the critical fourth term. We think that simply increasing the amount of postings probably will result in higher improvement rates, particularly if we have more work from the final semester of development to assess. In order to improve faculty and student buy-in to e-portfolios, we have been making a concentrated effort this term to encourage students to post their work and to encourage faculty to get students to post work. We took half of the first college-wide faculty meeting to discuss the results of our summer assessment and our need for more consistency in postings. We also showcased a feature of Digication (our e-portfolio platform) that makes it easier for faculty to check which students have posted their work. We sent all College of General Studies students emails at the beginning of the term with revised and clearly written instructions on how to set up their e-portfolios, and we've sent reminders to faculty and students about why we are using e-portfolios. We also have hired a peer-mentor for e-portfolios who has been helping students and faculty with various problems they have in setting up or adding onto their sites. In addition, we hosted an e-portfolio contest and showcase in the spring with cash prizes for the best portfolios, and we discussed the importance of e-portfolios with all incoming students during orientation sessions in Summer 2013. We hope these measures will result in fuller, more comprehensive portfolios both for our students' benefit and for our ongoing assessment work.

We also have begun discussing how well our course assignments reflect the competency areas targeted in our rubric. While our rubric was designed by a committee that included members from every division in the college and was revised with feedback from every division, there may be ways in which it isn't representing our program's goals as precisely as we might wish. We may eventually need to tweak the rubric to better reflect our program or work on changing some of our assignments to better reflect our goals—or both.

Electronic portfolios clearly have enhanced the interdisciplinarity of our program by encouraging reflections that integrate the coursework, by strengthening the collaborative aspects of the capstone project and assisting faculty in gauging individual's input in group work, and by enabling faculty to assess the impact of our interdisciplinary general education program. E-portfolios are not a magic pill that will solve every educational ill or a magic wand that will turn rags into ball gowns, but they are a useful tool for analyzing the effectiveness of a course or program, for facilitating group work, and for encouraging educators to think of new strategies to increase student learning and improve students' perceptions of their learning.

References

American Association of Colleges & Universities. 2009. "High-Impact Educational Practices." http://www.aacu.org/ leap/hip.cfm.

———. 2012. "VALUE: Valid Assessment of Learning in Undergraduate Education." http://www.aacu.org/value/rubrics/index.cfm.

Arum, R., and J. Roksa. 2011. *Academically Adrift: Limited Learning on College Campuses.* Chicago: University of Chicago Press.

Augsburg, Tanya. 2006. *Becoming Interdisciplinary: An Introduction to Interdisciplinary Studies.* Dubuque, IA: Kendall/Hunt.

Brown, Gary, Helen Chen, and Jayme Jacobson. 2012. "ePortfolios Changing the Learning Context: The AAEEBL Survey Report 2011." *AAEEBL Learner* 3(3): 1–11.

Dezure, Deborah. 2010. "Interdisciplinary Pedagogies in Higher Education." In *Oxford Handbook of Interdisciplinarity*, edited by Robert Frodeman, Julie Thompson Klein, Carl Mitcham, and J. Britt Holbrook, 372–86. Oxford: Oxford University Press.

Eynon, Bret. 2009. "Introduction." *In Transit: The LaGuardia Journal on Teaching and Learning* 4: v–xviii.

Finley, Ashley. 2012. *Making Progress? What We Know about the Achievement of Liberal*

Education Outcomes. Washington, DC: Association of American Colleges & Universities.

Klein, Julie Thompson. 2010. "A Taxonomy of Interdisciplinarity." *Oxford Handbook of Interdisciplinarity*. In *Oxford Handbook of Interdisciplinarity*, edited by Robert Frodeman, Julie Thompson Klein, Carl Mitcham, and J. Britt Holbrook, 15–30. Oxford: Oxford University Press.

Kuh, G. D. 2008. *High-Impact Educational Practices: What They Are, Who Has Access to Them, and Why They Matter*. Washington, DC: Association of American Colleges & Universities.

Newell, William H. 2013. "The State of the Field: Interdisciplinary Theory." *Issues in Interdisciplinary Studies* 31: 22–43.

Rodgers, C. R. 2002. "Defining Reflection: Another Look at John Dewey and Reflective Thinking." *Teachers College Record* 104 (4): 842–66.

Wexelblatt, R. 2012. "The Capstone Project of the College of General Studies, Boston University." *IMPACT: The Journal of the Center for Interdisciplinary Teaching and Learning* (Summer): 5–11. http://www.bu.edu/cgs/citl/impact/.

Chapter 11

The Problems and Possibilities of Integrating Professionalism and Liberal Education: A Case Study of the Senior Capstone Experience at Champlain College

Michael Kelly, PhD, Michael A. Lange, PhD,
and Katheryn Wright, PhD, Champlain College

Champlain College, in Burlington, Vermont, is a small, private, professionally focused, four-year school with majors ranging from accounting and graphic design to social work and digital forensics. There are no majors in the traditional humanities or social sciences, so the liberal arts/general education requirements for undergraduate students are delivered through the Core Division. The Core, first implemented in 2007, replaced a more standard, menu-type general education curriculum with distribution credits, and many of the faculty teaching in the old curriculum simply transitioned into the new Core when it was put in place. The curriculum in the Core Division is a four-year, integrated, explicitly interdisciplinary series of courses ("Core Division" n.d.). Unlike the standard menu of distributed requirements (two history courses, two math courses, three English courses, etc.), Champlain offers a series of courses that every student takes in sequence over the course of their four years at the school. Each course is interdisciplinary and integrative in some degree, and all are designed to build on one another from the beginning of the first year through to graduation. Thus, rather than learning about a single discipline in isolation, Champlain students take courses focused on relevant themes or topics like Ethics and the Environment (a second-year Core course). These courses examine a subject from multiple disciplinary perspectives and methodologies with an explicit emphasis on synthesis, rather than focusing on ethics in one classroom and science in another, perhaps in different semesters. A Champlain student pulls concepts and methods from both fields (and more) within the same class in order to create more synthesized and applicable knowledge.

The senior capstone experience at Champlain represents the culmination of their interdisciplinary curriculum and integrative learning, providing students the opportunity to apply the different types of integration utilized in Core classes to their major coursework. This chapter focuses on the senior capstone experience as a case study herein to identify what tensions arise when the rhetoric of professionalism collides with integrative learning practices. The authors of this chapter each teach a separate section of Champlain's senior capstone, each for a different professional major. Just as the school itself has a rhetoric of professionalism, each major presents a more focused definition of what being a professional in that field means. The variety of our experiences, as well as the particularities of the majors within which we teach, are examined here to gain some insight into the effects of the different understandings of professionalism. The majority of the salient academic literature explores integration in either professional fields or in educational settings. Because Champlain is a professionally focused undergraduate institution and because the school has an expressly interdisciplinary and integrative curriculum, we are able to examine integration uniquely at the intersection of the educational process and the professional world.

Integration in the Core Curriculum

As a small school, Champlain has greater flexibility in creating a distinctive, integrative curriculum for all its majors. "One of the defining features of small colleges is that it is possible at such places to think in terms of the coherence of the curriculum as a whole" (Schuman 2005, 140). Echoing Schuman's assertion about the possibility of a coherent course of study at small colleges, the core curriculum is required for all undergraduate students at Champlain College no matter their major. While their programs of study emphasize job preparation, the core curriculum focuses on the development of "habits of mind," or the critical thinking skills necessary not only in preparing students for a career but also in the fostering of an engaged citizenship. Klein (1990) discusses different approaches to interdisciplinarity in higher education:

> William Mayville spoke of three types of IDS [interdisciplinary studies]: *revolutionary* programs, which dispense with the traditional disciplinary apparatus; *professional* programs, which are committed to training specialists and use integrated approaches to acquaint students with the broader dimensions of their professional fields; and *programmatic* curricula, which seek to broaden the cultural and intellectual frameworks of students. (156)

Champlain, and particularly the Core, is a hybrid of all three of these forms. Core courses are built on themes rather than "traditional disciplinary apparatus," with each course having a topic around which the readings, assignments, and discussions are based. The overarching idea guiding the curriculum is a progression from the student outward into their local and global communities, broadening their "cultural and intellectual frameworks" by recognizing the value of diverse perspectives. Major programs tackle more specialized training by using applied, integrated approaches that "acquaint students with the broader dimensions of their professional fields." For example, a first-year course for all business majors titled Business and the Entrepreneurial Mindset asks students to explore intersections between "marketing, management, economics, etc." by running their own virtual business ("Integrated Business Experience" n.d.). This course leads into a four-year sequence of integrative courses that, like their Core courses, culminate with the senior capstone experience.

The sequence of Core courses for every undergraduate student at the college starts with a rhetoric series and two courses titled Concepts of the Self and Concepts of Community in the first year, followed by four courses focusing on the Western world in the sophomore year, four globally themed courses in the third year, and an integrative capstone course in the senior year. The themes begin in the first year focusing on the student as an individual (the "self" of Concepts of the Self) and then progress in steps conceptually further away from the individual as each semester and year pass (e.g., through the role of the individual in a group in Concepts of Community). Members of the Champlain faculty express the structure in shorthand as "individual-community-West-world." Courses are taught in multiple sections from a master syllabus, requiring each instructor to use certain texts, as well as common learning outcomes and one large, integrative common assignment per course. An example of an integrative common assignment is the self-portrait project in Concepts of the Self, where students create their own self-portrait from any medium and use concepts from psychology, neuroscience, literature, and art to analyze their concept of self and support the aesthetic choices they make. Like all of the common assignments in the Core, the self-portrait asks students to engage in interdisciplinary, integrative thinking by synthesizing multiple disciplines alongside their personal experience to create a cultural artifact, evaluate choices they make, and critically reflect on the creative process.

Much like the content of Core courses, the ability for students to integrate different knowledge bases, professional fields, and personal experience strategically builds from the first year to the third year. The first-year courses have "focus disciplines" embedded within them. For Concepts of the Self, the focus disciplines are visual art, literature, psychology, and neuroscience. In Concepts of Community, the focus disciplines are economics, history, and philosophy. Each focus discipline in the first year is represented by a text, such that the philosophy is meant to be delivered by reading Plato's *Republic*, while the neuroscience is examined by reading David Linden's *The Accidental Mind*. In the second year, courses have themes within a larger framework of providing a "shadow Western Civilization" curriculum by dividing the year among courses such as Scientific Revolutions, Aesthetic Expressions, Secular and Sacred, and Capitalism and Democracy. The approach in the second year is to present four threads that cover foundational aspects of Western life, namely, the particular forms of artistic, scientific, religious, and political/economic systems that can define the West. The second year relies more heavily on discipline-specific knowledge and approaches, shifting the priority for integration to the instructor's approach to the material.

In the third year of the curriculum, courses are again thematic, but the attempted shadow curriculum is gone so that the goal of the courses, exploring global issues, stands alone. The third-year courses include Technology and Globalization as well as Human Rights and Responsibilities, along with two courses with a geographic focus and a range of potential themes. These junior-level courses attempt to be disciplinary, with some texts rooted in a discipline (such as Kwame Anthony Appiah's *Cosmopolitanism*, which comes from philosophy) and others that are broad topical surveys (such as Rachel Louise Snyder's *Fugitive Denim*, which is a journalistic overview of the production of cotton and denim). The focus on an interdisciplinary field of global studies in the third year transfers the onus of integration to a synthesis of previous years' coursework into the topical discussions. These three years lead to a senior capstone, which is explicitly designed to integrate a student's first three years of general education with his or her professional major.

Every major runs its own capstone in the senior year, and the forms of those capstones can vary. Some majors hold a single course within either the fall or the spring semester of the final year, while a few distribute the work of the capstone across both semesters. Regardless of the structure, every capstone is designed to integrate the professional education and the liberal arts education that each student has received in their previous three years of college. The parallel strands of education are meant to intertwine in the capstone course, however it is delivered. In order to achieve that intertwining, the capstone courses are team taught by a professor from the appropriate major and a professor from the general education curriculum. The team-teaching model puts both professors (and both strands) in the classroom simultaneously, with the capstone course and projects being taught and assessed by both professors in tandem. This collegial relationship, with a major professor and a gen ed professor in the classroom together at all times, carries the burden of integration not only within the capstone course but also vertically across the whole student experience.

The Rhetoric of Professionalism at Champlain

Champlain College presents this unique integrative curriculum as providing students with an education that prepares them to be standouts in their careers: "passionate, career-minded students have been the focus of Champlain College since it was founded in 1878" ("About Champlain" n.d.). The rhetorical stance of the school foregrounds the job, the career, and the student as a future member of the workforce. This rhetoric of professionalism sometimes is understood to include critical, integrative thinking: "Academic rigor and professors who bring professional experience into the classroom are the norm at Champlain College" ("About Champlain," n.d.), but even when traditional academics are foregrounded, that emphasis is balanced with an adjoining stress on the *professional* experience of the faculty. Often, though, the rhetoric simply does not place any emphasis on the traditional higher education abilities of critical thinking, reflection, and synthesis. The school presents its Upside-Down Curriculum as a unique feature for prospective students ("About Champlain" n.d.). The Upside-Down Curriculum refers to students taking intensive classes in their major from their first college semester rather than taking liberal education courses for a year or two and then shifting toward major courses in their later years. Champlain presents the Upside-Down Curriculum early and often to students, but the upside-down-ness of it only applies to the professional major. Indeed, the rhetoric of the Upside-Down Curriculum is exclusively about the professional courses at the expense of the liberal education. In essence, Champlain is selling students on the idea that they will not be spending time taking courses that are not in their major. The presentation does not overtly devalue liberal education, but the stress and the excitement are placed with this rhetorical presentation entirely on the professional major. By exploring the rhetoric of professionalism that Champlain uses, both at the college level and within individual programs, this chapter examines the tension that can exist between professional education and integrative liberal education. In the process, we explain the pedagogical and institutional challenges of teaching an integrative curriculum at the school as well as exploring ways in which the rhetoric of integrative teaching and learning can be an integral part of the rhetoric of professionalism.

By exploring three examples of the college capstone, we demonstrate the varying understandings and approaches to this interdisciplinarity and integration. Students have the opportunity in the capstone to use the skills and content they learned in the core to develop a professional-quality product or complete an internship relevant to their chosen profession, or both. Here, integration takes center stage. Rather than focusing exclusively on the core curriculum, students are asked to consider the entirety of their college experience as they prepare to enter into the workforce. For some, the senior capstone experience is revelatory; for others, it is a challenge because this course lives out the struggle between Champlain College's emphasis on professionalism and the integration developed through the core curriculum. A focus on profession foregrounds the employer and employment in a student's mind, and the job is understood in relatively simplistic terms (i.e., as a set of skills put to use on a set of tasks). This understanding reflects a general trend in what Stark and Lattuca (1997) call "enterprising/production career fields" (156). The example they put forward—business administration—could be used as a representative of many majors at Champlain: "Business instructors did not strongly endorse a view of their field as a group of scholars; rather they characterized it as both an organized body of knowledge and a set of skills. . . . In contrast, learning the 'great ideas' is minimally important to business faculty" (Stark and Lattuca 1997, 156).

Although programs at Champlain like business use integrative pedagogies to introduce students to the profession, the emphasis on learning a particular skill set specific to a particular occupation counters the liberal arts mantra of a well-rounded general education that focuses on big ideas about the human condition. There can be difficulties getting the students to see the possibilities and the value of bringing the two sides of their education together at this summative point in their college careers. These difficulties come partially from the overall rhetorical position that Champlain takes when presenting the value of its education to prospective and current students.

Psychology Capstone

The American Psychological Association, the largest professional organization for psychology in the United States, adopted Principles for Quality Undergraduate Education to explore the teaching and learning of psychology at an undergraduate level ("Principles for Quality Undergraduate Education in Psychology" n.d.). The organization focuses on student responsibility for learning, the faculty member's role as scientist-educator, and the development of a coherent curriculum that contributes to the psychological literacy of the general public. These principles reflect the breadth of the discipline and its professional, political, and cultural applications. Although psychology is a popular major in many colleges and universities across the country, however, the rhetoric of professionalism heavily influences the psychology curriculum at Champlain. Much like other fields at the college, the program emphasizes career planning for a wide range of occupations in business, education, and the nonprofit sector, to name a few. Either students identify a career path they want to pursue and model their course of study to reflect their goals, or they discover their area of interest by taking electives in the field. Career readiness provides the framework through which students explore the discipline.

The psychology major takes advantage of the fact that students come into Champlain already declared when they enter the college, according to Dr. Bjarne Holmes, associate professor and director of psychology (personal communication). Psychology's interpretation of the Upside-Down Curriculum gives incoming students the opportunity to take courses like Cognitive Psychology their freshman year rather than waiting until after they take their general education requirements. By their senior year, students will have designed their own path to meet their goals or accommodate a specific career path. The curriculum is designed to create a more flexible and applied approach to the study of the discipline, exposing students from their first year in the program onward to the breadth of career options for which they will be prepared. By the end of their sophomore year, students should have a clearer idea about how they want to use the major to achieve their personal and professional goals'; then they can organize their upper-level coursework based on that knowledge. The fourth year is about application, with students going into the community through internships or taking courses in counseling or organizational psychology. The senior capstone experience is the final component of the curriculum.

For the capstone, students develop a project that integrates both their major coursework and general education. The project is independently designed and executed, with the primary requirements being that it needs to be professional in caliber and address the student's self-identified career goals. The relatively open-ended nature of the assignment is intended to promote discovery through integrative thinking and critical reflection where students consider the variety of ways they could apply the knowledge and skills they acquired over their college careers. Students write a proposal for a final project of their choosing that includes an ethical rationale, background research, audience analysis, and the identification of key stakeholders and experts. They then execute projects that range from grant proposals to children's books. The final stage of the capstone includes a poster presentation and community showcasing, and a critical reflection that analyzes how they integrated different disciplines, professional coursework, and personal experiences in their project's development and execution.

To support the development of the projects, students create a portfolio document that can change throughout the course of the semester as they adapt their project by integrating what they learn through the research and implementation phases. The explanation, rationale, and ethical consideration sections of the portfolio need to be refined continually in order to reflect the student's increasing knowledge of the broader cultural context of which their project is a part. With the portfolio, students defend the relevance and viability of their projects. Students identify issues they encounter throughout the research and development process, including the struggle to apply ethical decision making to their projects. A student writing a novella, for example, debated whether to use actual names and how to introduce psychological concepts to a more general audience. This record of each student's thought process became the starting point for his or her reflective essay at the end of the semester. The portfolio document and the reflective essay assignments invite students to integrate their education and personal experiences in an effort to locate and evaluate their creative and critical thinking processes.

In practice, students often struggle with scope throughout the course of the semester as they try to come to terms with the creativity and openness of the project in relation to the perceived inflexibility of having to integrate the core curriculum into it. Students in the capstone erroneously believe they have to create projects that include Michelangelo's Sistine Chapel or Thomas Kuhn's *The Structure of Scientific Revolutions*, two of their required Core readings. This belief that the content of their courses in the Core should directly correspond with their career preparation cultivated by the rhetoric of professionalism is, at times, counterproductive to other types of integration that occur in the senior capstone experience. For example, they often resist differentiating between psychology as a discipline (a component of liberal studies) and psychology as a professional field of study (a path to a career). Many students had an easy time picking a topic they were interested in but struggled with identifying a professional-quality product (like a grant proposal) that they would develop based on that topic. Why? In order to identify a product, they needed to draw on their ability to integrate disciplinary expectations of psychology with their own career goals. Echoing their seeming unwillingness to connect anything in their Core classes with their major, this process proved very tough for them to accomplish.

The trouble with integrating psychology as a discipline and a career path resurfaced in their portfolio documents. They struggled to see how the choices they made in terms of the proposal, execution, and presentation of their work involved anything related to both their liberal learning and their major discipline. Students could not effectively tease out the expectations associated with psychology as a career path and psychology as an academic discipline, a distinction that the rhetoric of professionalism at Champlain similarly downplays.

Looking back on what they accomplished during the capstone experience, however, proved much easier for students in the reflective essay assignment, for which they assessed their final project within the broader context of their academic careers. The essay asked students to reflect on how their personal and professional experiences at Champlain—not only their liberal arts education—coincides with what it means to be a professional in their chosen field. Psychology students were adept at explaining the narrative of the institution itself. Through the reflective components of the course, they explain how "critical thinking" and "inquiry" alongside "career preparation" are important without fully understanding how they can apply these decidedly integrative practices to their personal growth and professional goals.

While the psychology major at Champlain undoubtedly provides a high degree of psychological literacy as the APA's principles for undergraduate education in the field suggests, the college's emphasis on career preparation seems to undermine their ability to see connections between liberal studies and professional education. This dilemma is especially interesting in a discipline that is conventionally a part of the liberal arts and sciences, so presumably it would be fairly easy for students to see the relationship between these two sides of their education at Champlain. The rhetoric of professionalism should theoretically help students recognize what it means to be a professional, but that is not always the case.

E-Game Capstone

In a recent essay published in the *Atlantic*, pioneering game developer Jonathan Blow lambasted the current state of the gaming industry for its lack of risk taking and vision. Blow, the developer, designer, and producer of the megahit *Braid*, laments, "There are some smart people wallowing in there, but the environment discourages creativity and strength and rigor, so what you get is mostly atrophy" (Clark 2012, 43). Blow's contention that video games lack a degree of sophistication comes at a time when electronic gaming has risen in popularity across a wide cross-section of audiences, ranging from the teenage boy who spends hours in massively multiplayer online role-playing games (MMORPGs) to the suburban commuter who plays *Angry Birds* on the train ride home from work.

Game design is also a burgeoning academic discipline as well. The Entertainment Software Association lists 381 colleges and universities in the United States offering courses in game programming, game art and animation, and video game design. While the foci of these courses and programs ranges from a humanities-based theoretical study of the evolution of games to collaborative partnerships with established educational enterprises set on designing pedagogical technology, the sum of these efforts has resulted in increased academic credibility to a medium that is often wrongly dismissed as a child's toy.

The production of video games inherently requires a particular interdisciplinary combination of artists, computer programmers, and game designers who bring more traditional disciplinary backgrounds to project-based environments; professionals from disparate backgrounds are placed into teams and must translate their own disciplinary understandings to nonexperts in order to make the game project work. This type of interdisciplinarity manifests itself organically within the game industry, and the same type of creative production extends to the academic realm of game making fairly easily.

Champlain College has attempted to capitalize on the popularity of this growing entertainment medium by offering majors in a variety of electronic game production areas ranging from game art and animation to game programming. Consistent with Champlain's strategy of offering innovative and relevant majors, the Electronic Game Design (EGD) program is one of the most popular at the college, drawing more applicants than any other field. The capstone course that all seniors in the program take is a team-taught, five-credit course where a faculty member in EGD pairs with a faculty member from the Core Division. Students are assembled in four- to six-member teams with the semester-long charge of creating a playable video game. What differentiates this capstone course from a standard production course, though, is an intentional integration of knowledge from other realms brought to bear on the game itself. For example, a team may demonstrate how they incorporated what they learned from a specific demographic analysis into their creation of a particular mechanic that players of the game must employ, or they may research the art styles of a particular historical period in order to create a more authentic visual setting for their game. These examples highlight the ways in which a variety of academic subjects (marketing, history, and folklore in this case) might inform the technical production of an electronic game. When students are able to successfully integrate multiple disciplines into their work in this capstone course, they are better able to counter the trends in the gaming industry that Blow decries and lend academic credibility to the creation of video games since students, after all, will graduate with a bachelor's degree in majors like EGD and game art and animation.

The difficulty in doing this work successfully, however, rests within the tension students feel between concentrating on the technical aspect of making games and the integration they are charged expressly with demonstrating. For most of these seniors, the realistic demands of the workforce are at the center of their thinking, and they want to create as much slickly produced material for their portfolio as possible. They (rightly, to some extent) believe that the proof of their expertise is encompassed by the finished products they are able to show prospective employers. Especially as seniors, the idea of a college course asking them to perform tasks that fail directly to pertain to this end sometimes is seen as just another academic hoop to jump through instead of the thing that makes a Champlain College degree different from a job training site. As one anonymous student evaluation contended, "I don't feel ready to enter the game industry, and need more experience writing code that's actually used in the real world . . . and feel like I wasn't taught much that's actually relevant to the game industry."

This comment is indicative of an instrumentalist, skills-based logic that runs counter to the objective of the EGD Capstone as well as the larger, collegewide goal of integrating interdisciplinary knowledge within the framework of a professional field. Implicit in the student's statement that he "wasn't taught much that's actually relevant to the game industry" is the idea that time spent on integrating the liberal arts into the technical production of a video game was time ill-spent. While this example does not prove anything about the success or failure of interdisciplinary integration at Champlain, it does underscore how difficult integration can be when the rhetoric of professionalism at the college combines with a student's perceived impression of what it means to be a viable candidate for employment. The student went on to state in highly technical terms how the college's emphasis on a particular type of programming software is growing increasingly obsolete and why this limited his employment potential. His course evaluation does not mention the habits of mind that the interdisciplinary, team-taught structure of the course was supposed to foster. Furthermore, the student does not recognize that the very software programs he wishes the program taught will likely be obsolete very early in his career.

The irony here is that attending to big questions about the human condition that the liberal arts compel students to think about and, in turn, applying these ideas to the production of video games is consistent with Blow's argument about what the mainstream gaming industry needs to do in order to move forward as an entertainment and artistic medium. Put differently, a belief in the value of incorporating traditional liberal arts ideals into making games is shared by both an industry leader like Blow and the designers of Champlain's EGD capstone. Yet a fundamental disconnection remains between the integrative design of the course and what the students expect it to be. To be sure, other possible factors in this scenario include a student's own intellectual motivations, the material conditions facing students upon graduation, the course delivery, and his position as a game programmer; but it remains crucial to examine the gap that exists between how students perceive a professionally focused degree and how the curriculum offered at the college positions students professionally.

Within the context of the EGD capstone at Champlain, students are asked to strike a balance between a hands-on, real-world application of their specific disciplinary knowledge and the more intangible skills like critical thinking, teamwork, and analytical reasoning. However, the tangible product a student is asked to complete in this course often supersedes the process-based approach the curriculum advocates because of the immediacy of the task-oriented charge of making a playable electronic game.

Graphic Design Capstone

The graphic design program's senior capstone attempts to integrate the students' general education with their professional education. As with many majors, getting the students to see the possibilities and the value of bringing the two sides of their education together at this summative point in their college career can be difficult. These difficulties may come partially from the overall rhetorical position that Champlain takes when presenting the value of its education to students, as discussed in our introduction. Rhetorical devices such as the Upside-Down Curriculum ("About Champlain" n.d.) and the emphasis on preparing students for the professional world foster a greater appreciation for major classes than for liberal education. Graphic design, which usually sits within an arts or fine arts context in the academic world, is a field where one might not expect such a divide between the major and the liberal education. Champlain's graphic design program compares itself to other programs in the area, at schools such as the Rhode Island School of Design and the Pratt Institute. These programs are all housed in arts and fine arts contexts. However, Champlain does not have a traditional fine arts department. Graphic design at the school actually started in the Business Division, moving later to the Division of Communication and Creative Media. This history has influenced graphic design at Champlain since its inception, focusing as much on graphic design as a profession as it does on graphic design as an integrative artistic field.

The American Institute of Graphic Arts (AIGA), created in 1914, is the oldest professional organization for graphic designers. Their mission is to advance design "as a professional craft, strategic tool and vital cultural force" ("About AIGA" n.d.). While the first two parts of this mission statement relate directly to the skills-based approach of business administration, the third part, "vital cultural force," speaks to something much larger, to a holistic understanding of humanity. The AIGA is recognizing that design is a cultural process, integrated into the complex set of patterns, beliefs, understandings, practices, and contexts that make up human cultural life. In order to best prepare design students to become design professionals, the AIGA urges design educators to approach their task with an understanding of human contexts: "This environment of shifting control for design decisions results in concern for methods for understanding people's wants, needs, and patterns of behavior; recognition of social and cultural differences; and strategies for resolving competing values" (Grefe 2012).

Clearly, the AIGA places emphasis on more than delivering skills when educating designers. The organization takes an almost anthropological stance toward understanding the role of design, and it views as necessary that a student of design gains knowledge of how to integrate his or her design skills into a larger and broader understanding of human life. The view of the AIGA is in many ways strikingly similar to the approach to culture taken by the American Anthropological Association (AAA), and the similarity is no accident. Like the AIGA, the AAA is the oldest and largest professional organization for its field, and it describes the role of the anthropologist as examining "social patterns and practices across cultures, with a special interest in how people live in particular places and how they organize, govern, and create meaning" (American Anthropological Association n.d.). The two organizations are not using the same words, but they are presenting the same idea: In order to be a good designer/anthropologist, one must integrate understandings of a range of cultural contexts, understanding how people make meaning based on their own cultures. Indeed, many design fields understand the value of integration:

> Human design process, whether applied to hardware, systems, institutions, or interpersonal problems, is not mere analysis based on known science, although that may play an important part. Human design process is inherently synthetic, requires the human feedback mode, and often transcends the knowledge of any one discipline. (Kline 1995, 142)

The AIGA is a powerful voice in shaping the rhetoric of graphic design, but it is not the only voice. To be sure, many graphic designers approach their field as a set of skills employed on a task. However, the current trend within graphic design is to recognize that being a professional in the field requires holistic, theorized, and integrative thinking. As McLuhan states, the artist is a person of "integral awareness" (1964/1994, 65). While not all design schools and programs embrace these ideas equally in their pedagogy and curriculum, the field as a whole is moving in a direction that sees the value of these larger ideas. Between 2007 and 2009, the AIGA, working with the software company Adobe, conducted surveys and research to explore what graphic designers would need in order to succeed in the new millennium ("Designer of 2015 Timeline" n.d.). One of the results of this research was a list of thirteen educational competencies that the organization believes are necessary for the education of designers ("Designer of 2015 Competencies" n.d.). The first competency on this list, unsurprisingly, is "Ability to create and develop visual response to communication problems" ("Designer of 2015 Competencies" n.d.). However, ten of the subsequent twelve competencies deal primarily with integrative thinking, interdisciplinarity, awareness of cultural contexts, or ethics. The rhetoric of professionalism within graphic design more and more often includes a need for professional designers to think contextually and to integrate cultural knowledge into their design process. This being the case, there were comparatively fewer problems in the graphic design capstone integrating the broad, liberal education from the core with the professional education of the major.

Students see the value of this integrative thinking process. In the graphic design capstone, explicit use of AIGA's statements in the classroom makes students aware of the purpose of integrative thinking. It becomes a part of the rhetoric of professionalism—not just from the school's or the program's point of view but from a graphic design student's point of view. One student commented in the anonymous end-of-year course evaluation about the value of integrative class discussions,

> You help lead some very interesting discussions that I personally find very relevant to our field of study. . . . Love being in a classroom with my peers/students in my major and talking about our chosen career path. Some of the discussions we've had have really made me think about my own values as a designer and a person."

This student draws concrete connections between the liberal arts–oriented seminar discussions and a future career. Beyond simply discussing the worth of having a deep conversation, this student recognizes that such discussions can directly affect understanding of values as a designer.

At Champlain, the integration of liberal arts and major education happens in three main ways: integration of context, process, and product. The integration of product relies on some end result (e.g., an assignment outcome) to demonstrate that integration has happened within the capstone course.

Graphic design, while nominally a product-oriented field, recognizes the value of process, as evidenced by its integration of ethnographic methodology. The final project in the graphic design capstone is called a "process book," a collection of the various design choices made by a professional designer, along with a contextualized rationale for those choices. In the capstone, we ask the students to create a document fairly similar to a professional graphic designer's process book. We put particular emphasis on the students taking into account their audiences' cultural norms and how those norms shape the communication process—what anthropology calls the *habitus*, following Bourdieu (1997)—as well as the context in which their design will exist. In short, students must understand their project as a communicative process and that all participants in the communicative process shape the meanings that are transmitted. Students must be aware, to some extent, of the "native hermeneutics" involved in their project (Dubois, 1996). While students initially view the complexity of this assignment with skepticism, they come to understand the value of bringing both parts of their education together. Another student on the anonymous course evaluation recognized the value of "three teachers with COMPLETELY different backgrounds and teaching styles, all teaching a large class of designers. But like any 'real world' job, this class . . . *learned* to work together and to grow."

Students need to integrate their design choices with the cultural and interdisciplinary education they receive at Champlain. By calling the final project in the graphic design capstone a *process book*, the faculty has shaped the course to use explicitly the rhetoric of graphic design professionalism. As might be expected with such a final assignment, the integration found in the graphic design capstone is an integration of process. This integration reflects again a similarity between anthropology and graphic design methodologies. In 2011 the AIGA put out a publication titled "Ethnography/Design: An Ethnography Primer" ("Ethnography Primer" n.d.). It is a short booklet discussing how ethnography (a research methodology created by the fields of anthropology and folklore in the nineteenth century) can be a useful tool for designers to gain the integrated, contextualized understandings the AIGA deems necessary to a good designer: "Designers need to understand the relationship between what they produce and the meaning their product has for others. Enter ethnography" ("Ethnography Primer" n.d.). This description of holism and contextualized thinking is echoed in anthropology, which

> deals not only in knowledge about others, but also in the knowledge that others possess. More than any other field, anthropology tries to explore

> and understand the knowledge and knowledge-making processes of the subjects of their inquiry. Rather than simply overlay anthropological epistemologies onto the people we study, anthropology attempts to seek the insider, the emic understanding, allowing that to inform our own interpretations as well. (Lange 2013, 48)

Just as the AIGA's Ethnography Primer exhorts designers to learn about the knowledge of their clients and audiences, the discipline of anthropology requires a contextualized understanding of the knowledge of others.

Within the capstone's process book, students are required to work across epistemologies, presenting their design choices as well as what parts of their education (drawing on both their major and their liberal education) inform those choices. They must contextualize their project in the world to which, and within which, they are communicating their messages. Additionally, the students must set their professional education into the context of their integrative liberal education. As such, the process book actually combines integration of process with integration of context, following Irving's suggestion "that the concept of interdisciplinarity applies not only to learning across academic disciplines, but also to learning that links disciplinary study with learning through work, and to the development of pedagogies that facilitate learning in integrated, complex contexts" (Irving 2009, 85).

Why Resist Integration?

Champlain College is far from the only site of higher education where the rhetoric of professionalism permeates its identity. From university curriculum that champions "experience-based learning" to for-profit education sites, the idea that higher education should concomitantly provide students with specific career preparation and a more traditional liberal arts education is the contemporary standard in U.S. higher education. What sets Champlain apart from many U.S. colleges, however, is how explicitly this career orientation, combined with the promise of integration, manifests itself in the college's brand. Champlain College's vision statement reads, "By 2020, Champlain College will be the finest small, professionally and globally focused college in the United States" ("Vision" n.d.). At once a marketing tool designed to recruit students to a growing, expensive private college as well as a coherent innovation in the delivery of higher education, the emphasis on the professional has meaningful implications for the college's curriculum.

The focus on profession has several effects on students. For some students, it foregrounds the employer and employment in their minds, and the job is understood in relatively simplistic terms (i.e., as a set of skills put to use on a set of tasks). For students in many fields, this effect follows general trends:

> Notwithstanding widespread interest in the issues of race and gender, surveys conducted over the past decade in Canada and the United States indicate that university students tend to be more pragmatic, more vocationally oriented, and more politically conservative than those of the previous generation. (Axelrod 2002, 125)

The understanding that the practical parts of an education are more important than the less obviously applicable liberal arts portions reflects a general trend in what Stark and Lattuca call "enterprising/production career fields" (1997, 156). The example they put forward, business administration, could be used as representative of many majors at Champlain:

> Instructors teaching business administration courses least often considered either their scholarly or pedagogical training as an extremely strong influence on course planning. They drew instead on work experience and employer needs outside academe. Business instructors did not strongly endorse a view of their field as a group of scholars; rather they characterized it as both an organized body of knowledge and a set of skills. . . . In contrast, learning the "great ideas" is minimally important to business faculty. (Stark and Lattuca 1997, 156)

Not only does a curricular structure such as Champlain's compel students to think about the symbiotic relationship between integrated, interdisciplinary knowledge and professional practice, the case studies in this chapter argue that professional bodies value these same things. Why, then, do students often demonstrate an antipathy toward this type of thinking and, in some cases, an inability to do it meaningfully in the context of an upper-division class? The final section of this chapter examines some tentative answers to these questions in hopes that they will act as a bellwether for further examination into how institutional practices intersect with curricular decisions to shape how students experience higher education.

Political scientists sometimes use the term *policy lever* as an analogy to signify the practical significance of implementing a new institutional objective. As the analogy goes, the policy is the lever that will set in motion a change in human behavior or thinking. For higher education purposes, the term has been used to study matters such as student retention and motivation (Braxton and McClendon 2001–2002; Pascarella and Terenzini 1991). For Hossler et al. (2008) one notable policy lever is "using recruitment practices that support the fulfillment of students' academic and social expectations of college" (1). For example, a promotional video for accepted students describes the Upside-Down Curriculum at Champlain ("Upside-Down Curriculum" n.d.) solely as how early students get into their professional studies. For our purposes, it is worth questioning how the emphasis on professionalization in Champlain's recruitment strategy acts as a policy lever that works well for the purposes of enrollment but that simultaneously creates an unrealistic expectation about the reality of academic life at the college. The section of the college's website for prospective students works to entice students who, as Axelrod (2002) notes, "tend to be more vocationally oriented than those of a previous generation" (125). The website reads,

> Each Champlain College degree program has a single goal: to prepare the student for a leadership role in their chosen field. In a highly competitive world nothing less will do. Success depends upon distinction, and students must emerge from their education full-formed and ready to conquer the greatest challenges their profession can present. ("Career Focused" n.d.)

In fairness, the website comprehensively details how Champlain's interdisciplinary liberal arts curriculum and practical life-skills education provide the sum of a prospective student's experience. Nevertheless, the message that resonates for a high school senior far more interested in producing video games than making meaning from Plato is that Champlain will provide a skills-based education that renders the college different from other sites of higher education. Students who enroll at Champlain in part because of the explicit attention the college's recruitment strategies pay to the practical are often, as the narrative about the e-game capstone illustrates, resistant to the transferrable skills that an interdisciplinary education offers.

A Suggestion on Integrating Integration

Students at Champlain College explore the relationship of interdisciplinarity and integration in higher education, and one issue this chapter illustrates is that the two terms are neither synonymous nor automatically conjoined. Champlain has an avowedly interdisciplinary liberal education curriculum, and the realities of the courses, in large part, live up to that vow. The core curriculum described above introduces students to interdisciplinary thinking from day one of the first semester. As semesters pass, students learn to apply techniques from multiple fields to increasingly complex questions in increasingly complex ways. In the course of this process, students (ideally) learn to integrate ideas from one realm of knowledge into another. The experiences of the three authors teaching across the curriculum attest to the development of the students' abilities to integrate as they move through the first three years of their college education.

However, all of this interdisciplinarity and integration between liberal and professional education is contained wholly within the students' liberal education. Not until the senior year, in the capstone class, does Champlain ask the students to integrate *beyond* the liberal arts courses. For three years, the students experience a liberal education and a professional major education that exist as nearly parallel lines—tracking next to one another, but almost never meeting except on rare occasions fostered through the core and not the other divisions. In the second year of the core, a course titled Capitalism and Democracy contains a project that requires students to explore a constitutional issue related to their major. This class was the one explicit bridging of the gap between the major and the liberal education, as all students were required to integrate ideas from their major into a core class. However, as the core has undergone recent revision and expansion, Capitalism and Democracy has become one of a menu of courses that students may take within a semester, so that even this one explicit integration is no longer a common experience for all Champlain students. Beyond this course, core faculty are encouraged to integrate the liberal arts and the major in their individual delivery of their classes (although, interestingly, the reverse is not true: professional major faculty almost never seek to integrate ideas from the core into their lower-level classes). The encouragement to integrate liberal and major education is not codified in the master syllabi, though, and the degree to which it happens in core courses in the first three years varies from never to rarely, depending on the faculty member. Integration of the professional major with the liberal arts thus does not happen in any systematic way until a Champlain student's senior year, and then only in the capstone. The hope implicit in this arrangement is that the students, having been trained in integrative thinking as a tool unto itself, will be able and willing to apply integrative thinking as a habit of mind when asked to do so in their senior year. As the three case studies in this chapter demonstrate, that hope is not always fulfilled.

One of the most important reasons why the institutional emphasis on integration and interdisciplinarity fails to flourish is that simply relegating these habits of mind to the general education curriculum is insufficient. The authors suggest that the successful integration of professional-focused majors with liberal learning requires some type of campuswide initiative focused on making integration part of a college competency. Assigning an intellectual value or skill to a particular institutional domain creates an effect (real or perceived) among students and faculty that interdisciplinary and integrative thinking is something that matters only in core courses. In the same way that composition and rhetoric scholars have long argued that first-year composition courses cannot singularly cultivate a student's ability to write academically, we argue that placing integrative and interdisciplinary thinking into curricular silos is an impediment to delivering on Champlain's promise to meld interdisciplinary thinking with professionally focused expertise.

The case studies about the psychology, game development, and graphic design capstones speak to the ways that the professionally based academic work a student is asked to complete often competes with the kinds of thinking that Core professors ask of their students, as opposed to an integrative synthesis of professional and liberal learning. A course need not be interdisciplinary to facilitate integration, but the interdisciplinary teaching and learning that define the Core teaches critical skills necessary for successful integration. These skills can then be translated and applied into a student's major from their first year onward in the same way that a student's potential career path can be brought into the humanities and social sciences. The hopeful irony, though, is that what it means to be professional means being capable of integrating liberal learning into professional practice.

A 2006 Association of American Colleges & Universities (AAC&U) study found that 72 percent of executives in industry surveyed valued the same kind of balance between practical application and theoretical ideas that Champlain's curriculum, especially in the capstone, offers. As we see in the AIGA example, professional bodies want their students to be doing intellectual work that goes beyond mere technical competence. Graphic design falls under Stark and Lattuca's "Professional and Occupational Fields" designation, more specifically a hybrid of "productive/enterprise service" and "creative service" (1997, 148–49). As such, one might expect at least a partially skills-first approach in graphic design instruction, as described earlier with business administration. The creative side of graphic design would be expected reasonably to modify that approach, of course, but the reality is that graphic design as a field, and the graphic design faculty at Champlain, actively reject a skills-first approach, opting instead for explicit integration and promotion of interdisciplinary ideas and methods. The field and the faculty both recognize the value of integrating approaches established in other disciplines into the education of graphic designers, as evidenced by their professional association, the AIGA. Additionally, the Entertainment Software Association, a professional organization for video game designers, also champions the cultural and artistic advancement possible through video games and cites how they can influence education, public health, art, and other social issues. Implicit in the ESA's mission is the idea that in order to influence these bigger societal contexts, having an interdisciplinary, liberal understanding of them must be in place. The APA, the professional organization that integrates practitioners and scholars in the field, acknowledges the importance of both depth and breadth of a psychology student's education ("Principles for Quality Undergraduate Education in Psychology" n.d.). If fields that historically have been situated outside of higher education are making the case for integrated, interdisciplinary learning, more established academic studies like education should be able to do the same.

Media ecologist Neil Postman in *The End of Education* (1996) argues that underpinning cultural debates over public schools in the United States is a struggle over grand narratives about education. They create a sense of purpose for students, teachers, and institutions. Economic utility, the use of schooling as preparation for the workforce, is a reasonable yet ultimately unfulfilling narrative because it fails to develop curiosity, inquiry, creativity, and adaptability—all values for any professional occupation potentially in today's workforce (Postman 1996). Postman explains, as the authors of this chapter alongside professional organizations like the APA, ESA, and AIGA are apt to agree,

> Specialized competence can come only through a more generalized competence, which is to say that economic utility is a by-product of a good education. Any education that is mainly *about* economic utility is far too limited to be useful, and, in any case, so diminishes the world that it mocks one's humanity. (31)

Champlain College attempts to bridge the practical and technical with applied and inquiry-driven learning through the Upside-Down Curriculum of the professional programs alongside the interdisciplinarity of the core. The narrative of economic utility is far too narrow to encompass the integrative experience students are asked to play out in all three capstones that have been outlined, which is likewise at odds with the rhetoric of professionalism that Champlain College uses to attract current and future students. Likewise, the integration of a liberal education with professionalism needs to occur both within and between the student's general requirements and major coursework, lest it become another unfulfilling narrative sold to students about the value of higher education.

References

American Anthropological Association. n.d. "What Is Anthropology?" http://www.aaanet.org/about/WhatisAnthropology.cfm.

American Institute of Graphic Arts. n.d.. "About AIGA." http://www.aiga.org/About/.

———. n.d. "An Ethnography Primer." http://www.aiga.org/ethnography-primer/.

———. n.d. "Designer of 2015 Competencies." http://www.aiga.org/designer-of-2015-competencies/.

———. n.d. "Designer of 2015 Timeline." http://www.aiga.org/designer-of-2015-timeline/.

American Psychological Association. n.d. "Principles for Quality Undergraduate Education in Psychology." http://www.apa.org/education/undergrad/principles.aspx.

Axelrod, P. 2002. *Values in Conflict: The University, the Marketplace, and the Trials of Liberal Education*. Montreal: McGill-Queen's University Press.

Bourdieu, P. 1977. *Outline of a Theory of Practice*. Cambridge: Cambridge University Press.

Braxton, J. M., and S. A. McClendon. 2001–2002. "The Fostering of Social Integration through Institutional Practice." *Journal of College Student Retention: Research, Theory and Practice* 3 (1): 57–71.

Champlain College. n.d. "About Champlain." http://www.champlain.edu/about-champlain.html.

———. n.d. "Career Focused." Retrieved from http://champlain.edu/about-champlain/our-strengths/career-focused.

———. n.d. "Core Division." https://www.champlain.edu/academics/ academic-divisions/core-division.

———. n.d. "Integrated Business Experience." http://www.champlain.edu/academics/undergraduate-academics/majors-and-minors/marketing/curriculum-marketing/integrated-business-experience-marketing.

———. n.d. "Upside-Down Curriculum." http://www.champlain.edu/ undergraduate-studies/majors-and-programs/upside-down-curriculum-x14123.html.

———. n.d. "Vision." https://www.champlain.edu/about-champlain/vision.

Clark, T. 2012. "The Most Dangerous Gamer." *The Atlantic*: 40-46.

Dubois, T. A. 1996, Summer. "Native Hermeneutics: Traditional Means of Interpreting Lyric Songs in Northern Europe." *Journal of American Folklore* 109 (433): 235–66.

Grefe, R. 2012, August 16. "Evolving Expectations for Design Education." http://www.aiga.org/evolving-expectations-for-design-education/.

Hossler, Don, et al. 2008. *The Role of Institutional Practices in College Students Persistence: Results from a Policy-Oriented Pilot Study*. Paper presented at the May 2008 Annual Forum of the Association for Institutional Research (AIR), Seattle, Washington.

Irving, K. 2009. "Work-Based Learning as Interdisciplinary Study." In *Interdisciplinary*

Learning and Teaching in Higher Education: Theory and Practice, edited by B. Chandramohan and S. Fallows, 84–90. New York: Routledge.

Klein, J. T. 1990. *Interdisciplinarity: History, Theory, Practice*. Detroit: Wayne State University Press.

———. 1996. *Crossing Boundaries: Knowledge, Disciplinarities, and Interdisciplinarities.* Charlottesville: University of Virginia Press.

Kline, S. J. 1995. *Conceptual Foundations for Multidisciplinary Thinking*. Palo Alto, CA: Stanford University Press.

Lange, M. A. 2013. "The Particular Place of Anthropology in an Interdisciplinary Curriculum." *Teaching Anthropology* 3 (1): 43–54.

Lattuca, L. 2001. *Creating Interdisciplinarity: Interdisciplinary Research and Teaching among College and University Faculty*. Nashville: Vanderbilt University Press.

McLuhan, M. 1964/1994. *Understanding Media: The Extensions of Man*. Cambridge, MA: MIT Press.

Pascarella, E. T., and P. T. Terenzini. 1991. *How College Affects Students*. Volume 1: *Findings and Insights from Twenty Years of Research*. San Francisco: Jossey-Bass.

Postman, N. 1996. *The End of Education: Redefining the Value of School*. New York: Vintage Books.

Schuman, S. 2005. *Old Main: Small Colleges in Twenty-First-Century America*. Baltimore: Johns Hopkins University Press.

Stark, J., and L. Lattuca. 1997. *Shaping the College Curriculum: Academic Plans in Action*. Boston: Allyn and Bacon.

Chapter 12

Issues in the Assessment of Integrated Learning

Philip Craig Morton, PhD, Jennifer Shaulis Hughes, MS,
and Curtis Craig, MS, Texas Tech University

In order to improve student learning and meet accreditation requirements, educational programs are monitored in a process generally referred to as *assessment* (Palomba and Banta 1999). When properly implemented, assessment is ongoing, systematic, and grounded in social science research methodologies and professional standards (Allen 2004; Newcomer, Hatry, and Wholey 2004). Rather than just collecting data, assessment should be purposeful and goal-driven, linked to student learning and the goals of the institution, carefully reviewed, and used for program and institutional improvement (Palomba and Banta, 1999).

Good assessment, especially with regard to interdisciplinary courses and degree programs, may be challenging to achieve. For example, assessment usually occurs in reference to established program objectives. However, some interdisciplinary programs may have vague objectives, or the measurements employed may not be useful for determining if the program has met its student learning outcomes (Hatry and Newcomer 2004). An example of the latter may include course grades, which are frequently insufficient for measuring the quality of student learning when haphazardly collected and used for program assessment. Measures are best implemented when employed under a systematic evaluation model, such as a goal-based model in which the goals or outcomes are carefully clarified, criteria or standards are established, and then data are collected and compared against those standards (Conrad and Wilson 1985).

Given the limitations previously mentioned, assessment may be particularly challenging in the context of integrated learning. Integrated learning is an intellectually appealing approach to education that focuses on integration of insights from multiple disciplines, wherein students make connections between and synthesize dissimilar concepts, and effectively transfer and apply this knowledge to complex problems (Huber and Hutchings 2004; Klein

2005). The integrated learning approach is frequently employed in academic departments focused on general education (Wehlburg 2010a), and is gaining traction in other fields that require synthesis of disparate knowledge, such as engineering (Froyd and Ohland 2005). However, teaching students to critically think and effectively integrate insights from multiple disciplines involves complex skills that do not easily facilitate the establishment of clear and measurable learning outcomes (Wehlburg 2010b). Tackling this challenge requires consideration of previous efforts to develop and assess integrated learning curricula.

Development of any educational program should include assessment in the development process. For integrative learning, case studies in the field of general education have shown that development requires extensive collaboration among multiple stakeholders, including administrative personnel and faculty (Wehlburg 2010b). The fostering of dialogue is particularly important due to the disparate nature of integrated learning, whether in development of a curriculum and establishing objectives or in specifically establishing an assessment approach within the context of curriculum development (McNertney and Ferrandino 2010). One review of assessment development in three colleges found that development typically occurred in stages, although the exact sequence and initial motivation to begin assessment differed between colleges (Galle and Galle 2010). The impetus to begin development of curricula and corresponding assessment approaches may begin in faculty retreats, high-level discussions within a college, or even formal committees. These discussions generally result in broad integrative learning outcomes. A second sustained development phase follows in which those broad outcomes are refined, along with specific proposals for measures of student learning, such as embedded class assignments and other general performance indicators.

Before discussing measurement techniques, some thought on previously generated outcomes may be helpful. Integration itself may be treated as a single outcome for which to provide measurements (Mille, 2005). This approach may be the most common. Other approaches may divide integrated learning into multiple student learning objectives. An example of multiple outcomes for integrated learning is available in the Valid Assessment of Learning in Undergraduate Education (VALUE) rubric, which was designed by extensive coordination between multiple institutions and committees (Rhodes 2010). Key outcomes in the VALUE rubric include whether students are able to connect their learning to personal experience, whether they are able to connect concepts across disciplines, whether students can apply their learning to new situations, and whether students are able to effectively reflect and assess their own understanding and growth. Other potential outcomes that have been generated for integrated learning include whether students can identify multiple sources of knowledge, and whether they can compare or contrast multiple differing perspectives (Klein 2005).

Integrated learning has been assessed in a variety of ways, such as the aforementioned use of embedded class assignments (Galle and Galle 2010). Also, standard national assessment exams such as the Collegiate Learning Assessment (CLA) and the National Survey of Student Engagement (NSSE) have been used as indirect measures of integrated learning (Huber, Hutchings, Gale, Miller, & Breen 2007), either by finding evidence of activities related to integrated learning in the NSSE, such as community-based learning, or by analyzing writing samples in the CLA to measure critical thinking and integrative thought. Furthermore, the use of capstone courses, if designed with integrative learning in mind, may provide a useful measure of student ability to connect concepts across disciplines (Huber and Hutchings 2004). Performance on design projects or complex problems requiring disparate knowledge and synthesis may also provide another avenue to measure student learning (Froyd and Ohland 2005).

Two methods of measurement have been found particularly suitable to integrative learning assessment, although they have been employed in other areas: the use of portfolios, particularly electronic portfolios (e-portfolios), and concept maps. Portfolios allow the student to collect and synthesize knowledge in a concrete and analyzable product (Huber and Hutchings 2004). Furthermore, e-portfolios have been frequently used as the assessment method of choice (Arcario, Eynon, and Clark 2005; Flower and Rhodes 2005). E-portfolios are useful because they can store a variety of works in many different media formats, with minimal storage requirements, and can be analyzed by any interested faculty and assessment personnel. Normally portfolios are scored according to rubrics designed to assess integrative learning (Vars 2002), such as the aforementioned VALUE rubric (Rhodes 2010). The second method of assessment suitable for integrative learning assessment is concept mapping (Froyd and Ohland 2005). While not widely used, it holds promise as a flexible tool for assessing the conceptual integration of multiple domains of knowledge (Popova-Gonci and Lamb 2012). Concept maps are visual representations of student knowledge, consisting of concepts connected together with descriptive links. By counting the number of concepts a student generates, as well as the quality of links and number of cross-links between concepts, one may assess the degree of complexity and integration the student has for multiple domains. Some research has even synthesized the logic behind concept maps and electronic portfolios and effectively compared and contrasted knowledge profiles in students for different courses with some success by measuring page numbers (concepts) and cross-links in electronic portfolios (Birckbichler et al. 2012).

Key Issues

In this chapter, we use this information regarding the assessment of integrated learning and identify key issues that administrators and faculty should consider in developing an assessment plan. These issues have been identified from both the perspective of student learning and a broader institutional perspective. The identified issues incorporate institutional, political, and pragmatic concerns that often arise in the context of discussions concerning academic assessment. The following issues are discussed: (1) accreditation and reaffirmation, (2) strategic planning, (3) tenure and promotion, (4) promoting student success, (5) efficiency and human resources, (6) student engagement, (7) facilitating institutional communication, (8) student learning outcomes, and (9) navigating institutional politics.

Accreditation and Reaffirmation

Accreditation and reaffirmation are becoming central to many of the decision-making behaviors of higher education. Accreditors offer structured and peer-reviewed standards of best practices as well as opportunities for structured and strategic change. However, accreditation and reaffirmation also pose significant and high-stakes consequences for lack of planning, infrastructure, and goal attainment. Ensuring that institutions are considerate of these issues when implementing integrated learning strategies both provides valuable opportunities for effective collaboration as well as, and possibly more importantly, restricts the potential dangers that may be associated with non-compliance.

Accreditation is broadly defined as a voluntary method of quality assurance. Students, through degree completion, are assured of a quality education that validates academic goals. Students also are able to benefit from financial aid and other incentives. Institutions are able to maintain a reputable standing through accreditation. Accreditation is offered at the college and degree level as well as at the institutional level. Both these levels are important when considering assessment for integrated learning. At the college or program level, assessment methods and results need to be shared between institutional areas while being specific enough to the college that they meet specialized standards. At the institutional level, assessment for integrated learning needs to represent area and institutional goal attainment and evidence of best practices.

Practical approaches and suggestions. On a pragmatic level, integrated learning programs offer a special opportunity to highlight their uniqueness to accrediting agencies. While accreditation is often perceived in an adversarial light, preparing for accreditation or reaffirmation of accreditation is an opportunity to tell one's story about how integrated learning meets the changing face of higher education. For example, a looming accreditation visit may present administrators of integrated learning with an opportunity to write or speak about the transformative nature of this style of pedagogy. Integrated learning programs are indeed special; institutional periods of accreditation seeking or reaffirmation of accreditation are prime periods to spread the good news about the deep student learning that occurs in these programs. Tell your story with all the gusto you can muster!

Strategic Planning

Strategic planning is an institutional requirement for all institutions that are accredited. In fact, the basis of accreditation is institutional progress and integrity toward the institution's mission statement as it is identified within the strategic plan. While in reality, most decision making works independently of strategic planning, ultimately colleges and institutions will be expected to identify major strategies and goals for student learning within the strategic plan. The purposes for this expectation are broad—the political expectation that regulates institutional activities and promotes stability and accountability, the structural expectation that ensures that university activities extend beyond individual initiative, and a compliance expectation that requires identification of student learning strategies ensuring that certain initiatives are efficient, meaningful, and follow best practice. However, the primary reason for aligning strategies such as integrated learning into institutional strategic plans is so that a road map for what should be done, how it will be done, and how to know if it is done at the expected level is identified and well considered.

Strategic planning as it relates to integrated learning poses certain challenges. Addressing these issues thoughtfully and collaboratively will help, although not guarantee, that strategic plans meet the individual college's needs as well as the institutional needs. The issues related to strategic planning for integrated learning are unfortunately as much about navigating the political environment of assessment as they are about assessment best practices. However, this situation is not completely negative. Establishing benchmarking criteria early on, even if it is contentious, can negate future political issues down the road.

Practical approaches and suggestions. How much does your institution value integrated learning? Is your answer to this question quick, or do you need to pause for a few minutes to contemplate your response? The relative newness of integrated learning may mean that everybody's trying to jump on the same bandwagon at your institution, so you may have high buy-in but little organizational strategy. Perhaps there is little to no discussion on your campus because the institution is hesitant to raise the profile of its integrated learning programs for fear of appearing too biased toward a particular academic program or college. Perhaps funding issues and lack of resources are impacting the degree to which integrated learning programs succeed on your campus. Whatever the reason, administrators of integrated learning programs need to take stock periodically of the institution's commitment to these programs. One way to ensure that these programs remain on the executive leadership radar is to draft a succinct strategic plan for integrated learning and include the following suggested sections: mission, vision, action plan, resource plan, and adherence to university strategic plan. Make sure that your plan aligns with the university's goals and objectives, and then vociferously share that plan with whomever will listen. Take copies of your strategic plan wherever you go.

Tenure and Promotion

Few issues in higher education administration and higher education cultures are as volatile as tenure and promotion. From central administration to tenure-track faculty, these matters are highly personal and controversial. The institution has established specific and, ideally, standardized criteria for final approval. Colleges and departments devote significant resources into making the process as beneficial as possible for existing and potential tenure-track faculty. Tenure-track faculty invest countless hours into assembling their portfolio in the hopes of obtaining peer approval and other more concrete benefits that come with reaching tenured status. In broader terms, faculty credentialing and the subsequent associated accountability are more critical than ever before with higher accountability safeguards and expectations. Making sure that faculty are qualified to do the very things that they have spent their lives doing has broader and deeper ramifications than most people ever consider. The efficient and fair assessment of tenure and promotion as well as faculty credentialing is critical for an institution. However, if done in such a manner, all levels of the process will not only benefit from greater efficiency and transparency but the process will transpire with greater ease and higher levels of satisfaction.

These issues, as they relate to integrated learning, do pose significant challenges, but the potential payoff for faculty and tenure-track faculty is both immeasurable and incredibly measureable. Integrated learning possesses the capacity to measure faculty's broader impact on student learning, higher levels of collaboration, and greater opportunities for service and publication. By developing and implementing assessment strategies that capture faculty activity with integrated learning, faculty credentialing and portfolios have the potential to be more prolific and dynamic than existing models.

Practical approaches and suggestions. Faculty need to be reminded that integrated learning should be part and parcel of one's annual faculty review and tenure dossier. Documenting unique teaching pedagogies and strategies may create an additional time commitment for faculty; administrators thus should acknowledge this additional burden on faculty. Integrated learning faculty should be informed well ahead of institutional due dates, so that they have the time they need to dedicate to this task. Furthermore, integrated learning administrators might be well served to draft template statements for their faculty that they can then tweak into their annual reviews and tenure dossiers. Outside reviewers might be unfamiliar with the intent and scope of integrated learning programs, so providing these template statements could be helpful for promoting mutual understanding.

Promoting Student Success

Student success is often measured by degree completion and institutional retention rates. While a reasonable assumption is that student success extends beyond this description, the term has developed and addressed a nationally held concern on degree attainment. The general problem with addressing retention at the institutional level is the practically limitless number of individual reasons that a student may not complete a degree. A few primary reasons, however, include financial resources and homesickness. But even more complex than identifying reasons for student departure is identifying the impact that various levels within the institution have on improving retention. The standard at this time is typically limited to addressing the subunit impact of offices with specific missions on improving student retention, gathering data from colleges and departments on student retention, and then drawing conclusions on impact. This strategy may be suboptimal, but it is efficient and supplies an approach that shares responsibility across the campus while maintaining subunits with direct missions associated with improving retention.

Considering this strategy, integrated learning has the potential to provide rich data on factors contributing to student success. By identifying student variables that cross the boundaries typically associated with this form of assessment, integrated learning can help subunits with specific missions associated with improving retention as well as individual colleges working with those students. Additionally, integrated learning provides an opportunity for meeting specific student needs that may negate boundaries that have historically affected student departure. However, challenges are associated with student success and integrated learning. Student success becomes a shared responsibility. Strategies for assessment must be developed in such a way that subsequent actions for improvement are also shared.

Practical approaches and suggestions. Because of the dearth of understanding related to how faculty perceive their own role in student retention, institutions must work to train faculty on how their individual efforts are directly linked to improved student retention and student performance. Many faculty members may not be aware that their direct academic contact with a student has such a meaningful impact. Therefore, integrated learning administrators should consider the creation of faculty-directed public relations campaigns to inform faculty about how their involvement with students assists with institutional retention measures. Because faculty are integral to academic retention, it behooves university administrators to communicate this point directly.

Efficiency and Human Resources

An area often overlooked when developing assessment plans is efficiencies and human resources. Assessments seem often to be considered after the fact, using whatever resources are available. By developing assessment plans early in the process to ensure that adequate resources and measures of efficiency are in place, the assessment plan can additionally measure these issues. This approach not only assists in institutional reporting but may also give the department courses of action that can improve available resources and make the process of further developing the initiative or program more efficient. As it relates to integrated learning, this early assessment planning needs to be more complex and consider multiple stakeholders.

Another issue with assessment when considering resources and efficiency is with the assessment itself. Assessment has typically focused on student learning, as it should, but overlooks how efficient the initiative was in reaching its goal. Ultimately, this issue relates to student learning as well. The question is whether the resources students expended to meet the goal were efficient. While this issue might not be relevant to traditional learning environments, as it relates to integrated learning this issue may be very significant. Due to the multiple and potentially unrelated stakeholders involved in the student's learning experience, the student's continuing to invest the resources required for success may be unsustainable. Those resources may be related to the student's time and finances, but they may also be related to collaborating with the unrelated stakeholders. If the student finds that navigating the system is unmanageable, the student, while initially successful, may withdraw from the opportunity.

Human resources relates to managing the institutional workforce, including the posting of positions, paying of salaries, and at times, conflict resolution. A significant amount of institutional resources goes into the human resources department, but in a more informal use of the word, a significant amount of resources goes into departmental management of the workforce required for student learning. Because of fiscal responsibility and the need to ensure the best learning environments for students, it is important to establish assessment policies and practices that evaluate teaching, assess workforce growth needs, assess competitiveness of human resource issues, and conduct assessment that measures climate and levels of potential conflict.

With integrated learning this approach may difficult. While institutional policies govern many of these issues and a human resources department can and will handle potential problems, each subunit—college or department—has certain guidelines that direct how issues are to be handled and how it will make decisions. The potential issues that may arise with assessment of human resource issues for integrated learning are not so much about how difficult it may be to measure, but identifying what to measure that avoids potential conflict between subunits when an issue does arise.

Practical approaches and suggestions. When developing an assessment plan, discussing resource issues up front should be a natural. The following questions can help guide the conversation: How much time or staffing resources are required to run a meaningful assessment? What financial incentives should be provided to students to participate in these assessments? Are the required resources too burdensome, or do they provide an adequate ratio of time spent to information retrieved?

Student Engagement

Student engagement in any type of academic assessment setting, especially interdisciplinary assessment, can be problematic. First, students are unlikely to take institutional assessments as seriously as they do their coursework. Students may be less likely to make their best effort on a standardized test that has no bearing on their course grade. Second, incentivizing students to participate in institutional assessments is a challenge for faculty and assessment professionals due to institutional regulations. Many institutions are prohibited from offering their students financial incentives or even scholarships as a way to induce their participation in assessments. A small incentive, such as an institutional promotional item, may have little influence on a student's decision to participate in an assessment exercise.

Practical approaches and suggestions. Find unique ways to engage students in interdisciplinary assessments; perhaps a call to local school pride can be one way to get student buy-in. For example, what kinds of assessments encourage students to submit their best work? Are there particular forums in which students prefer to display their own learning? Would an interdisciplinary student learning portfolio be an appropriate method for capturing student performance? Perhaps a colloquium or student poster session might be an additional venue for highlighting student performance.

Facilitating Institutional Communication

Sharing information about how students perform on interdisciplinary assessments is critical, especially because information on student performance may be sensitive. Student performance may be low, high, or somewhere in between. Therefore, creating a standardized method of communication with institutional leaders is recommended. Integrated learning assessments may naturally be atypical, in the sense that standardized tests are not useful measures for assessing competency in multiple content domains. Therefore, providing institutional administrators with routine communication protocols on how students perform on interdisciplinary assessments is an important strategy for promoting integrated learning.

Practical approaches and suggestions. Create a blog, newsletter, or website that is regularly updated at meaningful and practical intervals. Posting information on student performance at the end of the semester is a strategy that trains institutional leaders to expect student learning–related information at a particular time of year. Also, regularly and routinely sharing this information promotes a dialogue about how students enrolled in interdisciplinary courses or degrees are uniquely assessed as compared to the rest of the student population.

Student Learning Outcomes

The creation of student learning outcomes that are focused on attaining interdisciplinary knowledge may be complicated, but not unreasonably so. Creating opportunities for faculty to engage in dialogue about specific knowledge, skills, and behaviors desired of students is also an opportunity to craft student learning outcomes that reflect the nature of integrated education. Student learning outcomes specific to integrated learning must be intentionally created and jointly agreed upon. Faculty consensus may take a long time to achieve, but once integrated learning outcomes have buy-in among faculty, collecting assessment data on these outcomes will be more meaningful, thoughtful, shared, and most importantly, doable.

Practical approaches and suggestions. Create an opportunity for faculty to communicate about what knowledge, skills, and behaviors are important for students to achieve. Creating a half-day student learning outcomes development workshop, or a monthly assessment meeting, can provide faculty an opportunity to focus their attention on crafting meaningful outcomes. If there is faculty buy-in at the outset, then collecting assessment data may be less arduous because faculty have already committed to the process. Thus, when first developing an integrated learning assessment protocol, include faculty in the process.

Navigating Institutional Politics

Assessment of interdisciplinary courses and degrees may not necessarily be a panacea for navigating the stormy seas of institutional politics. However, using assessment data to make curricular improvements and strengthen student learning is a useful strategy to help institutional administrators see the bigger picture of how interdisciplinary courses and degrees fit with the institution's mission statement. Using assessment data as a way to inform institutional leaders about the value of these assessments may help to diminish complicated institutional politics.

Practical approaches and suggestions. When appropriate, share the assessment results that have been collected while keeping in mind the interests of the institutional stakeholders. Frame the data as meaningful to the program as well as the institution. Use the data to highlight student performance and to highlight unique or excelling degree programs as a way of potentially marketing the institution's overall value. In this way, assessment data can help to redirect or even potentially neutralize institutional politics.

Conclusion

This chapter has highlighted (1) a background review on general assessment, integrated learning assessment, definitional issues, potential assessment techniques, and (2) a description of the key issues in integrated learning assessment followed by practical approaches and suggestions. This chapter has illuminated several challenges to assessing integrated learning and provided some practical approaches and suggestions for readers.

References

Allen, M. J. 2004. *Assessing Academic Programs in Higher Education.* San Francisco: Jossey-ass

Arcario, P., B. Eynon, and J. E. Clark. 2005. "Making Connections: Integrated Learning, Integrated Lives." *Peer Review* 7: 1–17.

Birckbichler, J., T. Bolt, C. O'Hara, A. Rinz, A. Rollo, C. Marshall, and B. Stephens. 2012. "Structural Measures of Undergraduate Eportfolios in Three Educational Contexts." *Proceedings of the Human Factors and Ergonomics Society Fifty-Sixth Annual Meeting,* October 27-31, Chicago, IL, 561–65.

Conrad, C. F., and R. F. Wilson. 1985. *Academic Program Reviews: Institutional Approaches, Expectations, and Controversies.* ASHE ERIC Report No. 5, ERIC ED 264 806. Washington, DC: Association for the Study of Higher Education.

Flower, M. J., and T. L. Rhodes. 2005. "Integrative Learning, E-Portfolios, and the Transfer Student." *Peer Review* 7: 21–23.

Froyd, F. E., and M. W. Ohland. 2005. "Integrated Engineering Curricula." *Journal of Engineering Education* 94: 147–64.

Galle, J. K., and J. Galle. 2010. "Building an Integrated Student Learning Outcomes Assessment for General Education: Three Case Studies." *New Directions for Teaching and Learning* 121: 79–87. doi: 10.1002/tl.390.

Hatry, H. P., and K. E. Newcomer. 2004. "Pitfalls of Evaluation." In *Handbook of Practical Program Evaluation*, 2nd ed., edited by J. S. Wholey, H. P. Hatry, and K. E. Newcomer, 547–70. San Francisco: Jossey-Bass.

Huber, M. T., and P. Hutchings. 2004. *Integrative Learning, Mapping the Terrain: The Academy in Transition*. Washington, DC: Association of American Colleges & Universities.

Huber, M. T., P. Hutchings, R. Gale, R. Miller, and M. Breen. 2007. "Leading Initiatives for Integrative Learning." *Liberal Education* 93: 46–51.

Klein, J. T. 2005. "Integrative Learning and Interdisciplinary Studies." *Peer Review* 7: 8–10.

McNertney, E., and B. Ferrandino. 2010. "Core Curriculum Revision at TCU: How Faculty Created and Are Maintaining the TCU Core Curriculum." *New Directions for Teaching and Learning*, 121: 59–68. doi: 10.1002/tl.388.

Miller, R. 2005. "Integrative Learning and Assessment." *Peer Review* 7: 11–14.

Newcomer, K. E., H. P. Hatry, and J. S. Wholey. 2004. "Meeting the Need for Practical Evaluation Approaches: An Introduction." In *Handbook of Practical Program Evaluation*, 2nd ed., edited by J. S. Wholey, H. P. Hatry, and K. E. Newcomer, xxxiii–xliv. San Francisco: Jossey-Bass.

Palomba, C. A., and T. W. Banta. 1999. *Assessment Essentials*. San Francisco: Jossey-Bass.

Popova-Gonci, V., and M. C. Lamb. 2012. "Assessment of Integrated Learning: Suggested Application of Concept Mapping to Prior Learning Assessment Practices." *Journal of Continuing Higher Education* 60: 186–91. doi: 10.1080/07377363.2012.726175.

Rhodes, T. 2010. "Since We Seem to Agree, Why Are the Outcomes So Difficult to Achieve?" *New Directions for Teaching and Learning*, 121: 13–21. doi: 10.1002/tl.384.

Vars, G. F. 2002. "Educational Connoisseurship, Criticism, and the Assessment of Integrative Studies." *Issues in Integrative Studies* 20: 65–76.

Wehlburg, C. M. 2010a. "Integrated General Education: A Brief Look Back." *New Directions for Teaching and Learning*, 121: 3–11. doi: 10.1002/tl.383.

———. 2010b. "Meaningful General Education Assessment That Is Integrated and Transformative." *New Direction for Teaching and Learning* 121: 89–97. doi: 10.1002/tl.391.

Epilogue

About this Book

The editors of this volume have provided a survey of contemporary perspectives of integrative studies and learning that are representative of the ways it is being incorporated into higher education. Additionally, we hope that this volume empowers people to address meaningful and complex issues in new and unique ways through the development of new programs or the enhancement of current programs. The contributing authors have provided chapters representative of the emerging discourses about theory, methodology, application, and assessment of integrative studies. We attempted to highlight integrative approaches to course development, pedagogy, and research.

We hope that this edition not only challenges students to integrate their learning into contexts outside of the classroom but also challenges administrators and educators to create and provide experiences where such learning may occur. Huber and Hutchings (2004) report that "an emphasis on integrative learning can help undergraduates put the pieces together and develop habits of mind that prepare them to make informed judgments in the conduct of personal, professional, and civic life" (13).

Expanding Interdisciplinarity

In addition to developing a volume of work on integrative learning, we wanted to provide some fodder for debate concerning interdisciplinarity and integrative learning. In 2013 the Association for Integrative Studies officially changed its name to the Association for Interdisciplinary Studies, stating that citing the term "integrative tends to be associated outside the U.S. with medicine, not education" (Newell 2012, 1). While this may be true, our argument is that integrative learning or integrative studies is distinct from interdisciplinarity and provides educational opportunities for students to synthesize learning and living. Klein (2005) discussed several distinctions between interdisciplinary studies and integrative learning, noting that integrative learning "is the broader of the two" (8). Newell (1999) discussed interdisciplinary study as providing "one form of integrative learning, but it is limited to drawing from academic disciplines" (19). Integrative learning comprises the structures, strategies, and activities that provide a passage between learning and living, pushing the parameters of interdisciplinarity by moving beyond developing a holistic framework for understanding complex problems and teaching students how they might apply interdisciplinarity. This process engages students in making meaning of connections between curricular and cocurricular experiences.

Defining Integrative Studies

Our intent was to show that integration is not only a concept embedded within interdisciplinarity but is also separate from and may be used to apply interdisciplinarity. Integrative learning is complex and multifaceted, drawing from different perspectives in such a way that synthesizes living and learning. In Bloom's taxonomy, "Integrative learning helps students develop higher-order thinking skills such as synthesis" (Newell 1999, 19). The American Association of Colleges & Universities and Carnegie Foundation (2004) defined integrative learning as "fostering students' abilities to integrate learning—across courses, over time, and between campus and community life" (1). Integrative approaches are transformative, moving beyond disciplinary and interdisciplinary practices, thereby modifying the processes of inquiry, instruction, research, and curriculum development.

Spotlight on Theory

Part 1 of this volume was dedicated to a theoretical perspective of integrative learning. Klein argued for a new model of interdisciplinarity that adds the concept of transdisciplinary integration and interprofessional skills and joins the model through four sets of skills. Klein's quadrangle and skill sets support and nudge the prospects for an emerging field of integrative learning. Her chapter set the stage for an epistemic discussion of integrative learning. Welch, Dreyfuss, Sasser, and Yeo provided an epistemological foundation for integrative learning.

Welch proposed a solid theoretical framework for integrative learning by considering learning theory, cognitive sciences, and neuropsychology. Integrative learning is a broader approach to knowledge that emphasizes the synthetic relationship between academic and experiential learning. Further, integrative learning is grounded in theories of learning, cognitive development, and interdisciplinarity. Welch's framework utilizes three foundational principles: the integrative nature of the mind, integrative learning engages metacognition, and integrative learning is holistic. The integrative learning process provisions students with the cognitive skills for fashioning holistic models that help them make sense of a complex world. Ultimately, synchronizing the internal and external facets of existence are the essential art and craft of integrative learning. Dreyfuss and Sasser argued that coming to a deeper understanding and creating meaning about complex phenomena is seldom a linear, discrete, or individual process. Rather, constructing environments for integrative learning requires three principles: inviting learners (1) into complexity, (2) to be curious about context and their own and others' epistemologies, and (3) into conversation and collaboration.

Yeo raised questions of integrative learning as a field because of its lack of epistemic concerns; we agree. However, this volume at least partially addresses many of the cautions Yeo raised and provides for an opportunity to further the discussion. He calls integrative learning a reform movement, intended to counter the fragmentation of the undergraduate curriculum and bridge the gap between educational institutions and an increasingly complex real world. Granting a redesign of curricula with integration as a goal, students would develop the capacity to better integrate their coursework with life outside the metaphorical walls of the university. The first part of this volume may raise more questions than it answers in terms of an epistemology of integrative learning. However, the authors provide a theoretical framework from which new research can come.

Applications and Practices of Integrative Learning

In the remaining chapters of this volume, we provided a survey of what other universities in the United States are doing to provide opportunities to apply integrative learning—the process that must be cultivated through curricular and cocurricular experiences. Whipps promoted an intentional integrative learning process in which educators teach students to synthesize their learning across curricula and assimilate it into the real world through (1) understanding integration as a problem-based active process, directed at resolving a perplexity; (2) embracing diversity: pluralism, multiple perspectives, differences, and contradictions; and (3) applying creativity to avoid either/or situations and compromise in favor of something new. We show, through this volume, how others are engaging in this intentional integrative learning process. Some are providing administrative and programmatic opportunities for students to learn the integrative process in an interdisciplinary environment.

Others are offering specific and unique training through integrative learning experiences. We highlight, just as many interdisciplinary programs do, the need to present integrative learners with a capstone and portfolio experience. The authors who contribute to these ideas support our argument that students must go beyond interdisciplinarity and demonstrate their ability to apply interdisciplinary learning.

In this volume, we attempted to show an expansion of interdisciplinarity toward integrative application. We maintain that integrative learning, as an emerging field, provides for a synthesis of study and life—an application of interdisciplinarity to complex problems—and invite further discussion on the topic.

References

American Association of Colleges & Universities and the Carnegie Foundation. 2004. "A Statement on Integrative Learning." http://www.aacu.org/integrative_learning/pdfs/ILP_Statement.pdf.

Huber, M. T., and P. Hutchings. 2004. *Integrative Learning: Mapping the Terrain.* Washington, DC: Association of American Colleges & Universities.

Klein, J. T. 2005. "Integrative Learning and Interdisciplinary Studies." *Peer Review* 7 (4): 8–10.

Newell, W. H. 1999. "The Promise of Integrative Learning." *About Campus* 4 (2): 17–23.

———. 2012. "Association for Interdisciplinary Studies is Official Name Starting January 1, 2013." *Integrative Pathways* 34.

Notes

Chapter 2

1. Although this movement has faced criticism, its ideas are widely utilized in many educational contexts, especially special education.

Chapter 3

1. This begins with its "Greater Expectations" Report (American Association of Colleges & Universities 2002), even though the scope of this report is much broader than integrative learning. The association's subsequent Integrative Learning Project (see Huber et al. 2007), in collaboration with the Carnegie Foundation for the Advancement of Learning, was the main catalyst. In 2012 the AAC&U announced a new Faculty for Integrative Liberal Learning program with a grant from the Teagle Foundation (American Association of Colleges & Universities 2012).
2. Klein (2005) and Newell (2010) have written about the relationship between integrative learning and interdisciplinarity. Although I essentially agree with the analyses they have given, I do not believe that they get to the key issues and concerns I raise in this paper, perhaps in some measure because of a greater sense of delicacy.
3. The theoretical literature on interdisciplinarity is extensive. Klein's pathbreaking 1990 work is dated but remains one of the most comprehensive treatments of the subject. Repko (2012) and Moran (2010) are two relatively recent book-length studies with very different approaches to the subject matter. Several useful anthologies have been published (for example, Newell 1998; Frodeman, Klein, and Mitcham 2012).
4. I have drawn from numerous sources regarding what initiatives are happening in integrative learning and included representative works by prominent proponents. Very few synoptic studies review initiatives. The study that DeZure, Babb, and Waldman (2005) covers is useful, but it is now somewhat dated. Huber, Hutchings, Gale, Miller, and Breen (2007) is a little more current but covers less ground and detail.

5. For a discussion of the institutional politics of disciplinarity, see Chandler (2009), who also has an interesting discussion of different senses of the term *discipline*.
6. The primary association representing the contemporary interdisciplinarity movement in North America, formed in 1979, was named the Association for Integrative Studies. As of January 13, 2013, it has changed its name to the Association for Interdisciplinary Studies. This name change had first been proposed in 1983 but at the time did not receive the two-thirds vote that the association's constitution requires (Newell 2008, 24).
7. *Application* is the term that Gadamer (1975), borrowing from Aristotle, uses to characterize all and any understanding, and he uses this term in the sense that it is employed here. Remarkably, there has been very little theorizing about interdisciplinarity from a hermeneutic perspective (and none at all about integrative learning).
8. Carp (2001) has criticized interdisciplinarity precisely because it has limited itself to disciplinary knowledge and has not taken into account such extradisciplinary knowledges.
9. I find it at least somewhat ironic that in the same issue of *Liberal Education* in which Huber et al. (2007, 51) celebrate the fact that "all six regional and four major specialized accreditors" are now "calling for some form of integrative learning as an outcome of college," Eaton (2007, 2) writes with indignation and profound concern about the "assault on accreditation" that began with the 'accountability' emphasis of the 2005–2006 Commission on the Future of Higher Education and continued in a series of government initiatives that, in the name of accountability and a variety of external goals, would transfer the responsibility for defining and judging quality from academic institutions to governments. Eaton notes that although a "federal schema" for this "has not yet emerged . . . The indicators of quality that are mentioned most frequently include graduation rates, job placements, course completion, pass rates on licensure and certification examinations, and successful transfer or entry to graduate school" (3).

Chapter 6

1. Reverence here is not meant to be religious. It is occasioned by something that reminds us of human limitations and that we do not totally control—for example, nature, genius, and an ideal such as freedom. Having reverence is having the feelings of awe, respect, and shame when these are the right feelings to have (Woodruff 2001, 65).
2. I thank my liberal studies majors for a spirited discussion around this point when a draft of this chapter was assigned in senior synthesis. In particular, Katherine Granath astutely pointed out that "truth" is often critiqued in feminist literature as a gendered, male concept. What I have in mind here is more of an existentialist conception of truth in the tradition of Martin Heidegger and Jean-Paul Sartre. Truth for these thinkers is a lighting, opening, or clearing within which phenom-

ena present themselves, and our authenticity hinges on owning our responsibility for this fundamental meaning-giving activity (see Heidegger 1962).

3. The Harvard Report of the Task Force on General Education states, "General education prepares students for civic engagement. Civic engagement means participation in public life. Harvard should seek, throughout the college experience and in its general education curriculum in particular, to inspire its students to become active and engaged citizens locally, nationally, and internationally" (Task Force on General Education 2007, 5).
4. This does not mean they will be docile, of course, if we take Socrates, Gandhi, and M. L. King as examples!
5. Autonomy is from the Latin *auto-*, which means *self*, and *nomous*, which means *rule* or *law*. In current English usage, *autonomy* has at least two meanings: common and philosophical. The common meaning, as used throughout this paper, is the freedom to do or not do something, open or free choice. The philosophical meaning is tied to the etymology: self-governing or self-ruling. This philosophical concept appears in the chapter in the term "self-discipline."
6. Titular changes are most variable with methods courses. Philosophy has logic, English has criticism or advanced composition, history has some sort of historiography. Psychology has statistics as well as research or research writing. Sociology, anthropology, criminal justice, political science—each explicitly or implicitly designates a course or series of courses for method.
7. The nature of these three courses in our program is a joint effort of faculty in addition to the author, especially Dr. Philip Barclift, Dr. Jennifer Schulz, and Dr. Christine Mower.
8. All examples in this chapter are actual student projects.
9. Programs at institutions where the mission is somehow not inspirational can still require a "mission" paper. Readings can be short, provocative articles about personal identity or the purpose of higher education, leading to a personal mission statement. Another alternative is to have students write their personal mission as their first page (a kind of manifesto), then for pages two and three, a critique of the personal mission from a third-person disciplinary perspective of their choosing, and then a final reflective page or two in first-person prose.
10. I am not here distinguishing interdisciplinary from integrative programs. I address this issue in the concluding section.
11. The idea of a disciplinary draft while using Repko's text did not originate with me, but I cannot remember from where I gained the idea. My best guess is that it was from the 2010 AIS meeting. Dr. Jennifer Schulz was the first to execute it in our program.
12. The content of the outline milestone can be arranged similarly, with separate outline sections for distinct disciplines.
13. The small group discussion task mentioned above, "How would you explain your project to a seven-year-old?" was drawn from one of the exercises. These exercises are inspired by the authors' work at Lincoln Center Institute in New York.

14. Students can choose an independent text that aids their disciplinary draft, or they can choose something unrelated.
15. In the past I have paired philosopher Martha Nussbaum's *Cultivating Humanity* (1997) or *Not for Profit* (2010) with biologist Edward Wilson's *Consilience* (1997) or psychologist Howard Gardner's *Five Minds for the Future* (2008).
16. The two examples that follow are used by written permission. Also, even though the point in what follows is the ability to build on research from one course to another in accordance with one thematic interest, it can be just as important for a particular student in an integrative program to be able to investigate something new, to be able to be intentionally flexible intellectually.
17. Interdisciplinarity is crucial for integrative programs like ours, but it is not enough. As the other two legs of the tripod, we stress community engagement and metacognition. Interdisciplinarity is compatible with these, but an interdisciplinary program is not necessarily an integrative one.

Chapter 7

1. Ten years later Follett said about the sentiment during and after World War I that "underneath was the exultant feeling that . . . the time had come when man was to awake to a great and new understanding of the possibility of human fellowship" (1928/1973, 309). For more about Follett's theory of democracy see Whipps 2012 and Mattson 1998. Also see "A Pragmatic Reading of Mary Parker Follett," submitted to *Transactions of the Charles Peirce Society*.
2. In Graham 1995 (240–45).
3. Jane Mansbridge (1998) notes that Follett's process of integration led to "win-win" theories of negotiation. "Integration," she continues, "has now become one of the best-known conceptions in modern negotiation," even though Follett is not generally credited (xxiv).
4. In this article Cabot says that in fact Follett was an idealist in philosophy and a strong believer in Christianity—a description that most accurately reflects his own position rather than what we see in Follett's writing.
5. Stephen Rowe says a very similar thing about education in "Access to a Vision" (2009). He points to the "paradox" of needing "an open mind, a clear mind to fairly and fully hear what others are saying . . . We also need to be definite, to take a stand or a position, to be committed and able to work toward the achievement of ends" (2009, 388).
6. Hoopes (2003) says that Follett did not acknowledge the "opportunities that corporate life offers for vicious tyrants" and so had an "inadequate suspicion of power" (120–21). Also see Nohria in *Prophet of Management* (Drucker, Kanter, and Graham, 1995).
7. Follett was fighting cancer during this last decade of her life, and she had long periods of time when she was unable to do any work at all.
8. According to Mansbridge (1998), feminist theorist Starhawk used the Follettian

terms "power-with" and "power-over" without citing Follett. She describes other ways that feminists described similar distinctions of power, and finds similarities between Follett's and Arendt's work.

9. A perspective often called transdisciplinary.
10. Huber et al. 2005.
11. Those words that were declared as "off-limits" were *intersectionality*, *psychology*, and even the *study of families*.

Chapter 8

1. Following Klein (2005), this chapter uses interdisciplinary research and education as a subset of integrative research and education. For Klein (2005), integrative learning is an umbrella term for "structures, strategies, and activities that bridge numerous divides," while interdisciplinary learning "fosters connections among disciplines and interdisciplinary fields" (8). As this chapter explores learning that integrates across disciplinary boundaries, we feel that both terms accurately describe the Carbon, Climate, and Society Initiative (discussed later in the chapter).
2. Wolfle (1981) also argued that the first real, theoretical call for interdisciplinary research (although it was not referred to as such) came from Francis Bacon's plans for research institutes that would unite scientists of different fields for collaboration. Bacon's plan, Wolfle (1981) continued, did not survive the peer review process.
3. There were several faculty members—at one count, eighteen—attached to the CCSI program in varying degrees. Core PIs refer to the two main faculty members who took responsibility for the program.
4. The main body of Cohort 1 operated during the fall of 2001 through the fall of 2003. However, several students received financial support from the IGERT grant during the 2000–2001 academic year. Additionally, three students (including the authors) received funding during the 2005–2006 academic year. Of Cohort 1, only the authors were actively involved with the CCSI grant at any point during Cohort 2.
5. During the time between the start of cohorts, the University of Colorado–Boulder began a graduate program in environmental studies. Thus, students in Cohort 1 came from traditional social science disciplines, while their counterparts in Cohort 2 came from an interdisciplinary program with a social science track.
6. The authors observed Cohort 2 during this third year. Our participant observation largely consisted of attending group meetings, reviewing materials they were developing for their course, and serving as an outside ear.
7. Although Cameron (1965) argued that communication between people should not be hampered by disciplines because disciplines are merely organizational categories, most interdisciplinary researchers and participants note that communication is among the most difficult skills to acquire.
8. Generating credible knowledge begs the question of whose standards of credibility

are appropriate for the project. Careful selection of individuals for peer review may help in this endeavor; quality might then be determined by a broader set of criteria rather than by the narrow, disciplinary criteria of the current review system (Gibbons et al. 1994). In other words, a discourse that is specific to interdisciplinary research ought to be incorporated into the language of scientific excellence (Klein 1996).

9. As Lattuca (2001) pointed out in a positivist model of interdisciplinarity, unresolved conflict and contradiction imply the failure of a project. In a postpositivist model, however, contradiction, conflict, and the like are required and expected because of the pluralistic nature of the reality and the disciplines involved in a project (Lattuca 2001). Groups with one-dimensional understandings can be problematic in many respects. First, the lack of conflict over what the group is and ought to be doing could indicate that the group is dominated by a single paradigm—either because the group itself is one-dimensional or because alternate views are being suppressed (i.e., groupthink). Second, the lack of conflict could be an illusion of amity. In this instance, there are multiple worldviews, yet participants are weary of creating conflict and thus choose to keep quiet and try to get along with everybody.
10. Because interdisciplinary groups are developing new knowledge, some of the ends may be unknown at the beginning of the project.
11. The growth of instrumental interdisciplinarity (see Winthrop 1966, for example) has created tension between those who believe that interdisciplinarity should be an epistemological search for unity and those who believe it is a practical method to alleviate society's unsolved problems (Klein 1990).
12. Gilbert (1998) notes two approaches to the formation of interdisciplinary groups. In the first, the problem is selected, and group members coalesce around it. In the second, a group forms and identifies an interdisciplinary problem. Gilbert argues that success is more likely in the first case than in the latter because, in the first scenario, all group members hold an underlying principle in common. This may or may not be the case; certainly, Gilbert provides little empirical evidence for it. In addition, we would add that the more likely case is some combination of the two approaches—a problem is identified, and people join to work on the problem. The problem, however, is likely large enough to encompass several problem definitions and research questions that the group, already formed, must develop together.

Chapter 10

1. Integration, of course, is essential to interdisciplinary studies, as many scholars have pointed out, including Klein (2010), Dezure (2010), and Newell (2013).
2. See Tanya Augsburg's (2006) "Becoming Interdisciplinary: The Student Portfolio in the Bachelor of Interdisciplinary Studies Program at Arizona State University" for an excellent discussion of how portfolios help students integrate their learning.

Bret Eynon (2009), in his publications and direction of the national Connect to Learning project, has demonstrated how useful e-portfolios can be in encouraging students to reflect on and integrate their learning. A recent survey published in the *AAEEBL Learner* highlights the "high value" educators are placing on the "attributes of ePortfolios [for] fostering reflection . . . [and] integrative learning" (Brown et al. 2012, 7).

3. For an excellent history of our college's capstone, see Wexelblatt's essay on the subject (2012).
4. At 106, this is a statistically significant sampling of the 554 sophomores who completed our program in May 2012.
5. In *Making Progress? What We Know about the Achievement of Liberal Education Outcomes*, Ashley Finley (2012) shows that other national tests of student progress, such as the Educational Testing Service Proficiency Profile and the Collegiate Assessment of Academic Proficiency (CAAP), also reveal low rates of student progress.

About the Editors

Patrick C. Hughes is associate vice provost for undergraduate education and associate professor of communication studies at Texas Tech University. He publishes extensively on interpersonal and family communication issues, including interfaith marriages and interethnic and interracial interaction, often from an interdisciplinary theory perspective. He teaches undergraduate and graduate courses in communication research methods, family communication, and intercultural communication.

Juan S. Muñoz is currently vice provost for undergraduate education and vice president for institutional diversity, equity, and community engagement at Texas Tech University. As a vice president and vice provost, he serves on the President's Administrative Council, Provost Staff, Dean's Council, Academic Council, Strategic Planning Council, Strategic Enrollment Planning Council, and University Budget Working Group, and is the Chair of the TTUS Outreach and Engagement System Priority.

Marcus N. Tanner is the program director for integrative studies at Texas Tech University. His education and life experiences are interdisciplinary. Before working in higher education, he earned a bachelor's degree in church ministries and spent thirteen years in full-time pastoral ministry. He earned a master's degree in education and an interdisciplinary doctor of philosophy degree in human development and family studies. His research interests include the interaction of work and family, work and health concerns, program assessment, and online learning. Dr. Tanner has published primary research on forced termination of clergy and its effects on clergy and their families. His publications can be found in peer-reviewed academic journals as well as trade publications and organizational newsletters. Dr. Tanner serves as the co-coordinator for the Association for Interdisciplinary Studies National Honor Society (Alpha Iota Sigma). He also serves as the founding president of a nonprofit organization, HealingChoice, that provides marriage and family therapy for their clients.

About the Contributors

Charlie Adams is an associate professor at Texas Tech University. He serves as the Restaurant, Hotel, and Institutional Management (RHIM) program's director of career services and is responsible for placing interns, graduating seniors, attracting hospitality companies, and educating prospective students about the RHIM program. He travels extensively, maintaining relationships with over seventy-five companies and industry recruiters. Dr. Adams has over twenty-five years of teaching, research, and consulting experience in the food service and lodging industry. His research interests are interdisciplinary, and publications cover the areas of consumer behavior, product innovation, human resources, rural tourism, and alcoholic beverage issues.

P. Sven Arvidson is director of liberal studies and Senior Faculty Fellow in the Center for Excellence in Teaching and Learning at Seattle University, where he is also the founding director of the Consortium of Interdisciplinary Scholars. His interdisciplinary research centers on human nature, ethics, and pedagogy. His most recent books include *Teaching Nonmajors: Advice for Liberal Arts Professors* (SUNY, 2008) and *The Sphere of Attention: Context and Margin* (Springer, 2006). He received his MA and PhD in philosophy from Georgetown University, an MA in psychology from Duquesne University, and a BA in human development from St. Mary's College of Maryland.

Curtis Craig is a doctoral student in experimental psychology—human factors at Texas Tech University. He received his bachelor's degree in cognitive science and his master's degree in applied cognition and neuroscience at the University of Texas at Dallas. His research primarily focuses on the psychological, environmental, and biological basis of executive function, cognitive control, and development of expertise.

Simeon Dreyfuss is chair and associate professor in the Interdisciplinary Studies Department and director of the Liberal Arts Core program at Marylhurst University, a historically Catholic university serving adult and nontraditional students in the Portland, Oregon, metropolitan area. He joined Marylhurst's faculty as an adjunct member of the English Literature and Writing program in 1988, and the full-time faculty in 1992, and later served as the director of the Prior Learning Assessment program. He led the team redesigning the university's general education program into the outcome-based liberal arts core in 1998, and has served as the program's director for the last fifteen years. He designed and managed the online Marylhurst Academic Portfolio, part of the liberal arts core; designed the university's first online course evaluation system; and oversaw the degree audit and advising system during the twelve years it moved from a paper-and-pencil system, to a homegrown centralized computer-based system, to one available to students online and integrated with central student data. He designed the university's first introductory course for interdisciplinary studies in 1994 and became the department chair in 1999; the department is now the largest undergraduate major by headcount at the university. His stories, poems, essays, journalism, and peer-reviewed scholarly articles have appeared in *Clinton Street Quarterly*, *Gero-Punk Project*, *Issues in Integrative Studies*, the *Neighbor*, *Northwest Magazine*, *Nuclear Times*, the *Progressive*, *Puget Sound*, and *Willamette Week*, among other places.

Jennifer Shaulis Hughes is director of the Office of Planning and Assessment at Texas Tech University. She is also a doctoral student in higher education, studying faculty engagement in assessment. Jennifer has held full-time teaching positions in the Rawls College of Business and South Plains College. Before moving to Texas, Jennifer worked in the Colorado Community College and Occupational Education System, where she held positions in institutional research and marketing. She earned her BS in speech from Northwestern University and her MS in communication studies from Illinois State University.

Michael Kelly is an assistant professor of rhetoric and writing center director at Champlain College. He holds a PhD in English from the University of Nebraska. His research interests include institutional literacy and interdisciplinary pedagogy.

Julie Thompson Klein is professor of humanities in the English Department and Faculty Fellow for Interdisciplinary Development in the Division of Research at Wayne State University. She was also Visiting Foreign Professor at Shimane University in Japan; a Fulbright Professor at Tribhuvan University in Nepal; a Foundation Visitor at the University of Auckland, New Zealand; and Visiting Professor and Mellon Fellow in Digital Humanities at the University of Michigan. Klein is past president of the Association for Interdisciplinary Studies and former editor of the AIS journal *Issues in Integrative Studies*. Her books include *Interdisciplinarity: History, Theory, and Practice* (1990); *Interdisciplinary Studies Today* (coedited, 1994); *Crossing Boundaries: Knowledge, Disciplinarities, and Interdisciplinarities* (1996); *Transdisciplinarity: Joint Problem Solving among Science, Technology, and Society* (coedited, 2001); *Interdisciplinary Ed-*

ucation in K–12 and College (edited, 2002); the monograph *Mapping Interdisciplinary Studies* (1999); *Humanities, Culture, and Interdisciplinarity: The Changing American Academy* (2005); and *Creating Interdisciplinary Campus Cultures* (2010). She was also associate editor of the *Oxford Handbook on Interdisciplinarity* (2010) and is the author of numerous chapters and articles. Klein is currently coeditor of the University of Michigan Press series *Digital Humanities@digitalculturebooks* and is currently completing a new book on *Interdisciplining Digital Humanities.*

Michael Lange is an associate professor in the Core Division at Champlain College. An anthropologist and folklorist, his PhD is from the University of Wisconsin–Madison. He has conducted ethnographic fieldwork in Norway, Scotland, Morocco, and the United States, and his research interests include the intersections of identity with various other categories, including food, narrative, and academic disciplines.

Elizabeth Lowham is an assistant professor of political science at California Polytechnic State University–San Luis Obispo, where she also serves as director of the Master of public Policy program. Elizabeth received her BA in geology from Carleton College in 2001. She received her MA and PhD in political science from the University of Colorado–Boulder in 2003 and 2007, respectively. Elizabeth's research interests center around collaboration and leadership in environmental policy and research methodology. While in graduate school, Elizabeth was a fellow in the Carbon, Climate, and Society Initiative, which was funded through the National Science Foundation's Integrative Graduate Education and Research Traineeship (IGERT) program. This initiative brought together groups of graduate students studying natural sciences, social sciences, and journalism to do collaborative interdisciplinary work on climate change.

Natalie McKnight is associate dean and director of the Center for Interdisciplinary Teaching and Learning at the College of General Studies, Boston University. She is also a professor of humanities. She has published multiple essays and three books on Victorian fiction: *Idiots, Madmen and Other Prisoners in Dickens* (St. Martin's Press, 1993); *Suffering Mothers in Mid-Victorian Novels* (St. Martin's/Palgrave, 1997); and *Fathers in Victorian Fiction* (Cambridge Scholars Publishing, 2011). She is also coeditor of *Dickens Studies Annual* and *IMPACT: The Journal of the Center for Interdisciplinary Teaching and Learning.* For the past three years, she has been making presentations on using e-portfolios for interdisciplinary work and assessment at AAC&U conferences and other higher education meetings.

Philip Craig Morton is the associate director for the Office of Planning and Assessment at Texas Tech University. He earned his doctorate in higher education administration from Texas Tech University in 2010. His previous degrees are from Texas Tech as well, with a BA in human development and family studies and an MA in educational psychology.

Heather Pinson has degrees in music, musicology, and interdisciplinary arts and teaches courses on art and music history at Robert Morris University. As the chair for the Department of Communication, Heather publishes predominately on popular music, jazz, aesthetics, and race theory and is the author of *The Jazz Image: Seeing Music through Herman Leonard's Photography*, released by the University Press of Mississippi, which examines photographs of African American jazz musicians during the 1950s and 1960s. Other publications include articles in *Rock Brands: Selling Sound in a Media Saturated Society*, the *Encyclopedia of the Blues*, and the *Encyclopedia of African American Music*. In addition to her training as a classical violinist, she performs regularly in the greater Pittsburgh and Ohio area in both popular and classical music ensembles.

Jennifer Sasser is chairperson and associate professor in the Department of Human Sciences and director of the Gerontology program at Marylhurst University, a private liberal arts university in the Portland, Oregon, metro area. She joined the Marylhurst faculty as an adjunct member of the Master of Arts in Interdisciplinary Studies program in 1997, and since that time she has been involved in the design and implementation of many on-campus and web-based courses and programs for adult learners, including the graduate and undergraduate certificate programs in gerontology. Jennifer served as chairperson of the Marylhurst University Faculty Council for six years, and she currently serves on several university committees and task groups. In 2008 she received the Marylhurst Award for Excellence in Academic Service and Teaching; in 2010, the Trustees' Award for Individual Achievement; and in 2011 a Faculty Excellence and Innovation grant to fund her research and writing. Jennifer is also a 2012 recipient of the Association for Gerontology in Higher Education Teaching Excellence award. Over the past twenty years Jennifer has been involved in inquiry in the areas of creativity in later life, older women's embodiment, sexuality and aging, critical gerontological theory, and transformational adult learning practices. Jennifer served on the Oregon Gerontological Association Board of Directors from 2005 to 2010 and was chairperson of the board for three years. In addition, she served on the Mary's Woods @ Marylhurst Board of Directors from 2008 to 2010.

Annalisa Schilla received her BS in geological sciences from the University of California–Santa Barbara in 1999 and her PhD in geological sciences in 2007 from the University of Colorado–Boulder. Her graduate research focused on reconstructing past global climate from an Antarctic ice core. While in graduate school, Annalisa was a fellow in the Carbon, Climate, and Society Initiative, which was funded through the National Science Foundation's Integrative Graduate Education and Research Traineeship program. This initiative brought together groups of graduate students studying natural sciences, social sciences, and journalism to do collaborative interdisciplinary work on climate change. Since completing her graduate work, Annalisa has been working on a variety of climate change and air quality research and policy issues at the California Air Resources Board.

Monica VanDieren earned her PhD in mathematical sciences through the interdisciplinary Pure and Applied Logic Program at Carnegie Mellon University. She held the Szegö Assistant Professorship at Stanford University and the T. H. Hildebrandt Assistant Professorship at the University of Michigan before arriving at Robert Morris University. VanDieren publishes in leading logic journals, and she has presented her research to audiences in Russia, Finland, Poland, Germany, Italy, Colombia, and Canada. Her transformative work has influenced several PhDs in the past decade and is featured prominently in the monograph *Categoricity*, where her work is cited over forty-five times. VanDieren is a principal investigator of NSF Grant 0801313, "RUI: Model Theory of Abstract Elementary Classes," which supports not only her research but also her teaching and outreach. Through hands-on workshops at events such as the Expanding Your Horizons conferences, VanDieren encourages middle and high school girls to pursue nontraditional STEM careers. As codirector of the University Honors Program, VanDieren has overseen a 100 percent growth in enrollment through a diversification of the curriculum. As part of the new honors curriculum, VanDieren and Dr. Heather Pinson developed a math, music, and art class, attracting students who would not otherwise take an elective course in mathematics or art.

James Welch, IV, is currently assistant professor in the Interdisciplinary Studies Program of the University of Texas–Arlington, where he has been a faculty member since 2004. He served as the program's interim director from 2011 to 2012. His research centers on the development of interdisciplinary and integrative theory and its application to contemporary complex problems. James currently serves as the vice president for development and on the board of directors for the Association for Interdisciplinary Studies.

Judy D. Whipps is professor of interdisciplinary liberal studies and philosophy at Grand Valley State University. She is a coeditor with Marilyn Fischer of *Jane Addams's Writings on Peace* (2003), a four-volume edited set of Addams's writings, and the editor of *Reflection and Engagement* (2009), now in its fourth edition. She has published articles in journals such as the *Journal of Speculative Philosophy*, the *National Women's Studies Journal*, and *Hypatia*. Her essays are published in *Contemporary Feminist Pragmatism* (2012), *Feminist Interpretations of Jane Addams* (2010), *American Buddhism as a Way of Life, Vol. 2* (2009), and in *Democracy as Culture: Deweyan Pragmatism in the Age of Globalization* (2008). She has received the GVSU Barbara Jordan Award for contributions to feminist scholarship and service and the Excellence in Teaching and Faculty Service Award from the University Continuing Education Association. She is a former board member of the Association of Integrative Studies.

Katheryn Wright is an assistant professor in the Core Division at Champlain College. She holds a PhD from Florida State University, specializing in media studies. Her research focuses on global screen culture, media convergence, popular forms of entertainment, and critical theory related to the body.

Michael Yeo is an associate professor in the Department of Philosophy at Laurentian University. In addition to teaching philosophy, he also teaches regularly in Laurentian's Interdisciplinary Master's in Interpretation and Values program and in its interdisciplinary PhD in human studies. His main area of specialization is ethics, but he has lectured and published extensively on a variety of subjects. Recent publications include "An Agenda for Service-Learning in the Humanities" (*Interdisciplinary Humanities*, 2012); "The Rights of Science and the Rights of Politics" (*Canadian Journal of Sociology*, 2011); "Propaganda and Surveillance in Orwell's *Nineteen Eighty-Four*: Two Sides of the Same Coin" (*Global Media Journal*, 2010); and as a contributor to the third edition of *Concepts and Cases in Nursing Ethics* (Broadview Press, 2010).

Index

Note: page numbers in *italics* refer to figures.

Index